Empson

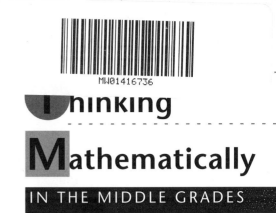

Thinking
Mathematically
IN THE MIDDLE GRADES

Designing Spaces

Visualizing, Planning, and Building

CREATED BY
EDUCATION DEVELOPMENT CENTER, INC.

Heinemann
A division of Reed Elsevier Inc.
361 Hanover Street   Portsmouth, NH 03801-3912
Offices and agents throughout the world

This project is based at Education Development Center, Inc. (EDC), 55 Chapel Street, Newton, MA, 02158, and was supported, in part, by the National Science Foundation (Grant No. 9054677). Opinions expressed are those of the authors and not necessarily those of the Foundation. The project is developing new mathematics curriculum materials for grades six through eight, and this unit is one of a series of transition units designed to fully address current standards and recommendations for teaching middle school mathematics.

Every effort has been made to contact the copyright holders for permission to reprint borrowed material where necessary. We regret any oversights that may have occurred and would be happy to rectify them in future printings of this work.

Library of Congress Cataloging-in-Publication Data

Designing spaces : visualizing, planning, and building / created by
  Education Development Center, Inc.
      p.   cm. — (Seeing and thinking mathematically in the middle
  grades)
    ISBN 0–435–08350–3 (acid-free)
    1. Mathematics—Study and teaching (Secondary)   2. House
  construction—Mathematics.   3. Project method in teaching.
  I. Education Development Center.   II. Series.
  QA11.D3785   1995
  728'.01'516—dc20   94–35412
                                                       CIP

Acquired for Heinemann by Toby Gordon and Leigh Peake
Produced by J. B. Tranchemontagne
Copyedited by Alan Huisman
Text Design by Jenny Jensen Greenleaf
Cover Design by Jenny Jensen Greenleaf and Darci Mehall
Cover Photo by Marlene Nelson
Spanish translation by Jaime Fatás Cabeza

Printed in the United States of America on acid-free paper
99 98 97 96 95 VG 1 2 3 4 5 6 7 8 9 10

Contents

Designing Spaces was developed by the following people on the Seeing and Thinking Mathematically project at Education Development Center.

Project Director
Glenn M. Kleiman

Project Manager
Karen Zweig

Curriculum Developers
Kristen Herbert
Susan Janssen
Glenn Kleiman

Editor
Dan Tobin

Graphic Production
Ellen Smith

Major Contributor
Marianne Thompson

Other Contributors
Rebecca Brown
Shelley Isaacson
Marlene Kliman
Kim Smart
Muffie Wiebe

Reviewers
Amy Brodesky
Dan Brutlag
Al Cuoco
Faye Ruopp
Bernie Zubrowski

Administrative Assistants
Andrea Tench
Albertha Walley

Teacher Consultants
Robert Bates, Brookline Public Schools, MA
Julie Dunkle, Freemont Public Schools, CA
Fred Gross, Sudbury Public Schools, MA
Yvelyne Germain-McCarthy, University of New Orleans, LA
Mark Rubel, Newton Public Schools, MA

Acknowledgments
STM would like to thank the teachers and students who field-tested the unit. In particular, we thank the students of Bill Rudder (Boston, MA), Carolyn Connolly (Brookline, MA), Mary Lou Mehrling (Cambridge, MA), Mark Rubel (Newton, MA), Oakley Hoerth (Brookline, MA), David Lawrence (Newton, MA), and Carol Mellet (Brookline, MA). Their work and pictures appear throughout this unit.

We would also like to thank the many teachers, students, and administrators of the California Middle School Mathematics Renaissance Project for their extensive field test of the unit. Their reflections and comments helped form the unit.

Additionally, we would like to thank the EDC staff and other colleagues who reviewed the unit. We would also like to thank Marlene Nelson, EDC staff photographer.

Foreword

With the Seeing and Thinking Mathematically (STM) materials, students learn mathematics by doing mathematics, by using and connecting mathematical ideas, and by actively constructing their own understandings. As a teacher, you'll find that these materials will put you closer to your goal of an inviting, exploratory classroom in which all students gain mathematical power. They are designed to help you as a sixth-, seventh-, or eighth-grade mathematics teacher, to accomplish the following goals.

Improve Your Mathematics Teaching

The reforms in mathematics education advocated by the National Council of Teachers of Mathematics (NCTM), the Mathematical Sciences Education Board (MSEB), and innovative state and local boards of education are challenging to implement in the classroom. The STM materials will support you as you carry out this reform, and are a step in the transition to a new curriculum that will prepare students for the complex technological world in which they will live and work.

Convey the Universal Importance of Mathematics

The STM materials center on the importance of mathematics in the human experience. In STM units, students use mathematics to accomplish things that have been important to all people in all places and all times: to design and build, to predict and plan, to analyze and decide, to imagine and create, to explore and understand, to play and invent, and to formalize and systematize their knowledge. This approach allows students to gain a deep understanding of central mathematical ideas, including patterns, representations, proportional reasoning, functions, and mathematical models.

Employ an Innovative, Hands-On Approach to Teaching and Learning

In each STM unit, your students will actively explore mathematical ideas using physical and pictorial models, and will apply these ideas in investigations and projects. Students pose their own problems; create their own strategies; build on their own knowledge and language; and reflect on their work by discussing and writing about it. In the process, they will build "mathematical habits of mind." They will visualize, represent, calculate, compute, model, invent, prove, systematize, and communicate about mathematics.

Provide Opportunities for All Your Students to be Successful with Mathematics

The STM materials provide opportunities for students from different backgrounds to contribute their ideas and experiences, thereby enhancing the mathematical learning experience for everyone in your class. They allow students to use and build on their own strengths and to deepen and broaden their areas of expertise.

Adapt Materials to Meet the Needs of Your Students

Each unit provides a rich set of resources that you can adapt to suit your classroom and teaching style. The lesson plans suggest variations and extensions and include From the Classroom vignettes from teachers who have taught the unit.

Employ New Approaches to Assessment

Performance assessment alternatives such as global scoring rubrics, portfolios, and student journals are embedded within the flow of STM learning activities.

Create a Community of Mathematics Learning

The STM units provide opportunities for your students to learn from one another as well as from you. In the STM approach, you become a resource guide, directing, encouraging, and supporting your students' learning.

Engage Your Students in Authentic and Exciting Mathematical Work

In an STM classroom, mathematics is placed in relevant contexts, so that it has a purpose and a motivation. Your students will produce things they value and want to share—products that reflect their own mathematical discoveries.

Build Connections to Other Disciplines and to Your Students' Lives Outside of School

STM units can be connected to all subject areas—art, literature, history, science, and social studies. By using mathematics to analyze, to decide, to plan, to design, and to create, your students will find that mathematics is useful in their everyday lives.

Dear Teacher:

As you and your students focus on *Designing Spaces: Visualizing, Planning, and Building,* an architect can be a valuable resource, demonstrating the "real world" uses of mathematics and suggesting building projects and architectural field trips. The tips below can help you build this kind of unique teaching team.

How can you contact an architect?

Members of The American Institute of Architects (AIA) have been told about this project, so they should not be surprised to get your call. There are over 300 local AIA chapters that would be happy to help you locate an interested member architect in your area. You may also contact the AIA national office at 1735 New York Ave., NW, Washington, DC 20006.

How do you decide on the architect's role?

Meet with the architect to discuss what the person's role will be during your *Designing Spaces* study. Will he or she teach from the materials in the unit? arrange a field trip? lead a discussion of a "case study" of an actual design project? Is the architect willing to work with students as they create house models, describe their building process, and represent their models in two dimensions?

Discuss the age and ability levels of your students, and ask the architect to suggest appropriate activities. Be sure to agree on the time commitment the architect will make to your class. The role you settle on will depend on the particular needs of your classroom and on the skills and availability of the architect.

As you and the architect discuss possible projects and activities, you'll want to review these key issues:

- How should you prepare your students for the architect's visit? What should they read or think about beforehand?
- How much hands-on activity will be involved? What materials are needed? Can the architect help supply those not available at school?

- What are some relevant field trips? Can the architect accompany the class? Can he or she suggest buildings to include on an architectural walking tour?
- Can the architect suggest enrichment projects for students who become especially interested in architecture?
- Will there be a culminating activity or presentation? What will it be and who should be invited? What role will the architect play in planning for it?

The success of this joint venture will depend to a large degree on these initial efforts to decide how the architect will work with students.

Good luck!

Sincerely,

Alan R. Sandler
Senior Director
AIA Education Programs

P.S. A lesson plan for architects, including a survey form for students, is available from the American Institute for Architects by calling 202-626-7573.

Unit at a Glance

In this unit, students use mathematics to visualize, build, represent, and describe models of homes for people around the world.

Grade Level
6–7

Length
Approximately 30 class periods

Prerequisites
Familiarity with common two-dimensional shapes

Ability to interpret two-dimensional representations of three-dimensional objects

Materials Required
Common objects for students to sketch

Cubes (wooden, plastic, or paper)

Shapes cut from poster board or card stock

String, yarn, or rope

Worksheets and transparencies made from masters provided in the unit

Mathematical Themes
Multiple representations of shapes and structures

Visualization

Properties and components of shapes

Communication

Specific Mathematical Concepts
Geometric properties of shapes: parallel, equilateral, regular, right angles, opposite angles, etc.

Isometric and orthogonal representations

Relating two- and three-dimensional objects

Spatial visualization

Overview

The igloos of the Arctic Inuits, the tipis of the North American Plains Indians, the castles built in medieval England, the thatched-roofed houses of Indonesia, the apartment buildings in cities around the world—these structures bring to mind particular geometric forms. We *see mathematically* when we visualize or communicate about the shapes of these structures. And the creators of these structures needed to *think mathematically* to design and build homes that made good use of available materials, provided protection from the elements, and met the needs of the inhabitants.

In *Designing Spaces: Visualizing, Planning, and Building*, students use geometry to analyze buildings from around the world, design and build their own house models, create plans for their designs, and build from each other's plans. Students start out the unit building with cubes and later move to other geometric shapes. As they learn to represent these three-dimensional structures with two-dimensional drawings and with words, students gain mathematical knowledge and proficiency. They develop their visualization skills, increase their mathematical vocabulary, and explore the properties of two-dimensional shapes and three-dimensional structures.

In the final activity, students begin with flat geometric shapes and build a model house for one of two climates—a hot, rainy climate or a cold, snowy climate. They then create plans that would enable someone else to re-create their models. As they design and represent their houses, students consider a range of questions: Which flat shapes can be combined to build a steep roof so that snow slides off it? How can the three-dimensional structure be represented in two-dimensional drawings that clearly show all of the shapes that were used in building it? What mathematical properties of the structure—such as equilateral sides, right angles, or parallel faces—should be conveyed in the plans to help someone visualize the structure?

To answer questions such as these, students engage in a form of mathematical thinking applied in all societies—designing living spaces to meet the needs of the people. In the process, students discover new ways to see, discuss, and make sense of their physical environment.

How This Unit Is Organized

Section 1 *Introduction*

Section 1 introduces students to the mathematical themes of visualizing, representing, and communicating about shapes and structures. Students make connections among perspective drawings, orthogonal views, and descriptions of the component shapes of houses from around the world. They also consider the functions of various three-dimensional shapes by matching these representations to explanations of how the house design is well suited to the climate or culture.

Section 2 *Visualizing and Representing Cube Structures*

In Section 2, students design and build model houses with cubes and explore different methods for representing them in building plans. Students first develop their own techniques for describing and drawing the cube structures and then learn to make isometric and orthogonal drawings. Students explore the relationship between two and three dimensions as they compare different ways to represent the structures.

Section 3 *Describing Properties and Functions of Shapes*

In Section 3, students use mathematical terms and concepts to describe model houses. Students design and construct houses from polygons and represent them in building plans. They then explore the properties of sides and angles in polygons as they create shapes to match given sets of properties. Students apply their knowledge of shape properties to creating building plans. When students use a classmate's plans to build a house, they explore the need for precision in mathematical communication.

Section 4 *Visualizing and Representing Polygons and Polyhedra*

Section 4 focuses on the properties of three-dimensional shapes. Students investigate techniques for creating, visualizing, and representing various polyhedra. After experimenting with ways of combining polygons to form polyhedra, students visualize and build specific polyhedra given sets of written and visual clues describing their properties. Students apply their knowledge of three-dimensional structures and properties to designing and representing a house for a given climate.

Appendix A *Designing Homes for Different Climates*

This article provides examples of how people from various cultures—and throughout history—have created innovative house designs for various climates. The article can be used as a resource for Lessons 7 and 14, when students design homes for specific climates, or assigned as homework.

Appendix B *Scoring Rubric*

This generalized scoring rubric can be used in conjunction with assessment criteria to evaluate student work in Lessons 6, 10, and 14.

Appendix C *Sample Final Projects*

These sample projects were created by students who participated in the field test of this unit.

Appendix D *Shape Templates*

These templates can be used to cut out all of the shapes that you will need for the unit.

Appendix E *Reproducible Blackline Masters*

Whenever a reproducible is required by the lesson, a master has been provided in both an English and a Spanish version. Depending on the structure of your classroom, you may prefer to copy the master onto an overhead transparency to be used with the whole class.

Mathematical Themes in This Unit

Throughout *Designing Spaces,* students will encounter four major, interconnected mathematical themes: *multiple representations of shapes and structures, visualization, properties and components of shapes,* and *communication.* These four themes are described briefly below. The section overviews provide additional specific information about how these themes are developed in the lessons of each section.

Multiple Representations of Shapes and Structures

Mathematical power begins with the ability to use appropriate representations to capture a wide variety of aspects of the world, such as quantities, locations, shapes, and sizes. Representations bring things into the world of mathematics, so they can be manipulated with mathematical techniques and analyzed with mathematical concepts.

Designing Spaces focuses on helping students develop ways to represent three-dimensional shapes and structures. Throughout the unit, students develop and use several forms of visual representations. For example, in Lesson 2 students create structures from cubic blocks and develop their own ways of visually representing these structures. In Lessons 3 and 5, they learn to represent their block structures with *isometric representations*, which show depth, and with *orthogonal representations*, which show the two-dimensional views of each side of the structure. They learn to build structures from both types of representation and to translate between the representations. Later in the unit, students learn to represent prisms and pyramids with drawings that show depth.

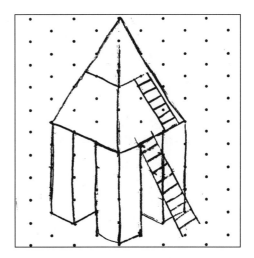

In addition to creating visual representations, students build physical models to represent their designs. They also create verbal representations, using the vocabulary of geometry to describe the shapes, properties, and construction of their structures. Each type of representation conveys different information about the structure. For example, isometric representations emphasize the three-dimensional nature of the structure while orthogonal representations highlight the individual, two-dimensional faces. Verbal descriptions communicate the step-by-step process of building the structure as well as the student's aesthetic sense of the structure.

Students investigate the uses and interplay of the multiple representations in several contexts within the unit. After building model homes from blocks and geometric shapes, students create visual and verbal building plans. Students then trade plans and each student builds a replica of another student's house. As students work to interpret the various representations, they gain new insights into the benefits of each. Students obtain further practice with the representations while playing and creating an answer key for the Mystery Structures game.

Visualization

Imagine designing a house for a very cold, snowy climate. Picture the front of the house in your mind's eye. What shape did you imagine to fit the climate? Now imagine viewing the house from one side. What shapes do you see? Finally, visualize a bird's-eye view of the top of the house. What do you see now?

Perhaps you visualized a dome shape, like an igloo, or a steeply slanted roof designed so that snow would slide off it. No matter what type of house you imagined, you used some of the visualization processes that are central to all areas of mathematics: using your knowledge to create a visual image and then performing "mental experiments," such as visualizing what your image would look like from different vantage points.

The ability to "see" and manipulate things in the mind's eye is essential for mathematical thinking. Throughout *Designing Spaces,* students develop and use their visualization skills in a variety of ways. Students use visualization as a basis for designing three-dimensional structures from blocks and from flat geometric shapes; for representing shapes and structures; for interpreting plans and clues to create structures; for transforming one shape into another; and for performing a variety of mental experiments, such as determining what the cross section of a three-dimensional shape would look like.

In these ways, visualization underlies the mathematical themes of multiple representations and communication. We visualize in order to determine the particular information we need to abstract and capture in our representation. We also visualize when we interpret a two-dimensional representation as the three-dimensional structure it represents. We then create messages to help others form mental images that are similar to our own.

The focus on visualization in this unit provides opportunities for some students to see mathematics in a new light and to demonstrate mathematical abilities that had previously been overlooked. Many teachers have reported being surprised that some of their students who have difficulty with other areas of mathematics are strong visualizers. The unit provides an opportunity for such students to build upon their strengths and to be successful in mathematics.

Properties and Components of Shapes

Shape is central to all the mathematical themes in this unit. When we represent three-dimensional structures in two-dimensional representations, we identify the component shapes in the structures and portray them on paper. When we visualize objects and perform mental experiments, we often imagine and manipulate geometric forms. When we communicate about structures, we use the language of shapes. This theme focuses on developing students' understanding of the properties of shapes, such as equilateral and parallel, and of how shapes can be built from component shapes, such as the triangles and rectangles that make up a triangular prism.

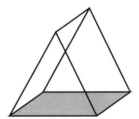

Designing Spaces offers students opportunities for both intuitive exploration and focused investigation of two-dimensional and three-dimensional shapes, their component parts, and some of their properties. Students arrive at an intuitive understanding of the properties of shapes by working with shapes and with the language that describes shapes. For example, as students build a house suited to a specific climate, they explore how and why certain shapes fit together. To create an initial set of building plans, students develop their own ways to describe the shapes that make up the house. In subsequent lessons, students make rope shapes to investigate properties such as parallel, equilateral, and right and opposite angles, and components of shapes such as sides, angles, faces, and edges. Students then apply these concepts in revising their building plans, making their plans clearer and more precise.

The work students do in the unit with shape, properties, and definitions culminates in the Mystery Structures game, in which students create structures from clues describing the two- and three-dimensional components of the structures.

Communication

The theme of home design places students in a context in which precise, mathematical communication has a real-world purpose.

Throughout the unit, students develop the precise mathematical vocabulary of shapes. For each key term, students first work with the concept and collect examples. For example, students construct various three-dimensional shapes and then group them into prisms, pyramids, and other shapes. Then they write informal descriptions of what is meant by the terms. They share and check their descriptions, determining, for example, whether their descriptions of *prism* include all of the sample prisms and exclude all of the pyramids and other shapes. Finally, the class agrees upon a definition for the term to be entered into the class glossary for the unit.

At three points in the unit, students apply both their developing vocabulary and their mastery of visual representations to communicate about the houses they've designed. For each set of building plans, students use new visual representations and geometric concepts to communicate in increasingly precise ways. Having others build from the plans provides a stringent test of the accuracy, clarity, and completeness of the plans. Students also learn to communicate constructive feedback to their classmates to help them improve their structures and their plans.

Letter to Families

A suggested letter to families, describing the unit and suggesting activities that can be done at home, is provided in an English and a Spanish version. See Appendix E (Reproducible 1).

Sample Lesson Schedule

The complete unit will require about 30 class periods, assuming class periods of at least 45 minutes. The table on pages xviii–xix provides a sample lesson-by-lesson schedule to help you plan. Suggestions for saving time, should you need to shorten the unit, are provided below.

Shorter Routes Through the Unit

This unit is designed so that all the lessons build and contribute to a whole that is greater than each part taken individually. For this reason, the ideal format is to use all of the lessons.

Approx. # of Classes	Lessons
	Section 1: Introduction
2	**1. Homes Around the World** Students solve the Homes Puzzle by matching illustrations of homes from around the world to corresponding description, view, and shape cards.
	Section 2: Visualizing and Representing Cube Structures
2–3	**2. Planning and Building a Modular House** Students design modular houses and represent their designs in building plans. They create their own methods of representation and compare them to a classmate's methods.
1–2	**3. Seeing Around the Corners—Isometric Drawings** Students find all the possible houses that can be made with three cubes. After experimenting further with their own methods of representation, students learn to use isometric drawings to represent their structures.
2–3	**4. Seeing All the Possibilities** Students find all the houses that can be made with four cubes and represent them isometrically. They then use isometric drawings to match rotations of different cube combinations.
2	**5. Seeing All Sides—Orthogonal Drawings** Students translate orthogonal drawings into (1) modular houses and (2) isometric drawings. They then learn to translate isometric drawings into orthogonal drawings.
2–3	**6. Picture This—Improving Your Drawings** Students redo their building plans from Lesson 2 to include isometric and orthogonal drawings. Students build from each other's plans and give feedback on their partner's plans. Students' building plans are assessed.

Approx. # of Classes	Lessons
Section 3: Describing Properties and Functions of Shapes	
1–2	**7. Planning and Building a House for Your Climate** Using a set of cardboard shapes, students design and build a house for the climate in which they live.
1–2	**8. String Shapes—Properties of Sides** Students work in groups using a loop of string to investigate parallel and equilateral sides in polygons.
1–2	**9. String Shapes—Properties of Angles** Students work in groups using a loop of string to investigate equal, right, and opposite angles in polygons.
2	**10. In Other Words—Improving Your Plans** Students apply what they've learned about the properties of shapes to improve their building plans. They are assessed on their improvements.
Section 4: Visualizing and Representing Polygons and Polyhedra	
2	**11. Beyond Boxes—Designing Polyhedra** Students explore various kinds of closed, three-dimensional structures by experimenting with combinations of polygons.
1–2	**12. Drawing Tricks—Prisms and Pyramids** Students explore methods for showing depth in representations of three-dimensional structures, including prisms and pyramids.
2–3	**13. Mystery Structures** Given written and visual clues, students work in groups to build polyhedra from polygons.
2–4	**14. Final Project—Putting the Pieces Together** Students design a house for a specific climate and create a set of building plans and design specifications.

However, if you do not have enough time to do the whole unit, we recommend shortening the unit in one of two ways. Choose option A or B below depending on the particular mathematics you would like to emphasize.

A. Focus on Visualization and Geometric Representations

In option A, students spend about half their time building with cubes and exploring different ways to represent their structures, including isometric and orthogonal drawing techniques. The remainder of their time is spent building with shapes and learning a perspective drawing technique for representing prisms and pyramids. The drawing techniques are chosen to encourage visualization of three-dimensional structures. Properties of two- and three-dimensional shapes are not covered.

Section 1: Use as is.

Section 2: Use as is.

Section 3: Cut.

Section 4: Use Lessons 11, 12, and 14. Omit or adapt the questions in Lesson 14 that use unfamiliar geometry concepts from Section 3.

Approximate time: 20 class periods.

B. Focus on Properties and Components of Shapes

In option B, students create more complex houses and building plans, since they use a variety of cutout shapes, instead of cubes. Emphasis is placed on investigating the properties and components of shapes: parallel; equilateral; regular; opposite, right, and equal angles; face; edge; and vertex, for example. While the houses students design in this option are geometrically more interesting than cube structures, students do not explore isometric and orthogonal representations.

Section 1: Use as is.

Section 2: Cut.

Section 3: Use as is.

Section 4: Use as is.

Approximate time: 19 class periods.

Key Features of the Lessons

An overview at the beginning of each section describes how the major mathematical themes are dealt with in the section's lessons. Each section also contains a Teacher Reflection that provides a more detailed picture of the kinds of student-student and student-teacher interactions that occur during the teaching of the unit.

The lessons contain the following elements:

- A brief overview of the lesson's goals and activities.
- The materials needed for the lesson. The reproducible masters for student worksheets are included in Appendix E.
- Preparation guidelines that describe essential steps to take before teaching the lesson.
- A suggested lesson plan outlining steps you might follow in teaching the lesson, with steps labeled to describe the nature of each activity. The key steps in a lesson are often labeled *investigation* or *problem solving*. An investigation is an open-ended and extended inquiry, in which students determine their own approaches and find their own solutions. Problem solving focuses on a question with a somewhat smaller scope and more specific parameters, but one that still requires students to devise their own solutions. Where relevant, the lesson steps include To the Student boxes containing information students must have to complete the activities.
- Suggestions for ways to introduce key terms. Several lessons in the unit contain mathematical terms that may be unfamiliar to your students. These terms are identified at the beginning of the lesson. Students encounter the terms as they work through the lesson and begin to develop their own understanding of each term's meaning. In the last step of the lesson, labeled *Writing: Add to the Glossary,* students create descriptions of the terms using examples drawn from the activities in the lesson, or provided in illustrations. Students share their descriptions and then the class discusses and refines them. This discussion leads to a class-generated definition of the term, which is added to the class glossary—a chart or poster containing the key terms and the class definitions. The poster serves as a reference for the class throughout the unit.
- From the Classroom vignettes. The lesson plans contain stories from teachers who taught *Designing Spaces* during the field-test phase of the unit's development. Some of the From the Classroom vignettes are a composite of several teachers' experiences, while others reflect what happened in one

teacher's classroom. The vignettes include such things as actual student work from the field test; stories of how an activity played out with one group of students; and teachers' descriptions of key moments—and key struggles—in student learning.

- Sample student work. Many of the lessons contain examples of actual student work that were gathered during the unit's field test. The extended examples of student work in Lessons 6 and 10 have been retyped to make them more legible and, in some cases, to create a composite of work produced by two different students.

- Answer Keys for questions and To the Student activities requiring answers that may not be self-evident.

- Criteria to help you assess your students' work. See Assessing Students' Progress on page xxvii for more information on assessment.

- Homework Possibilities. Each lesson plan ends with suggestions for activities that work well for homework. These optional activities reinforce and extend the material covered in the lesson. You can choose from a collection of activities for the purposes of practice, problem solving, writing about mathematics, and making connections. These different options will help you assign activities that are consistent with your homework policy and suited to your students' needs. Some activities are intended for individual work, while others are appropriate for group work. Activities labeled *Extensions* provide additional challenges at various levels of difficulty. Some of the extension activities may be used with students who need more practice, while others are most appropriate for students who would like a higher-level challenge.

- Multicultural Perspectives. The STM curriculum provides multicultural perspectives on mathematics in two ways: (1) The STM curriculum is designed to be "culturally open"—to create opportunities in the math classroom for students to bring their own experiences to bear, whatever their background and culture. For example, during the *Designing Spaces* field test, students from other countries designed houses based upon those in their homeland. They then shared with their classmates information about those houses and the climate and life in their homeland. In other classrooms, students interviewed parents and grandparents about their childhood homes and brought back stories and photos illustrating life in other time periods and cultures. In both examples, the students' own experience is relevant to the lesson and can be used to enhance the mathematics being taught. (2) There are lessons in which mathematical contributions from different cultures are researched and incorporated into the activities. For example, as part of their investigation of the functions and properties of shape in *Designing Spaces*, students learn how people from various cultures have designed homes that provide shelter from heavy rain, desert heat, or bitter cold and snow.

Materials to Obtain

The materials you will need to teach *Designing Spaces* are listed below. Most teachers have found it helpful to collect and/or prepare these materials before they start the unit.

Per class

- A paper cup, or other simple cylindrical object (two or three identical examples).
- A book, or other simple object with edges and vertices (two or three identical examples).
- Six to eight objects of different shapes (such as an orange, a glass, a chalkboard eraser, a stapler, a banana).
- A roll of masking tape.
- A couple of rulers, yardsticks, or metersticks, or measuring tape.
- Fourteen pieces of 22 cm × 28 cm poster board, oak tag or cardboard—two pieces each of seven different colors, cut into quarters.

Per group of three or four students

- Scissors.
- Loop of string or rope (string is preferable); these can vary from seven to fifteen feet each, depending on how the lesson is taught (see Lesson 8).
- Sets of shapes made from poster board (see above). Sets of the shapes are used for five of the lessons in the unit. The lessons work better if each of the six shapes is a different color. Templates for the six shapes are in Appendix D. You can prepare the shapes by photocopying the shape template onto card stock, or any other sturdy paper that will work in your photocopier. Alternatively you can have students glue copies of the shape template onto poster board and cut them out.
- Transparent tape.

Per student

- Blank sheets of paper.
- At least eight cubic blocks approximately one inch on a side (wooden cubes, sugar cubes, number cubes, Unifix cubes, etc.).
- Photocopies of reproducible worksheets.

Optional

- Graph paper.
- Modeling clay.
- Overhead projector.
- Protractors.
- A quarter-sheet of poster board or cardboard (base of final house).
- A one-sixth sheet of poster board or cardboard (for the additional shape in Lesson 14).

Storing the Models

Many of the house models that students build during the unit may need to be stored safely for several days while students create and revise their building plans. A good way to handle storage is to give each student a nine-by-twelve envelope at the beginning of the unit. Students write their names on the envelope and then store all of their work inside. Models made from paper cubes or cardboard shapes can be folded and stored flat by cutting the tape of a few of the edges. You can also use the envelope as a way to keep track of students' progress by attaching a checklist to the outside of the envelope for students to fill out as they complete activities.

Computer Possibilities

Designing Spaces is not accompanied by computer software, but there are a number of available programs that can provide good extensions and supplements to the unit. These include:

- *Building Perspective,* which provides good computer-based activities on orthogonal representations. This program is easy to use and provides an excellent extension of Lesson 5.
- *Logo,* or any similar program with turtle graphics, which provides a computer-based language for exploring properties of shapes. Students familiar with *Logo* can use it to create shapes to fit the clues in Lessons 8 and 9 as a replacement or

extension of the work with paper-and-pencil or string shapes. A more advanced use of *Logo* is to write *Logo* procedures to draw prisms and pyramids, as an extension for Lesson 12. Advanced *Logo* students can also explore creating procedures for making isometric and orthogonal drawings.

- Geometry construction programs, such as *The Geometric Supposer, Geometer's Sketchpad,* and *Geometry Inventor,* which enable students to make geometric constructions on the screen. These programs can be used to create shapes to fit the clues in Lessons 8 and 9 and to create prism and pyramid representations in Lesson 12. Most students will find these programs to be simpler to use than *Logo.*

Students can also use computer-aided design (CAD) programs, such as *Three-Dimensional Home Architect* and *Kid Cad.* While these programs provide powerful design tools, they are not designed to help students learn mathematics, and so are best used for optional projects following the unit.

Building Perspectives, The Geometric Supposer, and *Geometry Inventor* are available from Sunburst Communications, Pleasantville, NY. *Geometer's Sketchpad* is available from Key Curriculum Press, Berkeley, CA. Versions of *Logo* are available from several publishers. *Three-Dimensional Home Architect* is available from Broderbund Software, San Rafael, CA. *Kid Cad* is available from Davidson Associates, Torrance, CA.

Assessing Student Progress

Teachers in middle school mathematics classrooms today are using many assessment techniques. In addition to quizzes and tests, these include observations, embedded assessment problems, journal writing, portfolios, interviews, student self-assessments, and group assessments. This unit provides opportunities and support for many of these assessment techniques.

The activities in this unit marked as assessment opportunities gather information for two purposes: to inform daily instructional decisions and to help you monitor students' individual growth over the course of the unit.

From the students' point of view, the assessment activities are similar to other activities in the unit. The activities are designed to give all students an opportunity to demonstrate and apply what they know and can do. They are also designed to allow students to work at their own pace, since speed is almost never relevant to mathematical effectiveness. Most important, all of the assessment activities provide students with an opportunity to learn. In these ways, the assessment activities maintain rather than interrupt the flow of the unit.

You will encounter three types of assessment opportunities over the course of the unit: embedded assessment, student self-assessment, and the final assessment. You may decide to use all of these opportunities, some of these opportunities, or devise your own assessment methods.

Embedded Assessment	Lesson 6 Lesson 10
Student Self-Assessment	Lesson 1 Lesson 5 Lesson 10 Lesson 13 Lesson 14
Final Assessment	Lesson 14

Two of the lessons in the unit, as well as a few activities in other lessons, are identified as good possibilities for embedded assessment. Rather than introduce new content, these activities provide opportunities for students to learn through synthesizing and applying concepts from previous lessons. Lessons 6, 10, and 14 include suggested assessment criteria to facilitate scoring of student work. The assessment criteria can be used in conjunction with the generalized scoring rubric in Appendix B. For an example of how one teacher created a scoring system, see Teacher Reflection One, below.

The unit also provides opportunities for student self-assessment through a series of journal-writing activities spaced throughout the unit. Suggested journal-writing questions, which appear in the Homework Possibilities sections of Lessons 1, 10, and 14, are designed to encourage students to examine not only what they've learned, but how they've learned it. As they explore this connection between process and product, students will begin to think about how they might improve their methods in the future.

The student self-assessment activities—together with the embedded assessments—provide strategically placed opportunities to review and respond to student work and to make adjustments in your teaching. For example, if you receive student work indicating that the class has a good grasp on a central concept in a lesson, you may decide to assign some of the more challenging extension activities. If the class seems to be struggling with a central concept, you may want to help clarify the concept by creating a variation of one of the lesson steps or selecting a practice activity from the Homework Possibilities.

Overall learning for the unit is assessed through a final project (Lesson 14), which consists of a model house, a set of building plans, and "design specifications." The project is an open-ended assignment that provides all students with a creative and authentic application of the mathematical knowledge they have gained in the unit. The lesson plan includes suggested assessment criteria to aid in scoring student work on this project.

Portfolios are another assessment tool that is particularly well suited to the kind of work students produce in this unit. Students select work from throughout the unit to include in their portfolios and write about what they learned from working on each piece. The portfolios provide a vehicle for reviewing and assessing students' progress on both specific and global mathematics goals. For an example of how one teacher implemented the use of portfolios as assessment, see Teacher Reflection Two, below.

Teacher Reflection One: *Using a Scoring Rubric and Assessment Criteria*

Though I had heard a lot about new ways to assess students' understanding, I had never tried any of them before teaching this unit. I decided to try using assessment criteria and a scoring rubric—which I had learned about at a workshop I had attended—to evaluate student work. One of my colleagues, who was teaching the unit at the same time, agreed to use the same techniques. We decided to score our students on the three lessons marked as assessment lessons—6, 10, and 14.

After collecting student work from Lesson 6, we began our scoring by reviewing the assessment criteria in the lesson. We used the criteria to sort the work into three piles: Superior Response, Satisfactory Response, and Unsatisfactory Response. On our first pass through the student work, my colleague and I disagreed on our evaluations of some of the responses. By discussing our reasoning, we were able to reach consensus about the right pile for each response. More important, we learned a lot about what each of us thought constituted good work. I learned that I tended to give higher rankings to work that was neatly done. Since we had not specified neatness as a criteria when we assigned the task, I had to refrain from using it.

In the process of separating the papers into the three piles, we found different levels of work within a category. On our second pass through the papers, we subdivided the categories into two smaller categories—those at the higher end of that category and those at the lower end. We ended up with six piles, which corresponded to the six levels of the scoring rubric. [See Appendix B for a sample scoring rubric.]

We found that students responded to the task in a great variety of ways, and that the criteria and rubric allowed for these differences. For example, we found a few students responded in unexpected ways, but in ways that were consistent with the assignment and the assessment criteria. In such cases, we tried to judge the work on its own terms consistent with the rubric.

I originally thought that the students' papers would divide evenly among the piles. When we completed the assessment, however, we found that an overwhelming majority of the responses were in the Superior or Satisfactory categories. That makes sense to me now; I would like as many of my students as possible to be successful in their work.

The criteria and scoring rubric also helped me provide specific suggestions on each student paper. I think the comments helped a number of students produce even better work on the next assessment activities.

My colleague and I learned a lot about our students and our own expectations by giving this kind of extensive feedback, but we found that we didn't have the time to sustain that level of evaluation for the other assessments. For the next two assessments, we chose one or two aspects to give detailed feedback on—such as the written descriptions of the building process in Lesson 10 and the design specifications in Lesson 14.

I feel that the assessment criteria and scoring rubric allowed me to give a fuller and more accurate picture of what my students understood than a grade would have. Though I still have kinks to work out in the system, I will definitely work on refining it for the future.

Teacher Reflection Two: *Using Portfolios*

I have been working with a number of teachers in my system on using portfolios to assess student work. I found that this approach worked particularly well with this unit. At the start of the unit, I provided each student with a work folder for all the work they produced during the course of the unit. From this work folder, students would select pieces to go into their unit portfolio and their semester-long portfolio (which consisted of the best work students had done on this one large unit and on the smaller units we had worked on during the semester).

I began by evaluating students on the work they produced in Lessons 6, 10, and 14. I used a scoring rubric developed in our state to prepare comprehensive written evaluations and to assign grades to each piece of work. These three graded pieces went into students' work folders along with the other work they were doing in the unit.

At the end of the unit, I gave students time to revise any of their work from the unit and to place it in their mathematics portfolio, which would be a showcase of their work. In their portfolios, students were to include a table of contents, five to seven pieces of their best work (one piece had to be a project and no more than two pieces could be totally group work), a letter to their evaluator describing their strengths and weaknesses, and four illustrative pieces chosen by me.

The students knew that I would give them a written evaluation of their portfolio, along with a grade which would become 25 percent of their semester grade. I told them the breakdown of grades at the beginning of the semester. (All percentages are for work from throughout the semester, including *Designing Spaces,* except for the *Designing Spaces* portfolio.)

30%—An average of grades from all the work in the work folders

15%—*Designing Spaces* portfolio

25%—Semester-long portfolio

10%—My observations

15%—Homework

 5%—Group participation

Students also knew at the outset the seven criteria I would use to evaluate their portfolios: understanding the tasks, how they solved the problems, decisions made along the way, the outcome of the activities, their use of mathematical language, their use of mathematical representation, and their presentation of their portfolio. I included written comments on their work and a response to their letter to the evaluator.

Unlike a standardized test, portfolios are completely within my control. The portfolios gave me useful information about the growth of my students' understanding and abilities, as well as about the depth of my mathematics program. Those benefits were definitely worth the considerable time it took to evaluate the portfolios. Compiling portfolios was also worthwhile for my students because it caused them to reflect on the quality of their own work. I think a knowledge of their own abilities can help students feel more secure and self-reliant.

I showed parents their child's portfolio during parent-teacher conferences. The portfolios gave the parents a good sense of my mathematics program. They were also able to get a much better understanding of the child's work in mathematics than they got when I only had grades to show them. The parents came away knowing the areas of their children's strength and the areas in which their children needed to improve. I think this information helped parents focus their support for their children.

Sources of Further Information

BLACKWELL, WILLIAM. *Geometry in Architecture*. Berkeley: Key Curriculum Press, 1984.

COLE, DORIS. *From Tipi to Skyscraper: A History of Women in Architecture*. Boston: i press, 1973.

DUNN, SUSAN, and LARSON, ROB. *Design Technology (Children's Engineering)*. Bristol, PA: Falmer Press, 1990.

GRIFALCONI, ANN. *The Village of Round and Square Houses*. Boston: Little, Brown, 1986.

ISSACSON, PHILIP. *Round Buildings, Square Buildings, and Buildings that Wiggle Like a Fish*. New York: Alfred Knopf, 1988.

JAMES, ALAN. *Homes in Cold Places*. Minneapolis: Lerner Publications, 1989.

———. *Homes in Hot Places*. Minneapolis: Lerner Publications, 1989.

LEVY, MATTHYS, and SALVADORI, MARIO. *Why Buildings Fall Down*. New York: W. W. Norton, 1992.

MACAULAY, DAVID. *Unbuilding*. Boston: Houghton Mifflin, 1980.

"Movable Houses." *FACES: The Magazine About People*, March, 1985 (entire issue). Peterborough, NH: Cobblestone Publishing.

RICKARD, GRAHAM. *Building Homes*. Minneapolis: Lerner Publications, 1989.

SALVADORI, MARIO. *Building: From Caves to Skyscrapers*. New York: Salvadori Educational Center on the Built Environment, 1979.

SCULLY, VINCENT. *Architecture (The Natural and the Manmade)*. New York: St. Martin's Press, 1991.

WILSON, PATRICIA S., and VERNA M. ADAMS. "A Dynamic Way to Teach Angle and Angle Measure," *Arithmetic Teacher*, January, 1992.

Section 1

Introduction

In this section, which consists only of Lesson 1, students use mathematics to analyze representations and descriptions of houses from around the world. Students solve the Homes Puzzle, which introduces them to the idea of looking at houses as a collection of shapes with various functions. They make connections between orthogonal and perspective drawings of the houses and between the drawings and written clues describing the component shapes and their functions. The completed Homes Puzzle serves as a resource for students throughout the unit. The section also introduces the class glossary, which will guide students in creating definitions of key terms in the unit.

Mathematical Goals

- Identify two- and three-dimensional shapes in real-world objects.
- Identify orthogonal views of a structure.
- Relate the form of a shape to its function in buildings.
- Expand vocabulary for describing shapes and structures.
- Represent structures using orthogonal drawings and drawings showing depth.

Mathematical Theme 1

Multiple Representations of Shapes and Structures

The section introduces students to several different methods of representing houses. As they match perspective drawings of the houses with orthogonal drawings and written descriptions, students discover new ways to analyze three-dimensional

Approx. # of Classes	Lessons
2	**1. Homes Around the World** Students solve the Homes Puzzle by matching illustrations of homes from around the world to corresponding description, view, and shape cards.

Lesson summary and sample schedule for Section 1

structures. They also begin to explore the different uses of various methods of representation.

Mathematical Theme 2

Visualization

When students make connections between the drawings and descriptions of houses in the Homes Puzzle, they are visualizing two-dimensional representations as three-dimensional structures. In identifying orthogonal views and component shapes of houses, students form and manipulate mental images of each structure. In subsequent sections, students will use the skills of visualizing and describing orthogonal views and component shapes of structures to create building plans for their classmates.

Mathematical Theme 3

Properties and Components of Shapes

Lesson 1 provides an opportunity to find out how much students know about the mathematical names and properties of shapes as they begin the unit. After completing the Homes Puzzle, students create a list of all the two- and three-dimensional shapes they can identify in the puzzle clues. The shapes in the puzzle range from triangles, squares, and hexagons to pentagons, cubes, and cylinders. The Homes Puzzle also encourages students to think about the functions of the structures through description clues that explain how the house designs are well suited to the climate, culture, or geography.

Mathematical Theme 4

Communication

Mathematical communication is central to the activities in this section. Students come to view houses within a mathematical framework by learning to communicate about them through various mathematical forms. After interpreting written descriptions and drawings in the Homes Puzzle, students create their own written and visual clues for a new set of house illustrations. In the final activity in the lesson, students use the list of shapes they've identified in the puzzle to construct their own definitions for the terms *two-dimensional* and *three-dimensional*. As the class discusses and refines these definitions, students explore the need for precision in mathematical language.

Teacher Reflection

Identifying Shapes and Properties

I wanted to find out how much my sixth graders knew about shapes at the outset of the unit so that I could plan which concepts to emphasize in the first couple of sections. I handed the students the Homes Puzzle sheet with eight homes on it and asked them what shapes they could see in the houses.

"Triangles," replied Evan. "In the roof of the Russian house."

"And the whole Canada house is made of them!" Drina blurted out.

As the students called out the names of other shapes, I listed them in two columns, one for two-dimensional shapes and the other for three-dimensional shapes. I suspected my students would see and, on some level, understand the difference between the categories. I wondered if they would also have the language to describe the differences.

"There are squares in the Australian house," said Jeremy.

"Those aren't squares, those are rectangles!" responded Drina.

"Squares and rectangles are almost the same thing," Maya casually commented.

I drew a square and two rectangles on the board (Figure 1) and asked: "So, what is the difference?"

Figure 1.

"They all have two pairs of sides that are parallel. The difference is that the sides of a square are all the same size," concluded Evan.

"But squares do have two pairs of sides that are parallel, so they are rectangles. They are just a special kind of rectangle," concluded Maya.

"Right!" I said, making a note to myself that, at this point, the students were focusing exclusively on the properties of sides and ignoring the properties of angles—which is typical of sixth graders. I was glad that the unit would give them the opportunity to explore sides and angles and the relationships between them.

Distinguishing Between Two-dimensional and Three-dimensional

"What other shapes can you see in the houses on the sheet?" I asked.

"That house from the United States looks like it is made of cubes," said Joe.

Since students had studied only two-dimensional shapes in elementary school, I was not surprised that they hadn't mentioned a three-dimensional shape until this point. I started another column on the board and wrote "cubes."

When students stopped naming shapes, we ended up with a list of nine shapes (see Figure 2). I made a note to myself that some of the shapes in the unit—such as trapezoids, rhombi, and prisms—would be new to the students so I would want to plan the lessons accordingly.

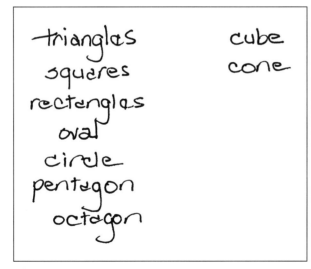

Figure 2.

"Why did I divide this list into two columns?" I asked.

"One is two-dimensional shapes and the other is three-dimensional shapes," said Evan.

"What is a two-dimensional shape?" I asked.

"It is flat, like a circle or a square," said Maya.

"How about three-dimensional?"

"Those are real things, like this desk or a person or the monster in *Godzilla in 3-D!*" said Farisa excitedly.

"Good. I think that you can all pick out examples of shapes that are two- and three-dimensional and you have started forming some ideas of what those terms mean," I said. "I'm going to ask you later to write your own definitions of those terms—so think about that while you work on the puzzle."

After students solved the Homes Puzzle, I asked if they had any new shapes to add to our list.

"Cylinders. The main parts of the castle are cylinders. I think that is where the guards lived, so that they could see all around. The townspeople lived in straw houses inside the walls," said Evan, who had been studying the Middle Ages in social studies.

"Also, the tipi looks kind of like a pyramid," Joe mentioned.

I added "cylinder" and "pyramid" to the list of three-dimensional shapes.

"The house from Canada is a dome," stated Jeremy.

"Good. Does anyone know another word for that shape?" I asked. I wanted to get students thinking about mathematical language without discouraging them from coming up with their names for the shapes.

"Sphere!" exclaimed Drina.

"Well, it is about half a sphere," replied Jeremy.

"That's called a hemisphere," I said.

Creating Mathematical Descriptions

For homework that night, I had students write their own definitions of the terms two- and three-dimensional—including explanations of what the *two* and *three* stood for.

Maya wrote: "Two-dimensional shapes are flat because they only have two dimensions you can measure, how long it is and how wide it is. Three-dimensional shapes are real things because they have three dimensions you can measure. Like you can measure how long it is, how wide it is, and how tall it is."

Daniel wrote: "Two-dimensional is anything on paper. Three-dimensional is everything else around, like the sofa or the TV. The 2 means vertically and horizontally and the 3 means it can be 2 inches high, 2 inches wide, and 2 inches long."

In class the following day, we used the students' descriptions to create a class definition for two-dimensional and three-dimensional. I planned to return to our discussion of the terms at key points in the lessons. I knew that my students' understanding of the terms would improve as they gained experience visualizing and representing shapes.

Lesson 1

Homes Around the World

How can you describe houses from around the world in words, with pictures, and in geometric terms? How are different shapes used in houses to meet the demands of climate and geography?

In this lesson, students complete a Homes Puzzle, which introduces them to the mathematical processes of visualizing, representing, and describing. Students match a picture of a home found somewhere in the world with (1) views of the base, top, or side of the home; (2) descriptions of the home; and (3) shapes that make up the home's structure. Discussion and writing activities based on the puzzle clues help reveal how much students know about shapes, views, and geometric concepts as they begin the unit. The final activity introduces students to the class glossary they will work on throughout the unit. They begin the glossary by creating definitions for the terms *two-dimensional* and *three-dimensional.*

The Homes Puzzle is designed to serve as a resource for students in subsequent lessons. The images of houses from around the world will give students ideas for the house models they design for different climates (Lessons 7 and 14). Students will also use the clues containing views and descriptions of shapes as they write about the function and properties of their house designs.

In Section 2, students learn to make and compare orthogonal and isometric drawings similar to the ones shown in the puzzle clues.

Mathematical Goals

- Identify two- and three-dimensional shapes in real-world objects.
- Identify orthogonal views of a structure.
- Relate the form of a shape to its function in buildings.
- Expand vocabulary for describing shapes and structures.
- Represent structures using orthogonal drawings and drawings showing depth.

Materials

Per Student	Per Group	Per Class
Reproducible 4, *More Homes*	Blank sheets of 8.5″ × 11″ paper	Reproducible 3, *Rules for the Homes Puzzle* (optional transparency)
	Scissors	
	Glue or tape	
	Reproducible 2, *Homes Puzzle* (four sheets)	
	Reproducible 3, *Rules for the Homes Puzzle*	

Suggested Lesson Plan

At the end of this lesson, students will add the terms *two-dimensional* and *three-dimensional* to the class glossary. As you work through the lesson, look for opportunities to draw out students' understanding of these concepts. See page xxi of the unit overview for suggestions on how to teach key terms in the unit.

1. Introduction: *Identify two- and three-dimensional shapes in homes.*

Ask students to list all of the shapes they can find in the homes shown on the first page of the *Homes Puzzle* (Reproducible 2). What are the shapes of the overall buildings? the roofs? the walls? the floors? the doors and windows?

As students call out shape names, write them on the board in two unlabeled columns. List all of the two-dimensional shapes that students identify in one column and all of the three-dimensional shapes in the other column. After students have named all the shapes they found, ask them to describe the difference between the two columns.

> Reproducible 2

▶ From the Classroom

We also discussed the shapes in homes students had lived in and compared them to the homes shown on the sheet. Some students who were born in different countries brought in photographs and illustrations of homes they had lived in throughout the world. That really opened up our discussion of different kinds of house designs.

These lists will help prepare students for Step 5, when they will begin to construct definitions for the concepts of *two-dimensional* and *three-dimensional*. The list of shapes also serves as an assessment of how much students know about shapes as they begin the unit.

2. Problem solving: *Solve the Homes Puzzle.*

The *Homes Puzzle* (Reproducible 2) encourages students to think both about houses as a collection of shapes and about the functions of various shapes. Students consider, for example, why a dome-shaped house is well suited to an extremely cold climate. The puzzle also provides an introduction to the kind of collaborative, hands-on problem solving that students will do throughout the unit.

Working in groups of two to four, students match pictures of homes from around the world with views of the top, base, or side of each home; descriptions of the homes; and shapes that can be found in each home.

Reproducibles 2 & 3

► **From the Classroom**

I have a number of students with limited English proficiency, so I created a version of the game that involved less reading. I removed the Descriptions and Shapes sheets and asked students to match the pictures of the homes with the views. Then I asked students to make their own shape clues by listing or drawing all the shapes they could find in each home.

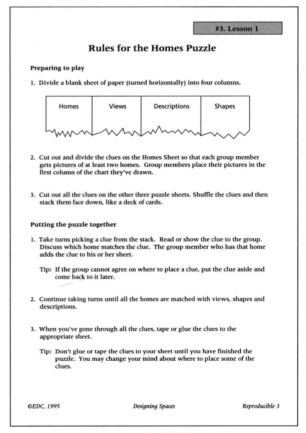

Reproducible 3.

If students do not know what a geometric term means, they may ask their classmates or look it up in a reference book. Save the finished chart to use as a resource throughout the unit.

The solution to the puzzle is provided at the end of this lesson.

3. Sharing: *Why are different houses shaped differently?*

The following questions help introduce the connection between the shape and functions of a house. This discussion will help students design and describe their own homes later in the unit. You may want to have students discuss the questions in pairs or groups and then report back to the class.

- Choose one home on the sheet. Discuss how the shape of this house fits the needs of the people who inhabit it.
- What are the most common shapes for houses in your area? Why do you think these shapes are used?
- Why do we find different shapes for houses when we look at pictures of homes from other parts of the world or different time periods? Describe some specific examples.

4. Investigation: *Design your own puzzle pieces.*

More Homes (Reproducible 4) contains pictures and descriptions of additional homes from the United States. Ask students to design view and shape puzzle pieces for two or more of the homes. This activity provides a good assessment of students' understanding of views and their ability to describe shapes. It also works well for homework.

Instead of using the homes on the *More Homes* sheet, students may want to make their own puzzle pieces by drawing their own homes or cutting out pictures from old magazines and postcards. These illustrations may include homes from countries or time periods that students are studying in social studies.

5. Discussion: *Begin a class glossary for the unit.*

Introduce the concept of a class glossary by identifying and discussing some key geometric concepts and terms from the Homes Puzzle, such as shape names and *two-dimensional* and *three-dimensional*. Have individual or small groups of students write descriptions of what is meant by the terms *two-*

▶ **From the Classroom**

I wanted to build on the multicultural connections in this lesson to provide a broader perspective for my class, which was not very culturally diverse. I provided students with old copies of National Geographic, Architectural Digest, *and* Life *magazine and encouraged them to think about the rich variety of house designs from different times and places. I had each student choose a house from a different culture and create a set of puzzle clues. We then played the Homes Puzzle with the student-made cards.*

▶ *I put up a large world climate map and asked students to find the location of each home. Students referred to the map many times over the course of the unit.*

I found that my students could easily identify examples of things that were three-dimensional (a basketball, a shoe). They also correctly identified squares and circles as two-dimensional shapes. However, they told me that a piece of paper was a two-dimensional object. At this point, I asked them what the difference was between a two-dimensional shape and a three-dimensional shape. After much discussion, the class agreed that a three-dimensional shape was one that you could hold, while you could only draw a two-dimensional shape. Then I asked what the "two" and the "three" stood for. One student mentioned that in 3-D movies the three meant that the things in the movie "came out at you; they weren't flat." I asked my students if a piece of paper was three-dimensional; they replied that it was since you could hold it. As we worked through the lessons, I found that students' understanding of the two concepts became a lot clearer.

dimensional and *three-dimensional*. Ask them to look back at the two lists of shapes the class created in Step 1 and think about such questions as:

• What do the two-dimensional shapes have in common?
• What do the three-dimensional shapes have in common?
• How are the two-dimensional shapes different from the three-dimensional ones?

Ask a couple of students from different groups to share their descriptions, and have the class discuss and refine definitions to add to the glossary.

Students will work with the concepts of two-dimensional and three-dimensional in almost every lesson of the unit. In Section 2, for example, students will learn to make two-dimensional representations of three-dimensional structures. You may want to refine the definitions the class comes up with as you work through the unit. At some point in the unit, for example, you may want to help students arrive at an understanding of what the "two" and "three" refer to in two-dimensional and three-dimensional.

A related point that you may need to explain to students during the course of the unit is the difference between *three-dimensional shapes* and *three-dimensional representations*. An illustration can never be three-dimensional, since it is drawn in two dimensions. Illustrations can, however, represent three dimensions by showing depth.

Homework Possibilities

Problem Solving

The activity described in Step 4 is well suited for homework.

Making Connections

Have students create four cards describing the structure they live in or another structure in their neighborhood: a picture of the building, a description card, a shape card, and a view card.

Journal Writing

Suggestions for journal writing appear in key lessons throughout the unit. The basic set of questions that follows encourages students to reflect on and communicate about what they've learned. (See page xxv for further discussion of journal writing in the unit.)

- What was the lesson about?
- Explain one math idea or concept taught in this lesson. Give an example.
- Which parts of the lesson were hard or frustrating? What did you do well as you worked on the lesson?
- What questions do you have at this point? Would you like help on any of them?

Answer Key: Homes Puzzle

Homes	Views	Descriptions	Shapes
A. Russia	b	3	IV
B. Canada	f	5	VII
C. Australia	h	4	I
D. Kenya	g	8	VI
E. England	a	1	V
F. Indonesia	d	7	II
G. United States	e	6	VIII
H. United States	c	2	III

Visualizing and Representing Cube Structures

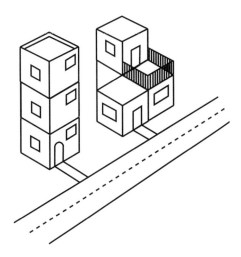

In Section 2, students develop, explore, and compare different methods for representing three-dimensional structures in two-dimensional drawings. Throughout the section, students build and represent a variety of modular houses made from cubes. (Cube structures are used in this section because they are relatively easy to represent.)

In Lesson 2, students build a modular house and create a set of building plans that includes drawings of the house and a written description of the building process. For this first set of plans, students create their own methods of representation. In Lessons 3–5, students learn to use isometric and orthogonal drawing techniques to represent their houses, and in Lesson 6 students apply these techniques when they revise their original building plans. Students interpret different methods of representations by building from each other's plans.

Students also find all of the possible houses that can be made with three and four cubes. As students try to show that they have found all of the possible cube combinations, they gain experience justifying a mathematical assertion.

Mathematical Goals

- Create two-dimensional representations of three-dimensional structures.

Approx. # of Classes	Lessons
2–3	**2. Planning and Building a Modular House** Students design modular houses and represent their designs in building plans. They create their own methods of representation and compare them to a classmate's methods.
1–2	**3. Seeing Around the Corners—Isometric Drawings** Students find all the possible houses that can be made with three cubes. After experimenting further with their own methods of representation, students learn to use isometric drawings to represent their structures.
2–3	**4. Seeing All the Possibilities** Students find all the houses that can be made with four cubes and represent them isometrically. They then use isometric drawings to match rotations of different cube combinations.
2	**5. Seeing All Sides—Orthogonal Drawings** Students translate orthogonal drawings into (1) modular houses and (2) isometric drawings. They then learn to translate isometric drawings into orthogonal drawings.
2–3	**6. Picture This—Improving Your Drawings** Students redo their building plans from Lesson 2 to include isometric and orthogonal drawings. Students build from each other's plans and give feedback on their partner's plans. Students' building plans are assessed.

Lesson summary and sample schedule for Section 2

- Compare and contrast various methods for showing three dimensions in two-dimensional representations.
- Visualize and build three-dimensional structures from two-dimensional representations.
- Visualize arrangements of cubes.
- Use and create isometric and orthogonal drawings of cube structures.
- Translate between orthogonal drawings and isometric drawings.
- Visualize rotations of cube structures.
- Develop arguments that all possible cube combinations have been found.
- Communicate properties of a structure through written descriptions.

Mathematical Theme 1

Throughout the section, students investigate the relationships among various kinds of representations of cube structures. Students make comparisons among their own methods of representation and the isometric and orthogonal drawing techniques they learn in Lessons 3 and 5. They also create written

Multiple Representations of Shapes and Structures

descriptions of their structures, and they begin to think about the different uses of words and drawings. That comparison of the usefulness of different methods of representation becomes clearer to students in Lesson 6 when they attempt to build replicas of another student's house using plans comprising isometric drawings, orthogonal drawings, and written descriptions. The activity encourages students to explore not only how the methods contrast with one another, but also how they complement one another. As students explore the interplay of multiple representations, they learn to use one method to interpret the others.

Mathematical Theme 2

Visualization

Creating and exploring methods for representing cube structures strengthens students' ability to visualize three-dimensional objects. Students compare various techniques developed in the class and discuss different ways to show depth in two-dimensional drawings. They then learn to make isometric and orthogonal drawings and to translate between the two, as well as investigate the relationship between the drawings and the cube structures. The process of interpreting and making orthogonal drawings teaches students to visualize structures from different vantage points. Students apply the ability to interpret drawings and written descriptions when they build a house from another student's plans.

Students engage in another kind of visualization when they find all of the possible cube combinations that can be made from three or four cubes. Students use isometric drawings to help them visualize which combinations of cubes are rotations of each other.

Mathematical Theme 3

Properties and Components of Shape

Students explore a variety of two-dimensional shapes—and the relationship between shapes—as they visualize and represent three-dimensional objects and structures from different vantage points. Students discover, for example, that both circles and rectangles can be used to create orthogonal drawings of a roll of masking tape. When they make and interpret isometric drawings of cube structures, they see how different shapes are used to represent the square faces of the cubes in order to show depth. (These ideas are explored further in Section 4, when students learn new techniques for showing depth in representations of various three-dimensional structures.)

Communication

Throughout the section, students learn to communicate through various methods and for various purposes. In creating a set of building plans, students use drawings and written descriptions to explain how to replicate a house they've designed. The focus of the building plans activities in this section is on visual communication, as students develop and learn various techniques for representing three-dimensional structures in two dimensions. The written descriptions in the building plans lay the groundwork for Section 3, when students learn new terms and concepts that will help them describe their building process in increasingly precise, mathematical language.

In addition to describing and representing their houses, students communicate their mathematical reasoning and reflect on their learning. In Lessons 3 and 4, for example, students create drawings and verbal explanations to explain how they know they have found all of the houses that can be made with three or four cubes. They comment further on their thought process, along with their feelings and questions about the material, in a journal that they will keep throughout the unit. The series of journal questions is designed to help students clarify their thinking about the material and their feelings about the progress they are making.

Finally, students investigate effective ways of communicating feedback to their classmates when they provide suggestions on a partner's building plans.

Teacher Reflection

Finding Combinations of Cubes

The first activity in Lesson 4—finding all of the modular houses (or combinations of cubes) that could be made with four cubes—provided an engaging challenge for my students. They spent a whole period searching for the combinations and then recording them on isometric dot paper.

The next day, I handed back their representations of the combinations of cubes and distributed cubes. "How do you know you've found all of the possible combinations?" I asked.

Using A Systematic Approach

"Well, the way I checked mine," responded Katie, "was that first I found all of the houses that were one story high. There are seven of those." (See Figure 1.) Katie drew each of these houses on the board. The other students checked off their own drawings of these houses on their own work.

Figure 1. Examples of Katie's one-story houses.

Figure 2. Examples of Katie's two-story houses.

Figure 3. Katie's three-story house.

Figure 4. Katie's four-story house.

Figure 5. Caleb's house.

Figure 6. Caleb's fifteenth house.

Figure 7. Todd's house.

"Next," continued Katie, "I found all of the ones that had two stories. There are six of those." (See Figure 2.) "Then I found all of the ones that could be made with three stories. There is only one of those." (See Figure 3.) "And, finally I found all of the ones that had four stories. Of course, there is only one of those. Add this up and I found fifteen possible houses." (See Figure 4.)

Katie's method of finding all of the possible combinations was very systematic. It allowed her to find all of the combinations in a short amount of time and with very little repetition. Her system was a good one to use as the class reviewed all of the combinations, since it was easy for the students to scan across their papers and find the one- and then the two-story houses. However, I held off praising Katie on her system. I wanted other students to share their strategies without feeling like Katie's was the "right one." And I wanted my students to see that there are many ways that this problem can be solved successfully.

So, I asked: "Did anyone find any other possible combinations?"

"Yes," said Caleb, "I found this one." Caleb drew it on the board (see Figure 5).

Visualizing Rotations

"Hey, wait a minute," Renee interjected. "I think the one Caleb just showed is the same as one of the two-story ones that Katie showed. Look, you can just rotate his around and you get the other one."

Caleb sighed since he was now down to only fourteen solutions. Renee looked at his drawings and said: "But you only have one laying down L-shaped house and Katie has two." She quickly demonstrated her point with the cubes (see Figure 6). "They can't be turned to become each other. So they count as two combinations." Caleb happily wrote down another combination; he was back up to fifteen combinations.

"I found a sixteenth combination," said Todd as he drew one of his combinations on the board (see Figure 7).

"Todd, your sixteenth combination is another laying down T, but you can rotate it to become Katie's laying down T," responded Kareem.

"You're right," said a deflated Todd. "There are only fifteen combinations."

"Do you now all think that there are only fifteen combinations?" I asked.

"Yes, because I got fifteen combinations and I did it another way," responded Renee. "I found all of the ones that could be made from two cubes laying down in a row with the other two cubes attached in different ways; there were eight of those." (See Figure 8.) "Then," continued Renee, "I found the houses that could be made with three in a row with the other cube attached in different ways; there were five of those." (See Figure 9.) "Then I checked four in a row—there was only one of these, of course, with all four cubes laying down in a row. And, then I remembered to count the one that only had one on the ground and three on top of that. That makes fifteen," finished Renee.

"Yeah," agreed Kareem, "I did it that way too. At first I thought I had found a lot more combinations, but then I saw that some of them were just rotations of the other ones."

Using a Geometric Pattern

"Did anyone try another strategy for finding the combinations?" I asked.

"I used one cube and found all the houses that could be built off of one face of that one cube, then I put two cubes standing up and found all of the combinations that could be built off of each face of that," said Todd. "This way is kind of like Katie's way except that I counted off each face of the stories. So, I had a lot more possible combinations and then I had a lot more to cross out as rotations. Anyway, I found fifteen combinations, too. So I think that there are only fifteen combinations."

Like Katie, Todd had used a systematic method of finding all of the cube combinations. His method was based on a geometric pattern involving the surface area of the cubes. The other thing that impressed me about Todd's reasoning was that he had recognized that his method was more time-consuming than the others.

I was excited by the different strategies my students had used to find the combinations of cubes. I was also glad that the students understood that "fifteen" was only part of the answer and that they had to communicate their strategy to their classmates. I was pleased to see how successful they were at communicating their strategies to each other.

Figure 8. Examples of Renee's houses made starting with two cubes.

Figure 9. Examples of Renee's houses made starting with three cubes.

Lesson 2

Planning and Building a Modular House

How can you draw a house model that you built from cubes? How can you show depth in your drawings?

In this lesson, students investigate how various kinds of drawing can be used to communicate about objects and structures. They experiment with their own techniques for drawing everyday objects and then move on to drawing a modular house they have built from cubes. As students compare drawing techniques, they explore different ways to visualize and describe three-dimensional structures in two dimensions.

Students complete their building plans by writing a description of how they built their houses. In Lesson 6, students will revise the plans they make in this lesson to incorporate the isometric and orthogonal drawing techniques they learn in Lessons 3, 4, and 5.

Students will make and revise two other sets of building plans later in the unit, as they learn new ways to communicate about shapes and structures.

Mathematical Goals

- Create two-dimensional representations of three-dimensional structures.
- Compare and contrast various methods for showing three dimensions in two-dimensional representations.
- Visualize and build three-dimensional structures from two-dimensional representations.

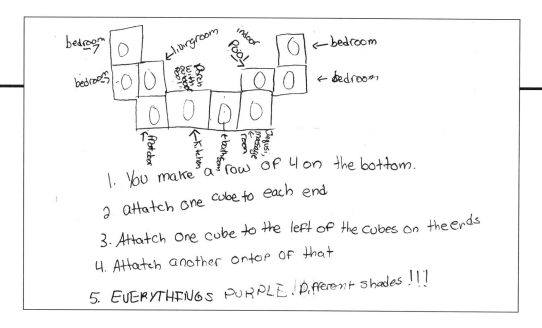

bedroom → □ ← livingroom   indoor pool → □ ← bedroom

bedroom → □ □   [sets of stairs]   □ □ ← bedroom

□ □ □ □

↑ porch ↑ kitchen ↑ bathroom ↑ dining/mud room

1. You make a row of 4 on the bottom.

2. attatch one cube to each end

3. Attatch one cube to the left of the cubes on the ends

4. Attatch another ontop of that

5. EVERYTHINGS PURPLE! Different shades !!!

Materials

Per Student

Set of 8–10 cubes, about one inch on a side (wooden cubes, sugar cubes, number cubes, etc.)

Graph paper (optional)

Glue, rubber cement, or tape (optional, for making cubes)

Reproducible 6, *Many Modular Methods* (optional)

Per Class

Four different objects representing a variety of two- and three-dimensional shapes, such as a chalkboard eraser, a sugar cone for ice cream, a coffee mug, a banana, a ball, or an egg

Reproducible 5, *Memo 1 to House Designers* (transparency)

Suggested Lesson Plan

At the end of this lesson, students will add the term *face* to the class glossary. As you work through the lesson plan, look for opportunities to draw out students' understanding of this concept. See page xxi of the unit overview for suggestions on how to teach the key terms in the unit.

1. Drawing: *Visualize and sketch common objects.*

Students choose their own techniques for sketching everyday objects and then compare their sketches with their classmates' sketches. This activity encourages students to think about different ways to represent three-dimensional objects before they begin building and sketching a modular house.

Choose four objects that will give students the opportunity to represent a variety of two-dimensional and three-dimensional shapes: an eraser, a sugar cone, a ball, and a coffee mug, for example.

Display the objects before students begin sketching and then put them away so that students must visualize the objects as they sketch. When everyone is done, have the class compare drawing techniques by discussing questions such as:

- Which objects were sketched the same way by everyone?
- Which objects were sketched in different ways? How did the sketches differ?
- What are the most common two-dimensional shapes in the sketches?
- Can you find two objects that look the same from certain views but different from other views?
- Do any of the sketches show depth? How?

Introduce the concept of depth by contrasting sketches that show depth with those that don't. You may also want to refer back to the illustrations in the Homes Puzzle from Lesson 1. Students will explore this contrast extensively in Lessons 3, 4, and 5.

2. Investigation: *Design a modular house using cubes.*

Students create a modular house, which they will go on to represent by using some of the drawing techniques they tried in Step 1. The transparency *Memo 1 to House Designers* (Reproducible 5) introduces students' role as house designers and describes the task of designing a low-cost house using just eight to ten cubes.

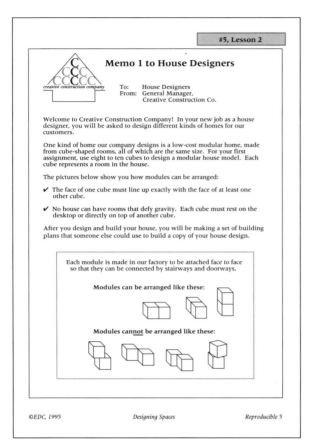

Reproducible 5.

Students use cubes to build this first house model because cube structures are relatively easy to represent. To help students think of the cubes as parts of a house, spend some time discussing the idea of a modular house. Refer back to the Homes Puzzle clues for a description and a picture of a modular house (see H. United States on the homes page and III on the shapes page).

You can reinforce the context of modular houses by asking students to think about the function of their design:

• How many people will live in this house?
• What rooms do you want to include?
• How should the rooms be arranged? For example, where would you put the kitchen or bathroom?

You'll notice that some of the student work shown and described in this lesson defies the "gravity constraint" in Memo 1. These samples were drawn from classes in which the houses were built from cubes that snapped together (Unifix cubes) and the gravity constraint was omitted.

► From the Classroom

Many of my students got very involved in imagining their house—labeling all the rooms and adding elaborate details. That helped other students think of the structures they were building as real homes.

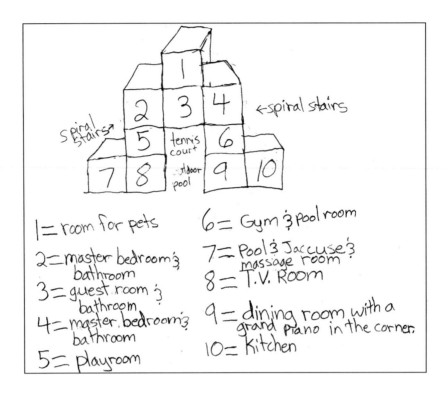

1 = room for pets

2 = master bedroom & bathroom

3 = guest room & bathroom

4 = master bedroom & bathroom

5 = playroom

6 = Gym & pool room

7 = Pool & Jaccuse & massage room

8 = T.V. Room

9 = dining room with a grand piano in the corner.

10 = Kitchen

► From the Classroom

I invited an architect to come speak to the class about the kinds of drawings she uses. She brought along a set of blueprints and described how they are drawn and how to read some of the information on them. The class was very interested in the blueprints. I heard several students refer back to some of her comments over the next few days as they made their drawings.

► From the Classroom

A few of my students had difficulty figuring out how to draw their houses. After giving them some time to develop their own methods, I suggested that they draw the structure from the top view and then label how many cubes are in each stack:

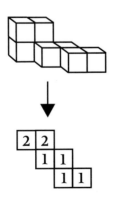

3. Investigation: *Make a set of plans for your house design.*

Students develop methods for drawing and describing their house models.

TO THE STUDENT

Make a set of plans that another student could use to build your model house. The plans should include:

- At least one drawing of the house.
- A description of the steps someone would follow to build the house.

► **From the Classroom**

My students' sketches showed a range of methods and abilities. Natasha tried to copy the kind of 3-D drawings that her friends were doing, but she had some difficulty. Anna kept the shapes from getting too distorted by using the lines on her notebook paper as a guide. Megan made up her own method of tracing one face of the cubes first as a way of keeping her drawing to scale. She eventually abandoned tracing in favor of drawing the cubes freehand.

Natasha's example.

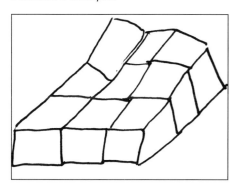

Anna's example.

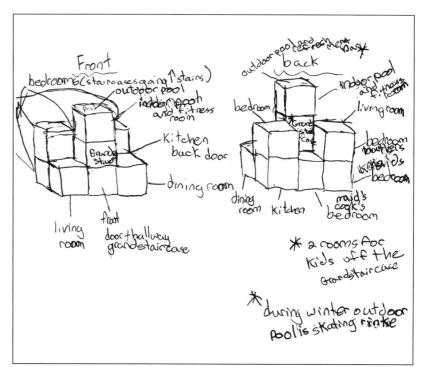

Megan's example.

4. Sharing: *Compare how you represented your structures.*

Pairs of students compare their building plans. Ask students to discuss the following questions and record their responses:

- How do the drawings differ? How are they similar?
- Which of the drawings show depth? How is the depth shown in the drawing?
- Which houses could you build just from looking at the drawings?
- Are some of the drawings difficult to understand? What suggestions would you give the person to make his or her drawing clearer?

▶ *From the Classroom*

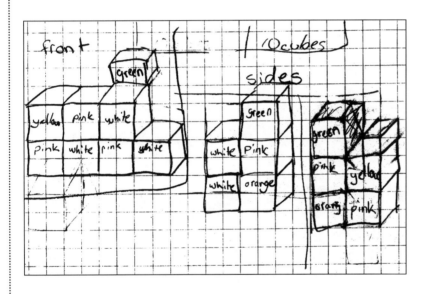

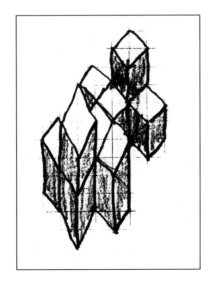

From the Classroom

Using Unifix cubes, one boy created a house with an eight-cube bottom layer with a hole in the center, and a two-cube upper layer (cube #10 sits on top of #5, #9 sits on top of the hole):

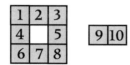

I overheard his partner say, "You should have done a bottom view so I could see there was a space." So he revised his drawings to include a bottom view.

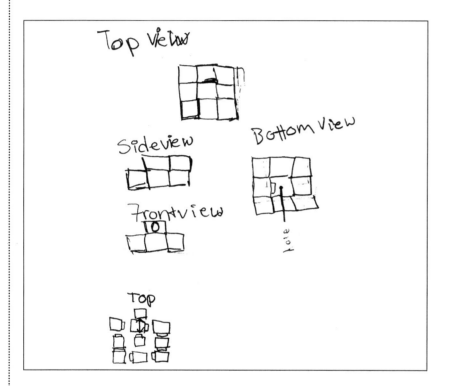

Usually three views are sufficient, but in this case, four were needed. I decided from that interchange to spend a little time in class talking about how many views were needed to show a structure accurately.

5. Writing: *Add to the glossary.*

Have groups of three or four students use the illustrations on *Memo 1 to House Designers* to write a description of what is meant by the term *face*.

Ask a few students from different groups to write their descriptions on the board and then have the class discuss and refine a definition to add to the glossary.

Homework Possibilities

Writing

If students haven't written a description of what is meant by the term *face* in class, have individuals or small groups write descriptions for homework. One student's pictorial representation of "face" is shown below.

Face
a face is a place where a flat surface, fully meets another flat surface forming a strong build. a face is a flat surface of a 3-D object.

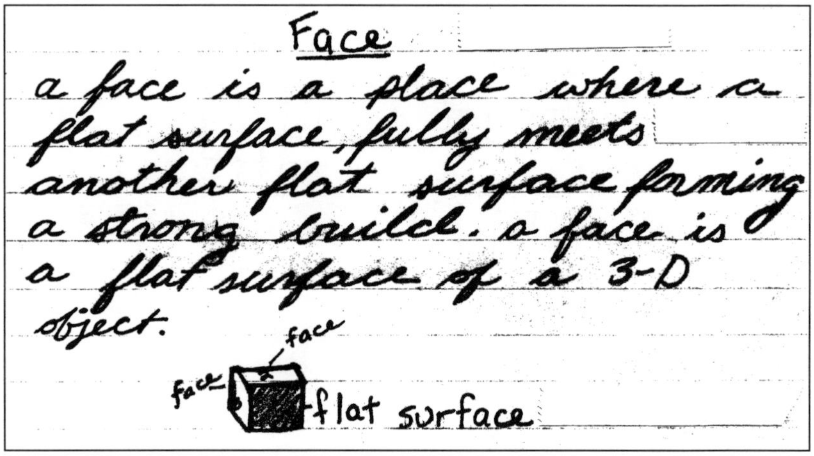

Practice

Use *Many Modular Methods* (Reproducible 6) to have students practice and compare drawing methods.

Making Connections

Have students find some illustrations in real estate magazines or the real estate section of the newspaper that represent houses or buildings in different ways. Have them find examples of a few different methods and ask them to write about why they think each method was used.

Lesson 3

Seeing Around the Corners— Isometric Drawings

How can you record all of the possible modular houses that can be made with three cubes? How can you use isometric drawings to represent cube structures?

In this lesson, students continue to explore different methods for representing modular houses. They find all of the possible modular houses that can be made with three cubes and compare techniques for recording the various designs. They then learn how to use isometric drawings to represent several sides of a structure in one sketch.

Students will use isometric drawings in Lesson 4 to record all of the modular houses that can be made with four cubes and to explore how structures look from different vantage points. In Lesson 5, students will make comparisons between isometric and orthogonal drawings. They will use both methods of representation in Lesson 6 when they revise their building plans from Lesson 2.

Mathematical Goals

- Visualize arrangements of cubes.
- Develop methods for representing cube structures.
- Use isometric representations.

Materials

Per Student

At least three cubic blocks

Reproducible 7, *Memo 2 to House Designers*

Reproducible 8, *Making Isometric Drawings*

Reproducible 9, *Isometric Dot Paper*

Reproducible 10, *Visual Glossary: Isometric Drawings*

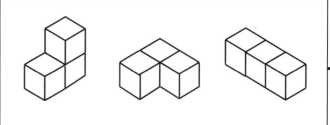

Suggested Lesson Plan

At the end of this lesson, students will add the term *isometric drawing* to the class glossary. As you work through the lesson plan, look for opportunities to draw out students' understanding of this concept. See page xxi of the unit overview for suggestions on how to teach the key terms in the unit.

1. Problem solving: *Build modular houses with three cubes.*

In *Memo 2 to House Designers* (Reproducible 7), students are asked to build as many different houses as they can with three cubes. Students develop methods for sketching the houses. Later in the lesson, they will consider the strengths and weaknesses of different recording methods and learn to make isometric drawings.

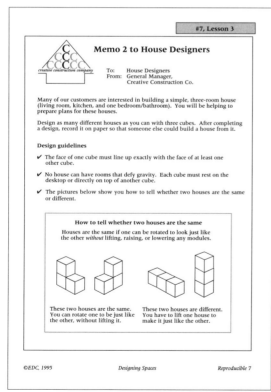

Reproducible 7.

2. Discussion: *How many houses did you build and how did you record them?*

Students reflect on the thought process they used to find the different cube combinations and to create a recording method. Having students exchange papers during the discussion highlights the differences between recording methods. As students examine their classmate's drawings, they will think about how clear their own records must be for others to use them. Some questions to begin the discussion include:

- How many houses did you build? How did you know when you had found all of the possible cube combinations?
- How did you record the houses? How did you decide on a recording method? Did you consider any others?
- Which kind of recording system would be the easiest to draw?
- Which kind of recording system would be the easiest for someone to build from? Why?

As part of this discussion, you may want to introduce the concept of symmetry—some students may notice that symmetrical houses look the same from some views.

The four houses that can be built with three cubes are shown at the end of this lesson.

My students came up with several interesting ways to record their block structures. Here, Alice has used two different techniques. In the first three representations, she has traced one face of the block to start her drawing, then she has added lines drawn at an angle to show depth. In the last representation, she has just shown a top-down view of the structure.

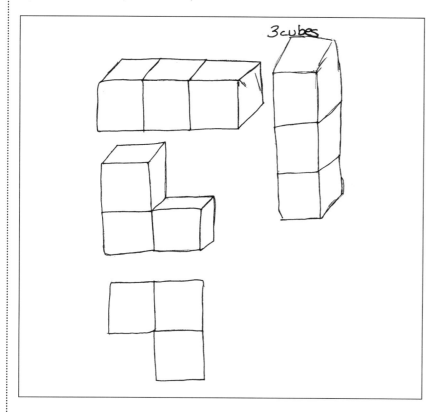

3 cubes

► *Some students focused on how easy or hard it was to create the representation. Others focused on how easy or hard it was to tell if two houses were the same from the representation. That contrast led to an interesting discussion of how different representations can be best for different purposes.*

3. Practice: *Make isometric drawings of cube structures.*

> *Reproducibles 8 & 9*

Isometric drawing is a particularly useful technique for representing cube structures because usually you can represent part of every cube in just one sketch. The practice exercises on *Making Isometric Drawings* (Reproducible 8) introduce students to isometric drawings. *Isometric Dot Paper* (Reproducible 9) helps students create and understand isometric drawings by providing a grid of evenly spaced dots on which to draw the cubes. You may want to assign some of the exercises in Reproducible 8 as homework.

Isometric drawing is just one of many methods for showing depth. The key characteristic of the method is contained in the word isometric—*iso,* same, and *metric,* measure. The elements in an isometric drawing maintain a consistent proportion—two objects that are the same size in real life will be represented as the same size. Thus, for example, all edges of an equilaterial cube will be drawn the same length in an isometric drawing.

Other kinds of drawings represent three dimensions by mimicking the way we perceive depth: objects that are further away from us appear smaller than closer objects. These nonisometric drawings use a "vanishing point perspective," so that two objects that are the same size in real life are drawn in different proportion depending on their "distance" from the viewer.

4. Writing: *Add to the glossary.*

After students have practiced making some isometric drawings, have groups of three or four students write a description of what is meant by *isometric drawing* using the illustrations on *Visual Glossary: Isometric Drawings* (Reproducible 10).

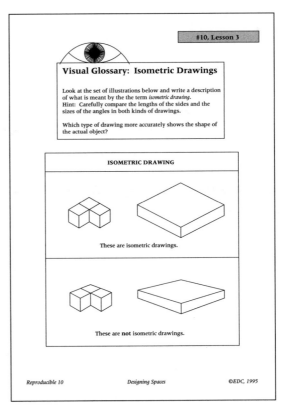

Reproducible 10.

Ask a few students from different groups to write their descriptions on the board and then have the class discuss and refine a definition to add to the glossary.

Homework Possibilities

Practice

- Assign parts or all of *Making Isometric Drawings* (Reproducible 8) for homework.
- Ask students to build a house using no more than six cubes and then make an isometric drawing of it.

Writing

Assign *Visual Glossary: Isometric Drawings* (Reproducible 10) for individual or small-group homework.

Making Connections

Ask students to find examples of isometric drawings and other kinds of drawings that show depth in newspapers, magazines, or books.

Answer Key

1. There are four different houses that can be built with three cubes.

Lesson 4

Seeing the Possibilities—Cube Combinations and Rotations

How many different modular houses can you build with four cubes? How can you use isometric drawings to record your designs and to identify houses that are rotations of each other?

In Lesson 3, students found all the possible modular houses they could make with three cubes and learned to represent them using isometric drawings. In this lesson, students make isometric drawings of all the possible modular houses they can build with four cubes. The additional cube makes finding and recording all the combinations much more challenging. Students also investigate the concept of rotation by making connections between isometric drawings that show the same structure from different vantage points.

In Lesson 5, students will make comparisons between isometric and orthogonal drawings. They will use both methods of representation in Lesson 6 when they revise their building plans from Lesson 2.

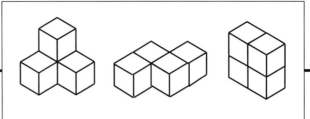

Mathematical Goals

- Visualize arrangements of cubes.
- Create isometric drawings of cube structures.
- Visualize rotations of cube stuctures.
- Develop arguments that all possible cube combinations have been found.

Materials

Per Student

At least four cubic blocks

Reproducible 7, *Memo 2 to House Designers*

Reproducible 9, *Isometric Dot Paper*

Reproducible 11, *Matching Rotations*

Suggested Lesson Plan

At the end of this lesson, students will add the term *rotation* to the class glossary. As you work through the lesson plan, look for opportunities to draw out students' understanding of this concept. See page xxi of the unit overview for suggestions on how to teach the key terms in the unit.

1. Investigation: *Design all possible houses with four cubes.*

Students repeat the activity from Step 1 of Lesson 3 using four cubes rather than three. The additional cube raises the number of possible houses to fifteen and makes the recording process much more challenging. Students should not be told how many combinations are possible; that is part of the discussion in Step 2. Solutions are shown at the end of this lesson.

TO THE STUDENT

- Using four cubes, design as many different modular houses as you can. Follow the guidelines on *Memo 2 to House Designers*.
- Record each different house using isometric drawings.

▶ **From the Classroom**

My class was confused at first about how to tell whether two houses should be considered the same. I demonstrated that if you can rotate one house to be identical to another, without lifting up the house, then the two are considered the same.

▶ *A few students used a variety of recording styles in representing their solutions. Here's Alan's drawing:*

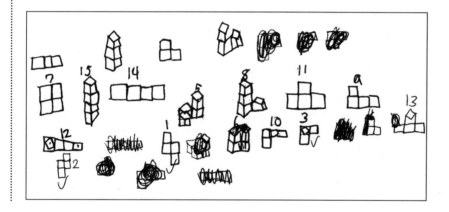

2. Discussion: *How many four-module houses are possible? How can we know whether we found them all?*

Allow time for students to do more experimentation as the class discusses how students know they have found all the combinations. Through this discussion, students gain experience creating an informal proof of a mathematical assertion (the assertion that they have found all the possibilities).

3. Problem solving: *How many different houses can you make with four cubes if you are allowed to lift the houses to rotate them?*

In Steps 1 and 2, students assumed that two structures were the same if they could rotate one to be just like the other *without lifting it*. That guideline was designed to introduce students to the concept of rotation on a vertical axis. In this activity and the next, students are introduced to the concept of rotation on a horizontal axis as well so that they learn to visualize rotations in two different ways. The gravity guideline is removed here so that students can explore all of the possibilities of horizontal rotation.

> **TO THE STUDENT**
>
> How many different houses can you make with four cubes if you assume that two houses are the same if they can be rotated either by turning or lifting them? (These houses *can* defy gravity.)

Solutions are shown at the end of this lesson.

4. Problem solving: *Find the rotations.*

The task of matching modular houses to rotations of those houses—presented in *Matching Rotations* (Reproducible 11)—helps students learn to interpret isometric drawings. It also strengthens their ability to visualize rotations.

Solutions are shown at the end of this lesson. This activity is appropriate for homework.

► *From the Classroom*

One group of students organized the process by dividing their structures into categories: 1 cube high, 2 cubes high, 3 cubes high, and 4 cubes high. They quickly found that there is only one structure that is 4 high and one that is 3 high. They then divided into subgroups, with one group working on all the 1-cube-high structures and the other on the 2-cube-high structures.

Reproducible 11

► *From the Classroom*

I encouraged students who were working on this sheet at home to find four cubes and recreate each house. Then, they could look at it from different directions to find the rotations.

5. Writing: *Add to the glossary.*

After students have completed Matching Rotations, have groups of three or four students use the illustrations on the reproducible to write a description of what is meant by the term *rotation*. An example of a description written by a student is shown below.

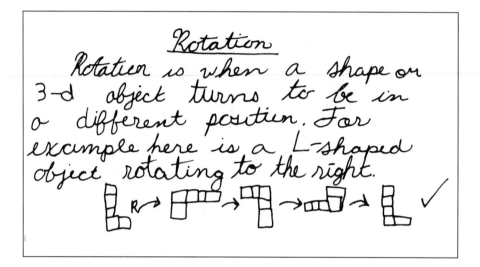

Ask a few students from different groups to share their descriptions and then have the class discuss and refine a definition to add to the glossary.

Homework Possibilities

Problem solving

Assign part or all of *Matching Rotations* (Reproducible 11) for homework.

Writing

If students haven't written descriptions of what is meant by *rotation* in class, have individuals or small groups write descriptions for homework.

Extension

After students have completed *Matching Rotations*, have them exchange work. Ask them to match up the rotations their classmates drew at the bottom of the page with the houses in Column A.

Answer Key

1. There are 15 different houses that can be built with four cubes.

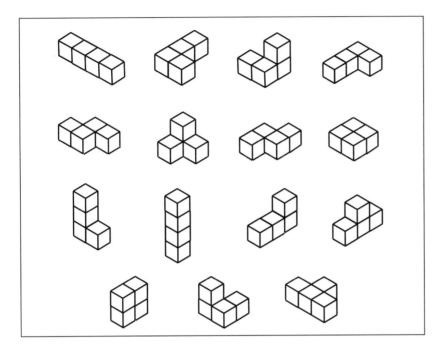

3. There are 8 different houses that can be built with four cubes.

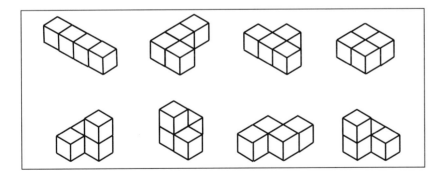

4. Here are the possible matches for the houses shown on *Matching Rotations* (Reproducible 11):
   1. c
   2. f
   3. a and b
   4. e
   5. d and g

Lesson 5

Seeing All Sides— Orthogonal Drawings

How can we use orthogonal drawings to represent modular houses? How are orthogonal drawings different from isometric ones?

In this lesson, students learn to interpret orthogonal drawings by translating them into (1) modular houses and (2) isometric drawings. They then learn to make orthogonal drawings by translating isometric drawings into orthogonal ones. As they explore the relationships between the two kinds of drawings, students deepen their understanding of the different uses of multiple vantage points and drawings that show depth.

In Lesson 6, students will use their knowledge of isometric and orthogonal representations to revise the building plans they made in Lesson 2.

Mathematical Goals

- Represent three-dimensional objects in two dimensions.
- Build three-dimensional structures to match two-dimensional plans.
- Translate between orthogonal drawings and isometric drawings.

Materials

Per Student	*Per Class*
Ten cubes	Roll of masking tape
Reproducible 9, *Isometric Dot Paper*	An orange or a marker and an ice cream cone (optional)
Reproducible 12, *Reading Orthogonal Drawings*	Overhead projector (optional)
Reproducible 13, *Making Orthogonal Drawings*	
Reproducible 14, *Visual Glossary: Orthogonal Drawings*	

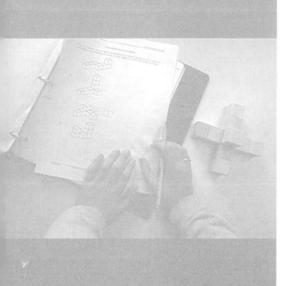

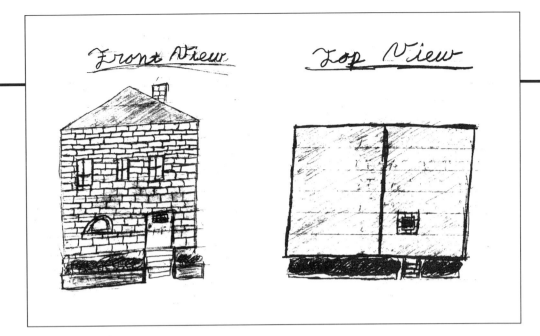

Suggested Lesson Plan

At the end of this lesson, students will add the term *orthogonal drawing* to the class glossary. As you work through the lesson plan, look for opportunities to draw out students' understanding of this concept. See page xxiii of the unit overview for suggestions on how to teach the key terms in the unit.

1. Introduction: *Make orthogonal views of a roll of masking tape.*

Hold up a roll of masking tape and ask students to sketch what they might see if they looked at the roll of tape from four views: straight down at the top of it; straight at the front of it; straight at the right side of it; and straight at the bottom of it. Explain to the students that they are now visualizing and representing the orthogonal views of an object.

A good way to help students see the orthogonal views is to place the roll of tape on an overhead projector and project the silhouettes of the four different views onto a wall. Students can decide which views of the tape roll that they want to label side, front, top, and bottom.

You may want to repeat this demonstration with a pair of objects—such as an ice cream cone and an orange—that look similar to each other from at least one view and very different from other views. Having students predict what they might see before they actually look at the view will help strengthen their visualizing abilities.

2. Problem solving: *Build houses from orthogonal drawings.*

Students build the modular houses represented in the top-view, front-view, and side-view drawings on *Reading Orthogonal Drawings* (Reproducible 12). Although these orthogonal drawings may seem less complex to students than the isometric drawings they worked with in the last lesson, the task of visualizing them as three-dimensional structures is more challenging. Interpreting the drawings in this activity will help prepare students to make their own orthogonal drawings of modular houses in Step 4 of the lesson.

There is more than one possible modular house for some of the sets of orthogonal views. Solutions are provided at the end of the lesson.

3. Drawing: *Make isometric drawings.*

TO THE STUDENT

- Create isometric drawings for two of the modular houses you built from the drawings on *Reading Orthogonal Drawings.*
- Compare your drawing to the orthogonal views. Can you find each of the views in your isometric drawings?

---

4. Problem solving: *Make orthogonal drawings based on isometric ones.*

On *Making Orthogonal Drawings* (Reproducible 13), students translate isometric drawings into orthogonal ones. Students may find it helpful to build some of the houses before representing them in orthogonal drawings. Possible solutions provided at the end of the lesson.

5. Discussion: *Compare orthogonal and isometric drawings.*

It is important that students understand that orthogonal drawings and isometric drawings serve different functions and that both are useful. For example, blueprints use orthogonal drawings because they can be easier to interpret than depth drawings. This example can help counteract some students' tendencies to see isometric drawings as being better because they seem fancier or more complex than drawings that don't show depth. On the other hand, depth drawings may communicate more or be more artistic than orthogonal drawings. Most of the illustrations of houses we see—such as those in books or real estate sections of the newspapers—show depth.

Encourage students to make their own comparisons between the two kinds of drawings:

- How are orthogonal and isometric drawings different? Are there any ways in which they are alike?
- Which type of drawing do you prefer? Why?
- If you are given an isometric drawing, how can you make orthogonal drawings of the same object?
- If you are given orthogonal drawings, how can you make an isometric drawing of the same object?
- When would you use orthogonal drawings? When would you use isometric drawings?

6. Writing: *Add to the glossary.*

Have groups of three or four students write a description of what is meant by the term *orthogonal drawings* using the illustrations on *Visual Glossary: Orthogonal Drawings* (Reproducible 14). If students are having trouble understanding the concept of orthogonal drawings, you can suggest comparisons to shadows or silhouettes.

Ask a few students from different groups to write their descriptions on the board and then have the class discuss and refine a definition to add to the glossary.

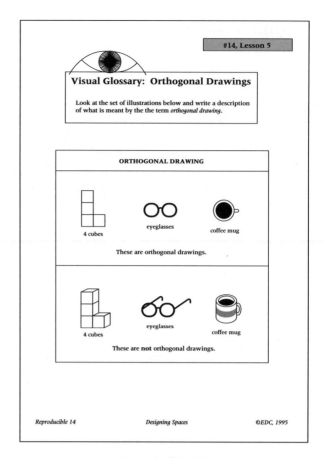

#14, Lesson 5

Visual Glossary: Orthogonal Drawings

Look at the set of illustrations below and write a description of what is meant by the the term *orthogonal drawing*.

ORTHOGONAL DRAWING

4 cubes   eyeglasses   coffee mug

These are orthogonal drawings.

4 cubes   eyeglasses   coffee mug

These are **not** orthogonal drawings.

Reproducible 14   *Designing Spaces*   ©EDC, 1995

Reproducible 14.

Homework Possibilities

Making Connections

Have students choose a building in their community to sketch using both isometric and orthogonal representations. Encourage them to sketch the building so that a visitor could recognize it from any view. As an extension of this activity, you could display the drawings in class and have other students try to identify the structure.

Writing

Assign *Visual Glossary: Orthogonal Drawings* (Reproducible 14) for individual or small-group homework.

Journal Writing

This lesson provides a good opportunity for students to reflect on the methods of representation they've learned in the section. See the journal-writing questions in Homework Possibilities in Lesson 1.

Answer Key: Solutions to Orthogonal and Isometric Representations

2. Problem solving: Build houses from orthogonal drawings

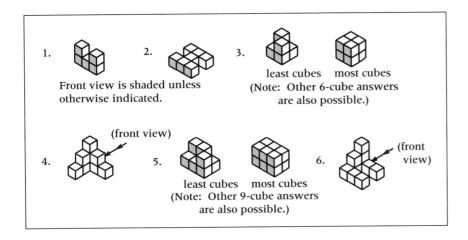

4. Problem solving: Make orthogonal drawings based on isometric ones. (Solutions will vary.)

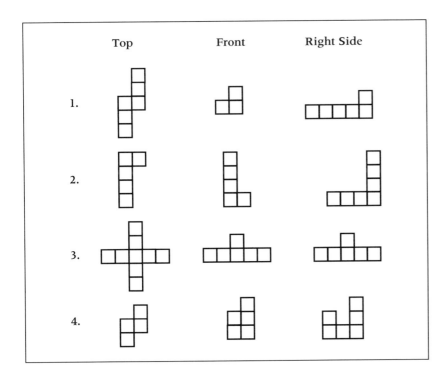

Lesson 6

Picture This— Improving Your Drawings

How can you improve your house plans from Lesson 2? Can someone else build a house from your revised plans?

This lesson serves as an assessment for what students have learned thus far in the unit about visualization, representations, and communication. Students use their knowledge of orthogonal and isometric views to revise the plans they made in Lesson 2. Students trade plans with a partner and build structures from their partner's revised plans. As students discuss ways to improve the plans, they learn about the process of giving and receiving feedback. The section ends with students turning the revised plans in to be assessed.

Mathematical Goals

Apply and extend knowledge of:

- Orthogonal and isometric representations of three-dimensional structures.
- Two-dimensional representations of three-dimensional structures.
- Visualizing three-dimensional structures from two-dimensional representations.
- Communicating properties of structure through written descriptions.

Materials

Per Student

Plans and house created in Lesson 2

Set of 8–10 cubes

Reproducible 9, *Isometric Dot Paper*

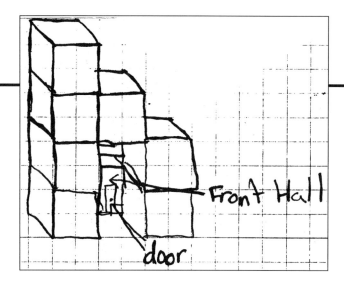

Reproducible 15, *Evaluating Plans*

Reproducible 16, *Giving Constructive Feedback*

Reproducible 17, *Hidden Cubes*

Preparation

You may want to prepare your own assessment criteria before class, depending on which of the options you choose in Step 1. See page xxv in the unit overview for more information on assessment.

Suggested Lesson Plan

1. Introduction: *Preparing for assessment*

The sample plans on *Evaluating Plans* (Reproducible 15) serve as a starting point for a discussion of assessment criteria. You may choose to go through the questions on the reproducible in a class discussion, or have students work on them alone or in small groups.

You can use the sample plans to help the class develop its own assessment criteria or to illustrate criteria that you provide for the class. Here are suggestions for each approach:

a. *Have the whole class establish the assessment criteria.* Give students some time in small groups to talk about the questions on Evaluating Plans. As a class, compare the two sets of plans and help students articulate the strengths and weaknesses of each set. Use these strengths and weaknesses to place each set of plans into one of three categories: Supe-

Reproducible 15

rior; Satisfactory; or Unsatisfactory. These placements may be based on such factors as clarity, accuracy, or inclusion of mathematical ideas. The class can then decide how to adapt these criteria to their upcoming task.

b. *Present your own criteria to the class.* Some suggested criteria is given in the margin as a starting point for developing your own.

It may help you to think of these assessment criteria in relation to the major mathematical themes in the unit. The criteria should help you evaluate a student's ability to *visualize, represent,* and *communicate* at this point in the unit: students use visualization to translate their modular house into drawings and written descriptions; they use orthogonal and isometric drawings to show multiple representations of the same structure; they communicate their building plans in words as well as drawings.

2. Assessment: *Revise the plans you made in Lesson 2.*

TO THE STUDENT

Revise the building plans you made in Lesson 2 to meet the assessment criteria.

Some students may want to rebuild their Lesson 2 house before making a new drawing.

▶ From the Classroom

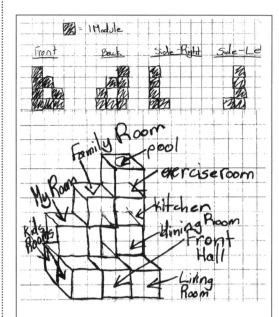

1) The bottom floor has 5 rooms shaped like a U that is symmetric. Snap 3 cubes together in a row then snap 1 cube on each end so it makes a ⌐⌐.

2) Snap 3 cubes together and stand them straight up. They go on top of the end.

Room on the right ⌐⌐.

3) On the other end room ⌐⌐, put one cube on top of it.

4) Attach one cube to the third cube up on the tall part. Put it on the left so it makes a space underneath it.

Superior

This student's orthogonal and isometric drawings are complete and consistent with each other. Her house could be built easily from the pictures alone. Her written instructions are clear.

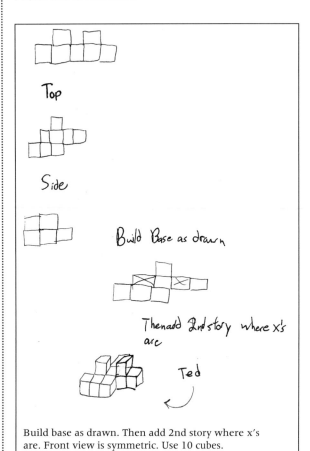

Top

Side

Build Base as drawn

Then add 2nd story where x's are

Ted

Build base as drawn. Then add 2nd story where x's are. Front view is symmetric. Use 10 cubes.

Satisfactory

This student's pictures and drawings together give enough information to build his house, but the written description does not include step-by-step instructions.

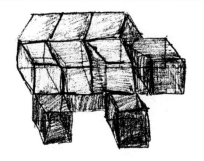

The first row has four cubes. The first color is black, the second is dark green, third light green and the fourth is light blue. The second row in the back has three cubes. The first color is white, the second is pink, and the third is brown. On the first row, there is one black cube. On the bottom of the black there is a brown. The third cube in the second line which is light green has a yellow cube at the bottom. In the second row there are three cubes. The second cube is pink, and at the bottom of it there's a dark green cube attached. The End.

Unsatisfactory

This student's plans include only an isometric drawing, which does not show clearly how the house is built. Though she gives a lot of detail about color in her written description, she conveys little about the building process or the shape of the house.

3. Sharing: *Trading plans, giving feedback, and revising plans.*

Students trade plans with a partner and build from the new set of plans without seeing their partner's house. As students build from another's plans, they think more deeply about different ways to communicate geometric ideas.

There are several ways to structure the trading of plans. The method suggested below ensures that students will not know whose plans they have been given. Keeping the identity of the designer unknown makes the building task more authentic. Students must work from the plans, rather than from any memory they may have of their classmate's structure.

Have each student put his or her plans in a manila envelope, labeled with a number or letter. Pass out the envelopes randomly so everyone gets a new set of plans. Usually, each student will review plans by a different student from the one that reviews theirs. Students build from these plans and write their comments and suggestions about the plans on a sheet of paper that is returned in the manila envelope.

Since this is the first time in the unit that students are commenting on each other's work, you may need to take some time to discuss the idea of *constructive* feedback. It is important that students make positive suggestions for improving the plans. You may want to use *Giving Constructive Feedback* (Reproducible 16) as a basis for the discussion, or simply hand it out to students as a set of guidelines. Having students write their feedback can minimize arguments between students and provide you with a record of students' suggestions.

Before students turn in their plans to be assessed, they should revise the plans one more time to incorporate their partner's suggestions. This final revision gives students an opportunity to submit their best work. It also ensures that part of what you are assessing is the student's ability to incorporate feedback.

Reproducible 16

▶ **From the Classroom**

I thought my students needed some additional guidance on giving feedback, so I had the class generate a list of questions and writing prompts for students to think about when reviewing their partner's plans, such as:

- *When my partner revises these plans, what would I like my partner to change?*
- *I found it hard to understand _____.*
- *One thing my partner did well in these plans is _____. One thing my partner could improve in the plans is _____.*

4. Writing: *Describe the changes you made in your plans.*

Have students write a brief memo to the directors of the Creative Construction Company in which they summarize the revisions they made to their plans. The memo can help guide you when you assess the revised plans and can give you a sense of how the students approached the revision process.

Homework Possibilities

Problem Solving

Have students draw orthogonal views of some of the homes pictured in the Homes Puzzle from Lesson 1. You can then compare drawings the next day.

Extension

Hidden Cubes (Reproducible 17) shows isometric drawings that could be interpreted in different ways, resulting in a couple of different possible house designs. Students make orthogonal drawings showing at least two different solutions for each isometric drawing. In a second set of problems, students make at least two different isometric drawings that could correspond to each set of orthogonal ones.

Answer Key: Hidden Cubes

1. This has three solutions, using 7, 8, or 9 cubes.

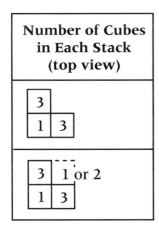

Number of Cubes in Each Stack (top view)
3 1 3
3 1 or 2 1 3

2. This has five solutions, using 6, 7, 8, or 9 cubes.

Number of Cubes in Each Stack (top view)
1 3 2
1 1 3 2
1 2 3 2
1 1 1 3 2
1 2 1 3 2

3. This has three solutions, using 9, 10, or 11 cubes.

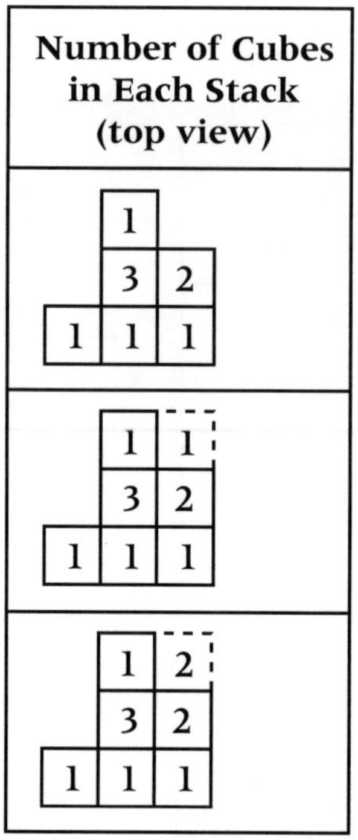

**Number of Cubes
in Each Stack
(top view)**

```
        1
        3  2
     1  1  1
```

```
        1  1
        3  2
     1  1  1
```

```
        1  2
        3  2
     1  1  1
```

4. This has three solutions, using 8, 9, or 10 cubes.

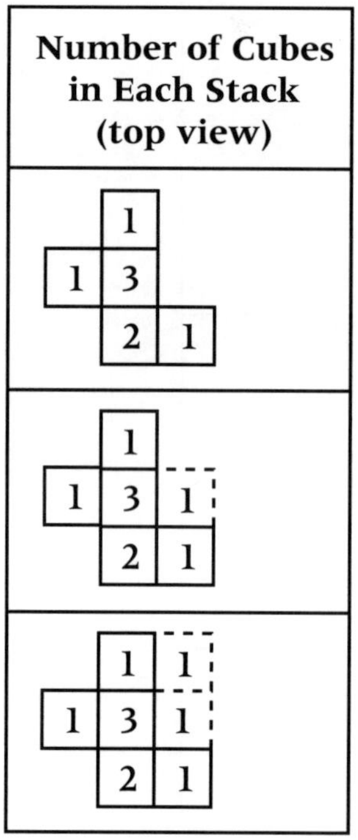

**Number of Cubes
in Each Stack
(top view)**

```
        1
     1  3
        2  1
```

```
        1
     1  3  1
        2  1
```

```
        1  1
     1  3  1
        2  1
```

5. This has five solutions, using 10, 11, 12, or 13 cubes.

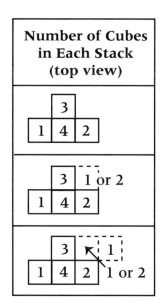

6. This has three solutions. The top view is shown, with the number of cubes in each stack given.

1	2
2	1

2	1
2	2

2	2
2	2

7. This has fifteen solutions. Four are shown here. To generate additional solutions, substitute two cubes where one cube is shown.

1	1	2
2	2	1

1	2	1
2	1	2

2	1	1
1	2	2

2	2	2
2	2	2

Section 3

Describing Properties and Functions of Shapes

In Section 3, students continue to explore new ways to communicate about three-dimensional structures through an investigation of the properties and functions of two-dimensional shapes. Students move from building cube houses to building houses made from cardboard shapes—including triangles, rectangles, squares, trapezoids, rhombi, and hexagons. The range of shapes makes the task of designing the houses and describing them in building plans more challenging. Students explore the properties of polygons by working in groups to create shapes that will match clues about the properties of the sides and angles in the shapes—such as a quadrilateral with two pairs of parallel sides that also have equal opposite angles. Through these activities, students discover new ways to communicate about shapes, which they apply when they revise their building plans at the end of the section.

Students explore further the concept of the function of shapes by designing a model house for the climate in which they live. In addition to revising their building plans in Lesson 10, students describe their model houses in "design specifica-

Approx. # of Classes	Lessons
1–2	**7. Planning and Building a House for Your Climate** Using a set of cardboard shapes, students design and build a house for the climate in which they live.
1–2	**8. String Shapes—Properties of Sides** Students work in groups using a loop of string to investigate parallel and equilateral sides in polygons.
1–2	**9. String Shapes—Properties of Angles** Students work in groups using a loop of string to investigate equal, right, and opposite angles in polygons.
2	**10. In Other Words—Improving Your Plans** Students apply what they've learned about the properties of shapes to improve their building plans. They are assessed on their improvements.

Lesson summary and sample schedule for Section 3

tions," which include explanations of how the houses are suited to the climate. The section ends with an assessment of the revised plans and the design specifications.

Mathematical Goals

- Visualize and build a three-dimensional structure from polygons.
- Create visual representations of a three-dimensional structure; apply and extend knowledge of orthogonal and isometric drawing.
- Use geometric terms to describe three-dimensional structures.
- Understand the meaning of the concepts *equilateral, parallel, regular, right angle, equal angle,* and *opposite angle* and apply them to create different shapes.
- Learn the formal geometric notation for equal and parallel sides, and equal and right angles.
- Describe the building process that results in a geometric structure.
- Perform visual and mental experiments with shape transformations.
- Devise tests for comparing sizes of angles and lengths of sides in a shape.
- Examine the relationship between properties of sides and properties of angles in a shape.

Mathematical Theme 1

Multiple Representations of Shapes and Structures

In the process of making, revising, and exchanging building plans, students continue to explore the uses of written descriptions and visual representations. While the section focuses on the written descriptions, students must adapt their techniques of representation to match the complexity of the houses they build in this section.

In the previous section, students learned isometric and orthogonal drawing techniques to represent cube structures. In this section, students must adapt these techniques—and develop some new ones—to represent more complicated structures. Whereas the orthogonal drawings of cube structures consist only of squares, the orthogonal drawings made in this section will include six shapes: triangles, squares, rectangles, trapezoids, rhombi, and hexagons.

Instead of making isometric drawings in this section, students develop their own techniques for showing depth. (It would be extremely difficult to represent the structures students build in this section isometrically—given the variety of shapes in the structures and the variety of ways they can be combined.) Students' ability to show depth will continue to grow in the next section when they learn techniques for making perspective drawings of prisms and pyramids.

Mathematical Theme 2

Visualization

In the cube structures students visualized in the last section, all of the pieces were the same simple shape. In this section, students visualize more complex structures made from a variety of shapes. As students build and represent house models in Lessons 7 and 10, they must visualize how two-dimensional shapes combine to form three-dimensional structures for which they have no previous mental image. Students must also visualize how to represent these structures in orthogonal drawings and drawings that show depth.

These visualization activities lay the groundwork for Section 4, when students will visualize how to combine polygons to form polyhedra—and how to represent those polyhedra.

In Lesson 8, students also visualize shape transformations. Groups of students convert one string shape to another by having one member of the group shift position while the rest stay stationary. As the group orchestrates its moves, students see the shapes as dynamic. As one side lengthens, for instance, the opposite angle grows larger, causing another angle to shrink. These activities teach students to visualize how the properties of shapes are interrelated.

Properties and Components of Shape

The hands-on activities in this section provide students with a new context for thinking about the properties of shapes and the relationship between different kinds of shapes. In creating string shapes to match given properties—and creating their own methods of measurement—students gain tangible experience with the components of shape. They also investigate the relationship between properties by trying to create shapes with pairs of inconsistent properties—such as a quadrilateral with two pairs of parallel sides and no opposite angles that are equal. Students also explore the relationships between shapes by transforming one string shape into another—such as converting a trapezoid into a triangle. In Lesson 10, students apply what they've learned about the properties and components of shapes to revise their building plans and write design specifications for their model house.

The emphasis on the properties of two-dimensional shapes lays the groundwork for an exploration of the properties and components of three-dimensional structures in Section 4.

Mathematical Theme 4

Communication

The focus of this section is on providing students with new tools for communicating—in writing—about two-dimensional shapes and three-dimensional structures. In Lesson 7, students develop their own techniques for describing the steps they used to build a house made up of triangles, rectangles, squares, trapezoids, rhombi, and hexagons. As students create string shapes from given properties in Lessons 8 and 9, they explore a range of geometric terms and concepts. In the process of developing and refining definitions of these terms, students clarify their thinking about the properties of shape. They also see the usefulness of mathematical language, as they apply the terms to revise their building plans in Lesson 10. The importance of precision in mathematical communication is reinforced when students exchange plans and build replicas of their partner's house from their partner's plans.

Teacher Reflection

Julia, Kelly, and Janine were three of the quietest girls in my class, though you'd never know it to see them with their friends. I wanted to see them show some of that effervescence in the class—and risk voicing their own ideas—so I assigned them to the same group for the string activities in Lesson 8. Since they had three in their group instead of four, I started them off with a triangle: "How would you make an equilateral triangle with your string?" The girls just looked at me, clearly hoping for some hints. I smiled. "That's it!" I said. "Go to it!" I then made my way across the room where I could unobtrusively watch what unfolded.

Measuring Qualitatively

They stood there for a moment, fidgeting with the string until Julia decided to take action. "Well, we need a meter stick. I'll go get one." She returned and started directing her partners to make a triangle, each of them holding the string to form a corner of their triangle. "Just take a corner and pull the string tight. Janine, move over. Yeah . . . no, Kelly, move back. . . ." and so on until they had a triangle that they estimated to be roughly equilateral (Figure 1). Julia struggled in vain to hold both her corner of the triangle and the meter stick steady so that she could measure the triangle.

Figure 1.

"Let's just put your corner around this chair," Kelly suggested to Julia (Figure 2). While Kelly and Janine held their vertices, Julia measured with the meter stick. She laid it along one side of the triangle, pinched the string at one meter to mark it, and measured the remaining length.

"It's five . . . what are those? Well, it's five," she announced. She moved around to the next side to measure the second side, using the same method.

"What did you measure those in? Centimeters or inches?" Kelly asked.

Janine said quietly, "It doesn't matter what they are, as long as you use the same thing all the time."

Figure 2.

However, Julia was intent on her task and ignored both of them. "Hey! Five again!"

"*What did you measure those in?*" Kelly tried again, more insistently.

"It's one thing and five somethings," Julia replied.

Julia was developing her own functional system of measurement made up of "things" (meters) and "somethings" (centimeters). Janine, on the other hand, seemed to have realized an important point that the other two girls had missed: it didn't really matter whether the meter stick was in inches or centimeters, since what they were interested in was the relationship between the sides rather than the numbers that represented their lengths.

Testing Equality by Vertices and Midpoints

"Here, you don't know how to read that. Let me try something," Kelly said.

Julia took her place, and Kelly started measuring one side of the triangle using her pen as the measurement unit. I smiled to myself, thinking that Kelly's method was really no different than Julia's, since they were both creating a unit of measure to test the equality of the sides. "Sixteen pens on this side," she announced, moving on to the next side. "Sixteen on this side too," she said. "Uh-oh. Eighteen on this side. We need to fix it," she declared.

"Well, you should move over and make this side shorter," Julia told Janine. Kelly and Julia took turns directing the group back and forth until they all agreed that the triangle looked more equilateral than before.

Figure 3.

Kelly started to take pen measurements again when Janine said, "Why don't we just put two sides next to each other to see if they're equal? We can do that with all the different pairs of sides."

"Hey! Yeah!" Kelly exclaimed. "Julia, move over next to Janine, like that. Now pull your sides straight (Figure 3). OK, now move over next to me. OK, that works" (Figure 4).

"OK, now Janine has to stand next to you," Julia directed Kelly. All three pairings checked out. "It works!" said Julia.

But Kelly clearly wanted to try one more thing. "Here, give me all your corners," she said. Janine handed hers over.

"What are you doing?" Julia asked.

Figure 4.

"Just give me your corners," Kelly insisted. When she had gathered them all in one hand, she let what had been the middles of the sides dangle down beneath her hand. "See!" she exclaimed, proudly. "They all dangle to the same length." I wondered whether she realized that the bottoms of the "dangles" were the midpoints of the sides. I made a mental note to ask Kelly about how she came up with the method later.

I notice that with hands-on activities like these, students often start from what they know best and then branch out; in this case, it was testing equality by comparing the lengths of the sides to some standard measuring tool. They then tried comparing the sides to Kelly's pen, an object that was not commonly used for measurement. Janine's simple suggestion of physically comparing the sides to each other to test for equality had seemed obvious to me but was something of a revelation to the girls. Watching this group in action reaffirmed my belief that, given the opportunity and permission to explore, students will break away from the familiar to explore their own ideas and gain confidence in their ability to be mathematically creative.

Lesson 7

Planning and Building a House for Your Climate

How does the shape of houses differ in different climates? What kind of house would you design for the climate in which you live?

In this lesson, students move from building and representing houses made from cubes to the more complex challenge of building and representing houses made from a collection of shapes (triangles, rectangles, squares, trapezoids, rhombi, and hexagons). An additional design guideline—asking students to construct a home to meet the needs of the climate in which they live—encourages students to think about the function of the shape of the house.

In Lessons 8 and 9, students will learn new ways to describe the properties of the shapes that make up these house models. In Lesson 9, they will use that knowledge to improve the plans they create in this lesson.

Mathematical Goals

- Visualize and build a three-dimensional structure from polygons.
- Use geometric terms to describe three-dimensional structures.
- Create visual representations of a three-dimensional structure.
- Describe the building process that results in a geometric structure.

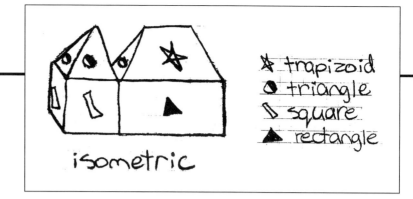

isometric

★ trapizoid
● triangle
◊ square
▲ rectangle

Materials

Per Student	*Per Group*
Drawing paper	Scissors
Sixteen assorted shapes made from poster board, including squares, triangles, rectangles, rhombi, trapezoids, and hexagons. Templates for the shapes are provided in Appendix D.	Masking tape or reusable tape
	Reproducible 18, *Considering Climate in House Design*
Reproducible 19, *Memo 3 to House Designers*	

Preparation

Make copies of *Considering Climate in House Design* (Reproducible 18) and cut out each of the cards. Each group of students should receive at least two cards with different climates.

Sets of assorted shape pieces are used in five of the lessons in the unit (Lessons 7, 10, 11, 13, and 14). See pages xxiii-xxiv in the unit overview for suggestions on cutting out the shapes for the unit and storing the model houses that students build.

Suggested Lesson Plan

Reproducible 18

1. Introduction: *How does climate affect the way we design houses?*

The climate cards from *Considering Climate in House Design* (Reproducible 18) encourage students to think about creative ways to design houses for various climates before they begin building a model house in Step 2. Pass out at least two different cards to each group of students.

TO THE STUDENT

Each of the cards you have been given describes a particular climate.

With your group, brainstorm and write down what kind of house you would design for each climate. What shape would you make the house? What kind of features would you include to protect against the climate?

If students need help getting started, you might pose some more specific questions, such as:

- What kind of roof would be best for this climate?
- What kind of walls and floors would be best?
- What about the overall shape of the house? Do some shapes provide more protection than others?

Students may also get ideas by referring back to the chart they created for the Homes Puzzle in Lesson 1.

2. Discussion: *Share climate solutions.*

When each group has completed at least two cards, have each group report on its solutions. This is a good opportunity to emphasize that different house designers can come up with different—but equally valid—solutions to the same set of climate conditions. You might point out that various cultures have found different and ingenious ways to protect themselves from extreme heat. For example, some Arab cultures have designed houses with wind tunnels to provide protection against the desert heat in the Middle East. In the Sahara Desert, the Tuareg tribespeople build tents with walls that do not reach the ground so that breezes can come into the homes.

▶ *From the Classroom*

As different groups reported on their solutions, I kept a running list of features for the three cards we did:

A desert	A very cold place	A place with lots of snow
Roofs that open up	thick roof to keep in heat	Slanted roof so snow falls off
lots of windows	double, or triple glass in windows	defrosters on roof
Shutters to keep sun out	lots of fireplaces	strong roof so it doesn't collapse from the height
Ceiling fans	round so it doesn't catch the wind	room to store food in case you get snowed in
underground	thick walls	doors on second floors so you don't get snowed in

3. Investigation: *Design a house and create a set of plans.*

Students design and build a model house according to the guidelines on *Memo 3 to House Designers* (Reproducible 19). In designing the house for their own climate, students apply their ideas about the connection between climate and the shapes of houses. They then represent and describe their houses in plans.

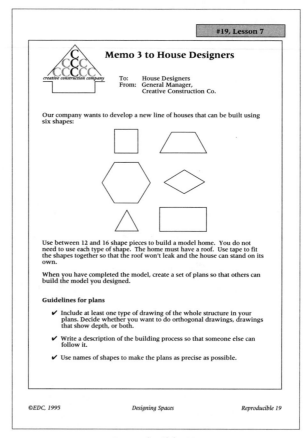

Reproducible 19.

In this lesson, students explore the properties of shapes in an informal way as they find their own ways to build with, describe, and represent each shape. In Lessons 8 and 9, they will investigate the geometric properties and learn the mathematical names of many of these shapes. Students will go on to incorporate these new terms when they revise their plans in Lesson 10.

It is best if students do not study each other's houses too closely now because they will try to build each other's houses from plans later in this section.

► *From the Classroom*

Students used a variety of approaches in their plans, which led to some interesting discussions. Some students traced the sides of their structure on a piece of paper and then labeled each view. Others made perspective drawings with written explanations of the shapes that they used to make their structure. In general, the class was split about the value of showing depth in their drawings. Some thought that trying to show depth was too confusing, while others thought that they could do fewer drawings if they showed depth.

4. Writing: *How is your house design well suited to the climate?*

After describing their house and climate conditions in their plans, students go a step further to reflect on the function of their design.

Some questions to help students explore the connection between climate and design include:

- What shape did you make your house so that it fits well with your climate?
- What special features did you add to your house to deal with climate conditions?
- Which climate conditions were you most concerned about when you designed your house? Why?

Homework Possibilities

Practice

- Students make four puzzle cards for the structure that they created: a picture of the building, a description card, a shape card, and a view card. (See the Homes Puzzle in Lesson 1 for sample cards.)
- If there is time, have students play a version of the Homes Puzzle with the cards they designed.

Extensions

Students research the ways that cultures in one specific climate have built their houses throughout history. They try to find pictures of different kinds of houses that are all appropriate for the same climate. Have students assemble these pictures into posters, which you can display in the classroom to give students ideas for their own designs.

Lesson 8

String Shapes— Properties of Sides

How can you tell if two sides of a shape are parallel? Can you make an equilateral shape with no parallel sides?

This is the first of two lessons in which students investigate the properties of the shapes they used to build their house models in Lesson 7. In this lesson, groups of students use a loop of string to create shapes with specific properties. As students solve clues based on the properties of sides in a shape, they explore the concepts of *parallel* and *equilateral*—as well as the relationship between parallel and equal sides. As an optional final activity, students explore how changing the lengths of the sides will affect other properties of the shape.

In Lesson 9, students focus on the properties of the angles in the shape rather than its sides. In Lesson 10, students will use their knowledge of shape properties when they revise the plans they made in Lesson 7.

Mathematical Goals

- Understand the meaning of the concepts *equilateral* and *parallel* and apply them to create different shapes.
- Perform visual and mental experiments with shape transformations.
- Learn the formal geometric notation for equal and parallel sides.
- Devise tests for comparing lengths of sides in a shape.

Materials

Per Student

Reproducible 22, *Visual Glossary: Parallel and Equilateral*

Per Group

Loop of string or rope (see Preparation for lengths)

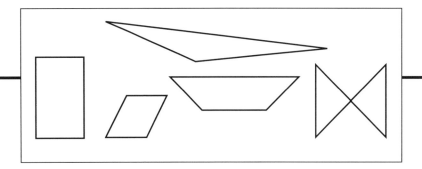

Reproducible 23, *Practice Shapes* (optional)

Reproducible 24, *Roping It Off, Method 1* (optional)

Rulers, yardsticks, meter sticks, or measuring tapes (optional)

Reproducible 20, *Can You Make This Shape?* Part 1

Reproducible 21, *Animated Shapes* (two pages; optional)

Preparation

The length of the string loops you need to prepare for this lesson depends on whether you choose to do the large-scale or small-scale versions of the string activities. In the small-scale version, students remain seated and work at tables or desks pushed together. In the large-scale version, students stand up and move around the classroom.

Large-scale version. This version, which students tend to prefer, may be done outside, in the cafeteria or gymnasium, or in an open space of the classroom. You will need to cut 8–12 feet of string (rope, yarn, etc.) for each group of four or five students. Knot the ends of the string to form a big loop.

Small-scale version. This version is done seated in the classroom. You will need to cut 4–6 feet of string for each group of students. Knot the ends of the string to form a big loop. Students may work seated around a table or a group of desks pushed together.

Suggested Lesson Plan

At the end of this lesson, students will add the terms *parallel* and *equilateral* to the class glossary. As you work through the lesson plan, look for opportunities to draw out students' understanding of these concepts. See page xxi of the unit overview for suggestions on how to teach the key terms in the unit.

1. Introduction: *Making shapes with string.*

Ask four students to help you demonstrate how to make a shape using the string. Each point where a student holds the string is a vertex of the shape. For the demonstration, ask the group of students to make a shape with four sides that has only one pair of parallel sides.

From this demonstration, you can check whether the class understands the term *parallel*, and if necessary, begin the discussion about what it means. During the demonstration, emphasize that students need to hold the string taut so that the side can be seen clearly. Each student should also try to form as sharp a corner as they can. Sharp corners are essential for measuring angles, which the students will do in Lesson 8.

▶ *From the Classroom*

In my first class, students would move from one shape to the next without stopping to examine the shape they had made. That made it very difficult for the group to draw the finished shapes. In my next class, I emphasized in the demo that each group had to have a leader to say stop when they had made a shape. Each student had to hold still until a group member had a chance to draw the shape. Then the leader would say go, and they could try something else.

When students are ready, draw their shape on the board so the class can see what they have created.

2. Investigation: *Making string shapes.*

Divide the class into groups of four or five students. To make sure the whole class understands the activity, discuss the directions before handing out the string to the groups.

Part of the purpose of this activity is for students to think about different ways that equal-length sides can be compared. Students need to be creative in developing a measurement test that does not involve a ruler or other measuring stick. This requirement encourages students to think about nontraditional units of measure, such as their hand, a pen, or one of the other sides of the shape.

TO THE STUDENT

- Using the string, make a shape that has four sides of equal length. The shape *cannot* be a square. The sides across from each other must be *parallel*.
- Figure out *two* different ways to test whether your sides are the same length. You may use a ruler or measuring stick for *one* of the tests. Describe your tests.

My students had fun spending some time just trying different shapes with the string. One group came up with an hourglass, which turned out to be surprisingly controversial.

A few students got into a debate about whether the hourglass had four sides or six. They had never really thought about what made a side. Those that insisted it was two triangles touching at the tip said it had six sides, while those who saw it as an hourglass claimed it had only four sides. The debate continued for several days, as the students consulted other teachers, books, and parents to try to figure out who was right. I was pleased to see them dig in like that!

Reproducible 20

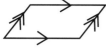

Figure 1.

Figure 2.

3. Problem solving: *Can you make this shape?*

Each group creates shapes to match the clues listed on *Can You Make This Shape? Part 1* (Reproducible 20). If they choose to make the shapes with the string (rather than paper and pencil), make sure they record the shape on paper.

The clues are written to highlight the concepts of *equilateral* and *parallel*. Introduce the notation for indicating parallel sides and equal sides used in geometry and ask students to add them to their sketches:

- Arrows drawn on the sides indicate parallel sides. Corresponding pairs of parallel sides have matching arrow marks. See Figure 1.
- Hash marks drawn on the sides indicate equal length sides. Corresponding pairs of equal sides have matching hash marks. See Figure 2.

The solutions to this exercise are presented at the end of the lesson.

4. Investigation: *Make animated shapes.*

Reproducible 21

In *Animated Shapes* (Reproducible 21), students convert one string shape to another by having one member of the group shift position while the rest stay stationary. Several moves may be necessary to get from one shape to another. This activity is more challenging than the stationary string shapes and may be difficult for students who have not had much background in geometry. You will need to decide whether to do this activity with the whole class or offer it as an extension for those who wish to try it.

5. Discussion: *How did you make the shapes?*

Ask students to discuss or write about the process they went through to make the shapes in Steps 2, 3, and 4. Questions such as the ones below can also be used to assess students' understanding of the properties of sides in a shape and the related terms and notations:

- How did your group decide that two sides were equal? Describe the different tests you used.
- How did your group decide when two sides were parallel? Describe the different tests you used.
- What is one idea you tried that didn't work? Why didn't it work?
- Did anyone in your group come up with a new idea about parallel or equal sides in a shape? Describe it. Draw some shapes and explain how your idea works with those shapes.
- In animated shapes, which clues needed only one or two moves?
- In animated shapes, which of the changes were hardest to predict? Which moves surprised you the most?

6. Writing: *Add to the glossary.*

Reproducible 22

Have groups of three or four students write descriptions of what is meant by the terms *parallel* and *equilateral* using the illustrations on *Visual Glossary: Parallel and Equilateral* (Reproducible 22).

Ask a few students from different groups to write their descriptions on the board and then have the class discuss and refine a definition to add to the glossary.

Homework Possibilities

Writing

Assign all or parts of *Visual Glossary: Parallel and Equilateral* as homework. A student's journal entry on the terms *parallel* and *equilateral* is reproduced below:

Parallel: 2 lines that run along eachother, that never meet, that have an equal mesurment between them.

Equiplateral: when all the sides on an object that are equal like a square.

Practice

Practice Shapes (Reproducible 23) extends the work begun with *Can You Make This Shape? Part 1.* Students solve new clues, write their own clues, and reflect on their thinking.

Making Connections

String or rope is often used in modern construction as a tool for marking off right angles. Two methods are commonly used. Students explore one method in *Roping It Off, Method 1* (Reproducible 24); the other method is part of a homework assignment in Lesson 9. Have students complete *Roping It Off, Method 1.*

Answer Key: Can You Make This Shape? Part 1

1. Any regular shape that has an odd number of sides greater than three will fit the criteria.
   Sample responses:

   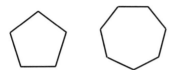

2. An isosceles trapezoid is the only quadrilateral that will work. Both concave and convex polygons with more than 4 sides are possible.
   Sample responses:

     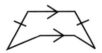

3. This claim is impossible. If a quadrilateral has two pairs of parallel sides, both pairs of sides must also be equal.

4. A parallelogram that is not a square or a rhombus is the only type of quadrilateral that will work. Other polygons with more than four sides are possible.
   Sample responses:

5. This claim is impossible. An equilateral quadrilateral can only be a square or a rhombus, both of which have two pair of parallel sides.

Lesson 9

String Shapes—Properties of Angles

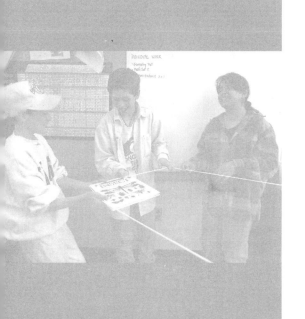

How can you tell when a shape has equal angles? If you know that a quadrilateral has parallel sides, what can you say about its angles?

As in Lesson 8, students work in groups to create shapes, this time focusing on the properties of angles in the shapes. Students solve clues based on the concepts of equal, right, and opposite angles. They apply these concepts, as well as the concepts of parallel and equilateral, in a game that focuses on the relationship between the properties of angles and the properties of sides.

Students will apply the concepts they learn in this lesson when they revise their plans in Lesson 10.

Mathematical Goals

- Understand the meaning of the concepts of *right angle, equal angles, opposite angles,* and *regular shapes* and apply them to create different polygons.
- Examine the relationship between properties of sides and properties of angles in a shape.
- Learn the formal geometric notation for equal and right angles.
- Devise tests for comparing sizes of angles.

Materials

Per Student

Reproducible 28, *Visual Glossary: Types of Angles and Regular Shapes*

Reproducible 29, *Roping It Off, Method 2* (optional)

Per Group

Loop of string or rope (see Preparation in Lesson 8 for lengths)

Protractors (optional)

Reproducible 25, *What Is an Angle?* (optional)

Reproducible 26, *Can You Make This Shape? Part 2*

Reproducible 27, *Sides and Angles Game Cards*

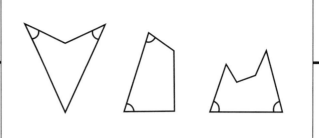

Preparation

Make one copy of *Sides and Angles Game Cards* (Reproducible 27) for each group of two to four students. Cut out the game cards.

Suggested Lesson Plan

At the end of this lesson, students will add the terms *equal angle, right angle, opposite angle,* and *regular shape* to the class glossary. As you work through the lesson plan, look for opportunities to draw out students' understanding of these concepts. See page xxi of the unit overview for suggestions on how to teach the key terms in the unit.

1. Introduction/Preassessment: *What is an angle?*

What Is an Angle? (Reproducible 25) serves as a measure of how well students understand certain concepts about angles. For this lesson, students will need to understand that an angle represents a rotation or a turn and that sizes of angles depend on the amount of rotation or turn rather than the length of the sides. If the class has already studied angles, you may want to skip this step.

This lesson focuses on methods for comparing angles so that students can understand the relationship between angles and sides of a polygon. The lesson is not intended as a complete introduction to angles. It does not, for example, address such topics as measuring with degrees or the concepts of acute and obtuse.

Reproducible 25

▶ *From the Classroom*

When I realized that my class had no real understanding of angles, I tried an idea I had seen in an article in the Arithmetic Teacher *(January 1992) by Patricia S. Wilson and Verna M. Adams. We made our own angle measurement tools out of bendable straws with sticks or pencils sticking out of the ends, and spent some time measuring rotations, such as how far the door to our classroom could open or how far apart we could spread our fingers. We didn't apply any numbers to our measurements, but simply marked the angles with the tools and compared each other's measurements. This helped some students understand that it's the amount of turn that matters.*

2. Investigation: *Make string shapes.*

Divide the class into groups of three students and give each group a loop of string. You will need to decide whether to allow your students to use protractors to measure the sizes of the different angles. The protractor can give them precise results, but some students may get a better understanding of angle measurement by creating their own tests and units of measure.

TO THE STUDENT

- Using the string, make a triangle with three angles that are the same size.
- Create two different ways to test whether your angles are the same size. Describe your tests.

▶ **From the Classroom**

Evan, William, and Luis first tried to compare the angles in their triangle by folding the base in half and holding two angles on top of each other, much like what they had done with the sides of quadrilateral. They liked this method as a quick test of equality, but they weren't confident of their answer. So, they got out a protractor to make sure the angles were, in fact, equal.

▶ *I watched a group of three girls struggling to use a protractor to measure the two base angles of a rope triangle. They had laid the rope on the floor in the shape of the triangle, but could not figure out which set of numbers to read off the protractor (see Figure 1). So they decided to "adjust" the angles to a measure that they could read off the protractor: they made two right angles and curved the sides up to the tip of the triangle (see Figure 2). I pointed out that they no longer had a triangle and I helped them straighten the sides and read the protractor. Later on, we did some practice with protractors.*

Figure 1.   *Figure 2.*

3. Problem solving: *Can you make this shape?*

Each group tries to create shapes to match the clues listed on *Can You Make This Shape? Part 2* (Reproducible 26). If they choose to make the shapes with the rope (rather than paper and pencil), make sure they record the shapes on paper. Classes that have access to geometry software may also want to try making the shapes on the computer.

The clues are written to highlight the concepts of *equal angles, right angles, opposite angles,* and *regular shapes* (shapes in which all sides are equilateral and all angles are equal). Introduce the notation for indicating equal angles and right angles used in geometry:

- Arcs with a hashmark drawn in the interior of an angle indicate equal angles. Any equal angles have matching arcs.

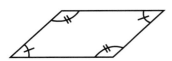

- A "box" or right angle drawn in the interior of an angle indicates right angles.

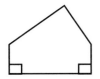

► **From the Classroom**

One group was trying to decide how many right angles they had in a six-sided shape they had created (below). The whole group wanted to count the exterior angle as one of the right angles in their shape. I told them that, in general, only the interior angles are counted and showed them how to draw arcs in each of the interior angles to distinguish them from the exterior ones.

4. Problem solving: *Play the Sides and Angles Game.*

The Sides and Angles Game integrates the concepts students have learned from making the string shapes in this lesson and Lesson 8. Provide each group of two to four students with a complete set of *Sides and Angles Game Cards* (Reproducible 27). Each set includes four "sides" cards and four "angles" cards.

There are sixteen possible card combinations. You may either give the class a certain number of rounds to play or you may have each student find a solution to a new pair of cards so that all combinations are tried. The letters in the right hand corner of the cards correspond to the solutions in the answer key, which is provided at the end of the lesson.

TO THE STUDENT

In this game, you will try to make shapes that fit two different clues. One of the clues describes the sides of the shape and the other clue describes the angles.

To play:

- Make a pile of "sides" cards and a pile of "angles" cards. Turn all the cards face down.

- Each player takes turns drawing one card from each pile and trying to draw the shape. Make sure your drawing fits the clues!

- If you can make the shape, draw it and label it using the notation you have learned for parallel and equal sides, and equal and right angles. Write the real name of the shape if you know it; if not, create a name for it. If you cannot make the shape, describe why you think it cannot be made.

- The next player tries to find another solution to the two cards until the group finds four shapes or runs out of possible solutions (whichever comes first). Then, draw two new cards and repeat the process.

- Your teacher will tell you how many rounds of the game to play.

To help students figure out ways to generate multiple answers for some of the combinations, I prepared the following hints for cards D, a:
Start with the easiest shape that fits the criteria.

Identify the essential part of the shape that fits the criteria (two equal angles and no parallel sides).

Keeping the essential part of the shape, draw a line that "cuts off" the unnecessary part of the shape.

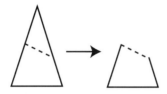

By adding more and more sides where the dotted line is, you can increase the number of sides infinitely and still have the shape fit the criteria.

5. Discussion: *What properties of sides and angles are related?*

Encourage students to make some general connections between the properties of sides and angles in a shape. Some questions to begin the discussion include:

- Which shapes from the clue game were impossible to make? Why? What would you need to change to make them possible?
- What was your strategy for finding more than one shape that fit a clue?

6. Writing: *Add to the glossary.*

Have groups of three or four students write descriptions of what is meant by the terms *equal angle, right angle, opposite angles,* and *regular shapes* using the illustrations on *Visual Glossary: Types of Angles and Regular Shapes* (Reproducible 28).

Ask a few students from different groups to write their descriptions on the board and then have the class discuss and refine a definition to add to the glossary.

Homework Possibilities

Writing

Assign all or parts of *Visual Glossary: Types of Angles and Regular Shapes* as homework.

Making Connections

Rope is often used in modern construction as a tool for marking off right angles. *Roping It Off, Method 2* (Reproducible 29) poses a problem based on one of these uses of rope. One student, Matthew, composed the following journal description of why the string shapes work:

You check this by using two pieces of string. and running them, corner to corner, in an angle so that they intersect in the center. (See drawing-1) If you cut the strings to the size of the angle (corner to corner) and measure them, then, if they are the same, your angles are perfect (Mrs. Mellett, I just today cut and built a picture frame. I did use this method to

① string

check it)
   This works because if you didn't have a perfect square, (see drawing 2) then the measurements wouldn't be the same.
   This method would also work with a rectangle and I'm not sure about a triangle. A triangle would probably work, but with a little different procedure.
   I tried a couple other kinds of shapes to try this with, on graph paper.

② $1\frac{1}{8}$" $2\frac{1}{8}$"

Practice

Have students write four of their own clues that involve equal angles, right angles, and/or opposite angles. If the shapes are possible, students draw a shape that fits the criteria. If the shapes are impossible, students try to explain why.

Journal Writing

This lesson provides a good opportunity for students to reflect on what they've learned about the properties of shapes. See Homework Possibilities in Lesson 1 for sample journal writing prompts.

Extensions

- Have students investigate "paired properties"—properties that always exist together. For example:

If a four-sided shape has two pairs of parallel sides, . . .

. . . it will always have opposite angles that are equal to each other.

 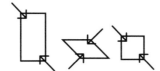

- See if students can identify paired properties involving the concepts of *equilateral, parallel, equal angles, opposite angles,* or *right angles.* Students might pick their favorite pair and make a poster to illustrate and explain the concept. They could even give it a name, such as "Susan's Theory of Parallel Sides."

Answer Key: Can You Make This Shape? Part 2

1. A trapezoid with two adjacent right angles is the only quadrilateral that will fit the criteria.

2. This clue describes an impossible shape. If two opposite angles of a quadrilateral are right angles, both pairs of opposite sides must be parallel. Therefore, the remaining pair of opposite angles must also be right angles.

3. This shape must have more than four sides to be possible. In most cases, the shape will look like a rectangle with the fourth side changed in some way.

4. This clue is impossible. One pair of opposite angles means that the opposite sides will be parallel, therefore the remaining opposite angles will also be equal.

5. The only shape that fits this criteria is a regular pentagon. The sides will also be equal.

6. If one pair of opposite angles are right angles, the remaining pair must be as well. Rectangles and squares are the only shapes that fit this criteria.

Answer Key: The Sides and Angles Game

Many geometric terms are used in this answer key. Students are not expected to know all these terms. They are used here for the teacher for the sake of clarity.

Sides Clues		Angles Clues		Answers
Equilateral	A	Exactly two equal angles	a	Impossible
Equilateral	A	Two pairs of opposite angles	b	Square, rhombus
Equilateral	A	At least one pair of opposite angles	c	Square, rhombus
Equilateral	A	At least two right angles	d	Square
Two pairs of parallel sides	B	Exactly two equal angles	a	Shape must have more than four sides. One example:

Sides Clues		Angles Clues		Answers
Two pairs of parallel sides	B	Two pairs of opposite angles	b	Any parallelogram (includes square, rhombus, and rectangle)
Two pairs of parallel sides	B	At least one pair of opposite equal angles	c	Any parallelogram (includes square, rhombus, and rectangle)
Two pairs of parallel sides	B	At least two right angles	d	Square, rectangle; other shapes with more than five sides are possible. One example:
Equilateral; at least one pair of parallel sides	C	Exactly two equal angles	a	Impossible
Equilateral; at least one pair of parallel sides	C	Two pairs of opposite angles	b	Square, rhombus
Equilateral; at least one pair of parallel sides	C	At least one pair of opposite equal angles	c	Any regular shape with an even number of sides

Sides Clues		Angles Clues		Answers
Equilateral; at least one pair of parallel sides	C	At least two right angles	d	Square
No parallel sides	D	Exactly two equal angles	a	Many answers, including isosceles triangles. Some examples:
No parallel sides	D	Two pairs of opposite angles	b	Any quadrilateral that is not a parallelogram or trapezoid. An example:
No parallel sides	D	At least one pair of opposite equal angles	c	Many answers, including a symmetric quadrilateral. An example:
No parallel sides	D	At least two right angles	d	Many answers, including a quadrilateral with nonadjacent right angles. An example:

Lesson 10

In Other Words— Improving Your Plans

How can you apply your knowledge of shapes and representations to describe your house?

Students use the concepts and terms they learned in Lessons 8 and 9 to revise their house plans from Lesson 7. Students trade plans and use the plans to build replicas of their partner's house model. They then compare structures and give each other suggestions on how to revise their plans further. After making their final revisions to the plans, students write a memo explaining the features of the house—including the shapes that make up the design. The lesson concludes with an assessment of the plans and the accompanying memo.

Mathematical Goals

Apply and extend knowledge of:

- Concepts about sides and angles.
- Geometric terms and notation.
- Orthogonal and isometric drawings.
- Visualizing and communicating a building process.

Materials

Per Student

Students' house models from Lesson 7

Cardboard shapes from Lesson 7

Students' plans from Lesson 7

Drawing paper

Per Group

Masking tape, transparent tape, or reusable tape

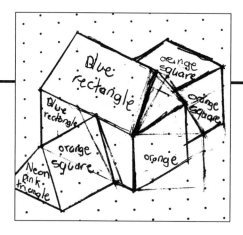

Reproducible 30, *Memo
4 to House Designers*

Reproducible 31, *Sample
House Plans*

Suggested Lesson Plan

1. Introduction: *Preparing for assessment.*

Students will be assessed on the revised plans they write in this lesson as well as on the design specifications they write as outlined on *Memo 4 to House Designers* (Reproducible 30).

Sample House Plans (Reproducible 31) serves as a starting point for a discussion of the assessment criteria. You may want to go through the questions on the reproducible in a class discussion, or have students work on them alone or in small groups. Additionally, have students review the questions on *Memo 4 to House Designers* (Reproducible 30 in Lesson 14).

As in Lesson 6, you should decide whether to use the assessment criteria provided at right, present your own criteria, or create the criteria with the class (see page 49). If you choose to use the criteria provided, students should notice that the plans on *Sample House Plans* do not meet all of the criteria.

Reproducibles 30–31

ASSESSMENT CRITERIA

- *The plans are written clearly so that the house models can be replicated. The plans include a step-by-step description of the building process.*

- *The plans and design specifications include geometric concepts and terms that help make the written description clear and precise.*

- *The correct terms for names of shapes and the components of shapes (side, angle, face) are used. The work exhibits a clear understanding of the properties of shapes (equilateral, symmetrical, regular, comparing angles, parallel).*

- *Geometric notation (equal-length sides, parallel sides, right angles, equal angles) has been used appropriately.*

- *The plans include both orthogonal drawings and drawings that show depth. Both types of drawings provide complete and accurate information about the structure.*

- *At least three orthogonal views have been drawn or described and labeled.*

- *The orthogonal drawings are consistent with the drawings that show depth.*

2. Problem solving: *Revise the plans for the houses.*

Once they understand the assessment criteria, students revise their plans.

TO THE STUDENT

Revise both the drawings and the written description you made in Lesson 7 to meet the assessment criteria.

- Use geometric concepts, terms, and notation in your written description. The terms should make your plans clearer and more precise so that someone else can build from them. Concepts and terms that you should consider include the names of the shapes, parallel sides, equilateral sides, opposite angles, right angles, equal angles, and rotation.

- Redo the drawings of the structure you created in Lesson 7. Your drawings should include both orthogonal views and drawings that show depth. They should show if the shapes in your structure have parallel or equilateral sides, right angles, or equal angles.

► From the Classroom

Below are examples of student plans along with notes on how they relate to the assessment criteria.

Instrushens -- Prisimid house
Supplies 12x ▭ 12x △

1.) Tape three rectangles together in a

shape. None of the rectangles
should be parallel. The shape at the
end should be a equillateral triangle.

2.) Then add two triangles to the ends.

 like this and tape them

3.) Make four more of these
Make sure that the ends are
equilateral triangles.

4.) Then place them together like this
and tape them together.

5.) you know you have finished making
the prisimid house, when the front and
back views are this

and the side views and the base view
are this

This house would be good for a climate
which gets snow because the snow would
roll right off the roof.

This student has fulfilled all the requirements for a set of building plans. There is a complete written description of the building process that someone could use to replicate the structure. There are also isometric and orthogonal views of the structure.

Additionally, this student correctly uses the geometric concepts and notation introduced in this section of the unit (parallel and equilateral sides, equal angles) as well as the previous section (labeling the views of the house).

► *From the Classroom*

Leaning Tower of Piza
with a few corrections
House
1.) Get 6 diamonds, 4 triangles, 2
Use tape to attach the shapes.

2.) Take the ⬡ and at each corner
attach a diamond. Like this

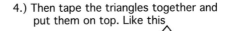

3.) Then attach the other one to the
opposite corners of the diamonds like
this

4.) Then tape the triangles together and
put them on top. Like this

Our house is for a desert because it gives
shade but lets the wind through.

This student has included a step-by-step description of the building process along with some orthogonal views of the structure. However, the orthogonal views are incomplete and not labeled.

This student does not use the geometric concepts introduced in this section of the unit and uses only some of the concepts from the previous section correctly (triangle, views that show depth).

3. Building: *Build from another's plans.*

Students exchange plans and attempt to build replicas of the original structures using their partner's plans. See Step 1 of Lesson 6 for suggestions on how to structure the exchanging of plans.

4. Sharing: *How could the plans be improved?*

The students compare the replicas they built to the original structures and determine whether the structures are identical and, if not, how they are different. They then make suggestions about how the plans could be revised.

Decide whether you want the class to give written or verbal feedback to each other. You can help students structure their suggestions by providing them with questions such as:

- Is the written description easy to follow?
- Are the mathematical terms and notations used correctly?
- Is any information missing? What else would you suggest including?

► *From the Classroom*

Before they wrote their suggestions, I reminded my students of the conversations we had on giving feedback. I encouraged them to be positive by having them list what they liked about the plans and then asked them to give suggestions for improvement. To give them a better idea of what I was talking about, I read examples of comments that students had written in other classes, including some that were particularly insensitive. I asked the students which of the comments were most helpful and which ones needed to be rephrased. This discussion took time, but it helped my students become more sensitive when they critiqued each other's work.

- Are the drawings accurate and consistent with one another?
- Would it help to add other drawings?
- Was some part of the plans especially helpful in your building process? Which part?

5. Writing: *Improve your plans.*

Students use their partner's suggestions to revise their plans. They may decide to rewrite their plans completely, to change a few words or drawings, or to keep their plans the same. In any case, students should understand that this is the last opportunity to revise the plans before turning them in to be assessed.

6. Writing: *Create design specifications.*

Memo 4 to House Designers (Reproducible 30) asks students to write design specifications that will provide the directors of the Creative Construction Company with more detailed information about the features of their house design. This writing assignment, which will be assessed along with the revised plans, gives students an additional opportunity to demonstrate what they've learned about shapes. Part of this activity may be done as homework.

Homework Possibilities

Journal Writing

Have students write answers to the following questions regarding the feedback and revision process:

1. What suggestions did your partner give you about how to improve your plans?
2. What suggestions did you follow when revising your plans and which ones did you decide not to follow? Why?
3. How do you feel about your final version of the plans? Do you think they come out well? Why or why not?

Visualizing and Representing Polygons and Polyhedra

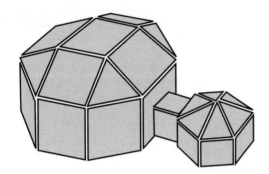

Section 3 focused on the properties of the two-dimensional shapes that make up three-dimensional structures. Section 4 focuses on the properties of the three-dimensional structures themselves. Students investigate the properties of a range of polyhedra through building, representing, and describing three-dimensional structures.

Students begin the section by exploring how shapes can be combined to form a variety of three-dimensional structures. Since these structures are not intended as model homes, students are free to experiment with whatever kinds of polyhedra they can imagine. Students compare the structures by creating a table of properties that includes the number of vertices, edges, and parallel faces in each structure. They also learn to identify which of the structures are prisms and pyramids and they practice techniques for representing the two kinds of common polyhedra.

The final two lessons require students to synthesize material from the entire unit. In Lesson 13, groups of students build a mystery structure by solving clues that contain views and descriptions of its properties. As they do so, they must visualize the structure, communicate their image to the group, and build it from shapes. In Lesson 14, students visualize, build, and represent a home for one of two possible climates; create building plans; and write design specifications. The unit ends with an assessment of the plans and the design specifications.

Approx. # of Classes	Lessons
2	**11. Beyond Boxes—Designing Polyhedra** Students explore various kinds of closed, three-dimensional structures by experimenting with combinations of polygons.
1–2	**12. Drawing Tricks—Prisms and Pyramids** Students explore methods for showing depth in representations of three-dimensional structures, including prisms and pyramids.
2–3	**13. Mystery Structures** Given written and visual clues, students work in groups to build polyhedra from polygons.
2–4	**14. Final Project—Putting the Pieces Together** Students design a house for a specific climate and create a set of building plans and design specifications.

Lesson summary and sample schedule for Section 4

Mathematical Goals

- Explore and describe polyhedra in terms of the number of edges, faces, and vertices.
- Visualize ways of building polyhedra from polygons.
- Define, describe, and identify different types of prisms and pyramids.
- Visualize and draw prisms and pyramids.
- Visualize and represent objects from different vantage points.
- Create two-dimensional representations showing depth.
- Communicate steps of a building process.
- Solve problems by:

  Identifying two-dimensional and three-dimensional shapes: triangle, square, rectangle, rhombus, trapezoid, hexagon, prism, and pyramid.

  Recognizing properties of shapes: equilateral; regular; parallel; number of faces, edges, and vertices.

  Interpreting orthogonal representations of polyhedra.

  Visualizing and building polyhedra.

Mathematical Theme 1

Multiple Representations of Shapes and Structures

Students learn new techniques for representing three-dimensional structures to add to the orthogonal and isometric drawings they learned to make in Section 2. Students are shown how to use perspective drawing techniques to represent prisms and pyramids. These techniques help broaden students' understanding of the two kinds of polyhedra and expand their ability to make and interpret drawings that show depth. Students apply their growing knowledge of multiple representations when they interpret and describe orthogonal drawings in the mystery structures games and when they represent their model house in building plans as part of the final project.

Mathematical Theme 2

Visualization

Just as the structures students build in this section are more complex than those they have built previously in the unit, the visualizing required to design and represent the structures is also more demanding. In Lesson 11, for example, students must visualize various ways to combine up to fifteen polygons to form polyhedra. In Lesson 14, students build with up to twenty-four shapes and then create a set of plans in which they must visualize the building process in order to describe it in words and drawings.

Students apply the visualizing skills they have developed throughout the unit when they play the mystery structures games. Students form pictures of polyhedra in their minds as they listen to classmates read a series of clues describing the properties and components of a structure. Students also improve their skills at representing three-dimensional structures through activities that teach them (1) how to draw prisms and pyramids and (2) how to rotate structures in their minds in order to see them from different vantage points.

Mathematical Theme 3

Properties and Components of Shape

In this section, students investigate the properties of polyhedra as they build, visualize, and represent three-dimensional structures. Students learn to identify which of the structures are prisms and pyramids and to categorize them according to the shape of their base. They also investigate the concepts of edge, vertex, and face by creating a table of properties to compare the structures.

When students assemble structures from clues in the Mystery Structures games in Lesson 13, they explore the relationships between the properties of two- and three-dimensional shapes. For example, students use the clues "This shape is a prism" and "This shape has a square base" to deduce that the bases and faces will be parallel, and, from the shape of the base, that the prism will have six faces. In creating design specifications for their final project, students describe their model house in terms of the properties and components of its shapes.

Mathematical Theme 4

Communication

In this section, students combine the language they have learned for describing structures mathematically with the knowledge they have gained about creating clear descriptions. Students create definitions of *prism, pyramid, edge,* and *vertex* and then apply those terms in the mystery structures games to convey a mental image of a structure to their classmates. Some of the game clues are visual, which students are required to describe—not show—to their partners.

The mathematical communication that students have practiced throughout the unit culminates in a final set of building plans in Lesson 14. The building plans for the final project are the most challenging in the unit because (1) the houses they describe are the most complex and (2) the assignment calls for more detailed information about the design. Students create a clear, written description of their house, including a set of design specifications describing the properties, components, and functions of the shapes in the structure.

Teacher Reflection

Daniel, Karen, June, and Carlos were seated together around a table scattered with a pile of colored shapes and a roll of tape. "We're ready for the next set of clues!" June announced, as they proudly displayed the structure they had built from Clue Set 1 in the Mystery Structures Game. I handed them the second set of clues, and decided to stay and watch since I knew this set was more challenging than the first set, which they had easily solved.

The difficulty with the second clue set lay in figuring out that the structure was a hexagonal prism, in which one of the hexagonal bases was made with three rhombi. The clues indicated that the structure was a prism with 18 edges, that it required 11 pieces to build, that there were half as many rhombi as rectangles, and that the bottom of the structure was a hexagon made from two isosceles trapezoids placed edge to edge. (See Figure 1.)

A base with 3 rhombi

A base with 2 trapezoids

Figure 1.

Deciding When to Intervene

Karen passed out the clues, and each group member read a clue out loud. "Well, I've got the easy one," she said. "Here's what the bottom looks like," and she put two trapezoids together.

"My clue says the structure is a prism, so the other base also has to be a hexagon," said Carlos, laying two more trapezoids edge to edge.

"Wait, how come it can't be one of these?" asked June, picking up a hexagon. After some brief discussion, the group agreed that maybe it was a hexagonal piece, but for now they were going to stick with 2 trapezoids so that the bases would be identical.

"OK, my clue says 'The number of rhombi in this structure is half the number of rectangles,' " read June. She paused for a moment, thinking, then started laying out four rhombi and two rectangles. I cringed slightly—she had reversed the relationship. *They should be able to interpret that clue correctly,* I thought. I wondered if I should intervene to correct them, but decided to wait a moment to see if any of them caught the mistake. This is a familiar dilemma for me. I want to encourage my students to pursue their own ideas rather than looking to me for all the answers, but I don't want them to waste their time needlessly. In this situation, since they were working with incorrect information, I decided to interrupt.

"June, would you please read your clue one more time?" I asked. They all stopped and looked at me, with that uh-oh-we-missed-something look. June read her clue again and, after a momentary pause, I heard a couple of ohhhhhhhs. Daniel rearranged the collection of shapes to have four rectangles and two rhombi. June reached over and added the two dual-trapezoid bases to the collection and counted the pieces.

"June, what are you doing?" Karen asked, looking on. "I'm doing guess and check," she replied, counting the pieces. ". . . 8, 9, 10. That's not right—we need 11 pieces. So let's try six rectangles and three rhombuses," she suggested, laying them out. Again, they counted the rectangles, rhombi, and four trapezoids.

"Thirteen. Too many," Carlos said. "We can't do eight rectangles, and four rhombuses because that's already too many pieces," added June. *Shouldn't you say something now?* that little voice inside my head spoke up again. *What if they don't figure it out? No,* I thought, *this time they have correct information and it's all there in front of them. I'll wait a while longer.*

This episode emphasized for me the difficulty of knowing when to intervene. Every situation is different, and I followed my instincts here. I suspected that this group could come to a solution if allowed time to explore; I might have made a different decision with a different group.

Observing Students Learning to Visualize

After studying the two bases for a few minutes, Daniel reached over and took one of them apart. While the others were engrossed in rearranging the pile of shapes, he seemed to be pondering another question entirely. He took three rhombi, and started turning them in different directions, fitting them together. "Hey!" he announced. The group stopped and looked at his creation. "Look! You can make a hexagon using these things. Then you could use six rectangles and it would work!" It sounded to me as if he could now visualize the finished structure in his head. He reached for the other base, and held the three-rhombus hexagon over it. "See?? If you do it like this, you have 11 pieces." June picked up some rectangles and held them up as sides. "Yeah!" she agreed. "That's five pieces in the hexagons, and then six rectangles!"

"Daniel, how did you decide to use three rhombi for the base?" I asked.

"Well," he explained, "after we tried all the different combinations of rectangles and rhombi that could have worked, and none of them did, I realized that that wasn't the only variable. So I started trying to find some other shapes that would make a hexagon for the base." We had only used the term *variable* with equations, so I was interested to see that he was using it in a new situation. I was also impressed with the mathematical nature of his decision. He had operated from an assumption that provided no correct solution: that the remaining base was made from two trapezoids. Instead of giving up, he had gone back to his original assumption and adapted it.

The thing that impressed me most about the episode, however, was the student's ability to visualize the structure. I could see from Daniel's pensive expression and his seemingly abrupt realization that he had "assembled" the complete hexagonal prism in his mind before doing it with his hands. And his comment about the bases seemed to provide enough of a description for June to visualize the structure as well.

I also realized how important it is to observe students at work solving problems in order to assess their abilities to visualize. I would have learned little about their visualization skills if I had looked only at their finished work. Of course, I would have learned even less if I had intervened to tell them what was wrong with the first bases they made.

Lesson 11

Beyond Boxes—
Designing Polyhedra

What closed, three-dimensional structures can you visualize and build from a set of two-dimensional shapes? What properties can you use to describe and compare these three-dimensional structures?

In this lesson, students explore various kinds of closed, three-dimensional structures by experimenting with different combinations of polygons. After visualizing and building various structures, students record properties of the structures in a table that includes the number of vertices, edges, faces, parallel faces, and parallel edges contained in each structure. This method of recording helps students see how the properties of two-dimensional shapes that they examined in Section 2 relate to the properties of three-dimensional structures. Students use the table of properties to begin exploring and comparing different kinds of polyhedra—particularly prisms and pyramids.

In Lessons 12 and 13, students will learn various techniques for visualizing and representing polyhedra. In Lesson 14, students will apply the properties of three-dimensional structures that they learn in this lesson when they write about their model houses.

Mathematical Goals

- Visualize ways of building polyhedra from polygons.
- Explore and describe the properties of polyhedra, including edges, faces, and vertices.
- Distinguish prisms and pyramids from other polyhedra.

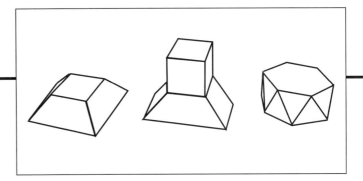

Materials

Per Student	*Per Group*	*Per Class*
Reproducible 32, *A Stack of Pennies*	Set of shapes made from poster board, four of each shape (square, triangle, rectangle, rhombus, trapezoid, and hexagon). Templates for the shapes are provided in Appendix D.	Modeling clay (optional)—about the size of a small fist
	Scissors	
	Tape	
	Sample prisms and pyramids made from shapes	
	Glue—for gluing template sheets to poster board before cutting shapes (optional)	

Preparation

Starting with any leftover shapes from Lessons 7 and 10, prepare (or have students prepare) sets of shapes for each student group. Alternatively, you can have students take apart the models they made in previous lessons and reuse those shapes. Students can cut out additional shapes as needed during the lesson. Any leftover shapes from this lesson can be used in Lessons 13 and 14. See pages xxiii-xxiv for further suggestions on preparing shapes and storing the house models.

Set up stations and labels for three groups of shapes: Pyramids, Prisms, and Neither. Prepare some sample prisms, pyramids, and other polyhedra of different sizes and shapes and place them in the appropriate groups.

Suggested Lesson Plan

At the end of this lesson, students will add the terms *vertex, edge, prism,* and *pyramid* to the class glossary. As you work through the lesson plan, look for opportunities to draw out students' understanding of these concepts. See page xxi of the unit overview for suggestions on how to teach the key terms in the unit.

1. Introduction: *Visualizing polygons into polyhedra.*

The activities on *A Stack of Pennies* (Reproducible 32) help students learn to visualize polyhedra by beginning with familiar shapes and objects—such as a penny, a rhombus, and a square. They will apply these visualization skills in Step 2, when they build three-dimensional structures from two-dimensional shapes.

Encourage students to use the concepts they have learned to this point in the unit to write descriptions of the shapes they visualize. This activity can serve as a quick assessment of how comfortable students are with the shape names and properties at this point. Students' results may differ depending on how they visualize the building process and how they mentally "cut" the objects.

You may want to have some modeling clay available for students who are having trouble visualizing the shapes. For example, a student could build the imaginary penny stack for the first situation and then cut it with a wire or piece of thread for the second one. This will give students a concrete image to connect to the abstract situation.

A Stack of Pennies

For each of the situations described below, draw the shape you would end up with and write answers to the questions on a separate sheet of paper.

1. Imagine a penny. Now imagine ten pennies stacked right on top of the first one so that the edges of each one line up perfectly with the one below it.

    Describe this shape. What would you call it? What properties does it have?

2. Imagine the shape you thought of in #1. Now imagine slicing that shape from top to bottom right through the middle. Open up the two halves of the shape.

    What two-dimensional shape is the face in front of you?

3. Imagine a rhombus-shaped piece of cardboard laying on your desk. Now imagine fifteen of them stacked on top of this shape so that all the corners and edges line up.

    Describe this shape. What would you call it? What properties does it have?

4. Imagine the shape that you thought of in #3. Now imagine that you sliced it from the top to the bottom through the center.

    What is the two-dimensional shape of the face?

5. Imagine a square. Imagine a point in space above the square. In your mind, draw a line from each of the corners of the square to the point. Now imagine this shape as a solid shape.

    Describe this shape. What would you call it? What properties does it have?

6. Imagine slicing the shape you made in #5 from top (the point) to the bottom (the square) right through the middle.

©EDC, 1995   *Designing Spaces*   *Reproducible 32*

Reproducible 32.

2. Investigation: *Construct closed three-dimensional structures.*

Provide each group of students with a set of shapes. If each set includes at least four of each kind of shape, students will have a variety of shapes to choose from. Students can build the structures individually or with other members of the group. Have students cut out additional shapes as needed.

► **From the Classroom**

I revised the lesson to ask each group to make one structure with each of the different pieces as the floor. Some of my students recognized that it is impossible to make a pyramid with a rhombus-shaped based using the pieces they had. Another group found it was impossible to make a pyramid with these pieces if the base was a hexagon, but that they could make a prism. One member of the group commented that if the triangles were taller and skinnier, they probably could make a pyramid. I was impressed with his visualization of such a pyramid.

What kinds of structures can you build from a set of shapes that includes triangles, rectangles, squares, rhombi, trapezoids, and hexagons? Build *at least two* different structures.

You may use 3–15 pieces for each structure that you build.

Tape the shape pieces together to build the structures. If you need more pieces, cut out additional ones that are the same size and shape as one of the given pieces.

Building Rules:

- The base or bottom of the structure can be made of only *one* piece. The base can be any of the six shapes.
- The pieces *cannot* overlap.
- The structure must be *closed*. No gaps allowed. (Use tape to hold the shapes together.)
- No hidden pieces allowed. You need to be able to see all the pieces.

3. Writing: *Create a table of properties.*

Have students record information about their structures on a table of properties similar to the sample below. The table helps students make comparisons among different kinds of structures. As students study the sample and begin to fill out the table for their own structures, they will begin to form definitions for the terms *vertex* and *edge*. They will write descriptions of these terms in Step 6.

Sample Table

Shape of Base	Shapes Used	No. of Faces	No. of Vertices (Corners)	No. of Edges	Parallel Faces?	Parallel Edges?
Rectangle	1 rectangle 2 triangles 2 trapezoids	5	6	9	No (0)	Yes (2)

The sample table on page 108 describes a structure that looks like the one below:

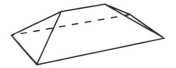

There may be some confusion about the relationship between the number of shapes used and the number of faces. For example, Ann could have used two squares for one side of the structure instead of the rectangle. This would change the number of *shapes* but *not* the number of *faces*. Also, the number of edges would not change.

► *From the Classroom*

I set up stations with the following signs: Square Base, Triangle Base, Rectangle Base, Rhombus Base, Trapezoid Base, and Hexagon Base. I asked students to take their structures to the appropriate station and compare them with the other students' structures at that station.

Examples of polyhedra with square bases.

4. Writing: *Describe one of your structures.*

In describing one of their structures, students apply the knowledge they've gained in Steps 2 and 3 about the properties of polyhedra.

TO THE STUDENT

Write a description of one of the structures you built. Include enough information so that your classmates would be able to pick out your structure from all the others. You can include drawings in your description.

Questions to think about when you write your description:

- What shapes did you use in the structure? What shape is the base?
- How many faces, vertices, and edges does the structure have?
- How many of the faces and edges are parallel?

---

5. Problem solving: *Sort prisms and pyramids.*

Show the class the sample prisms and pyramids you made and ask students to place their own structures in one of the three stations you have set up in the classroom: Prisms, Pyramids, and Neither. (See Preparation.)

6. Writing: *Add to the glossary.*

Have groups of three or four students write descriptions of what is meant by the terms *prism* and *pyramid* using the structures in the three stations as examples. The following questions may help students construct a definition:

- What do pyramids have in common?
- What do prisms have in common?
- Can you build a pyramid with any shape as the base? Can you build a prism with any shape as the base?

Discuss and refine some sample student descriptions and then add the class definition to the glossary. You may want to have the class refine these definitions further in the next lesson after students have learned techniques for drawing prisms and pyramids.

Ask the class to point out examples of *vertex* and *edge* in the student structures. Have students write descriptions of what is meant by the two terms by thinking about what the examples of vertex and edge have in common. Other questions that may help students understand the terms include:

- What makes an edge or vertex different from a side?
- What makes an edge or vertex different from a face?
- How are an edge and a vertex different from each other?

Discuss and refine some sample student descriptions and add the class definitions of both terms to the glossary.

Homework Possibilities

Practice

- Have students write two visualization problems of their own, using *A Stack of Pennies* (Reproducible 32) as a model. Students should think about creating situations in which (1) shapes are put together to form a different shape (such as pennies combined to form a cylinder) or (2) a shape is sliced so that another shape results from the cut (such as the circle that may result from cutting an egg). You can help students get started by suggesting they use household objects in their situations.

- Ask students to draw possible solutions to their problems. You may want to try a few of the students' examples as a warm-up in class the following day. Examples of visualization problems created by a student are shown below:

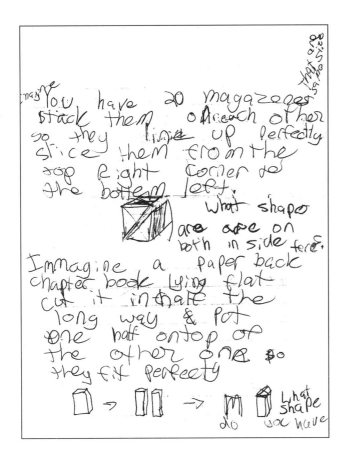

you have 20 magazenes stack them on each other so they line up perfectly slice them from the top Right corner to the bottem left. What shape are are on both in side faces.

Immagine a paper back chapter book lying flat cut it in half the long way & put one half ontop of the other one so they fit perfectly
→ → what shape do you have

2. Think of 15 equilateral triangles stacked up on top of eachother. Cut the stack directly down the center. Open it up. On one side you will see

(on the part that was split) a rectangle. Now, turn it around in your head so that the part that wasn't cut down the middle you will see. What do you see?

Extensions

- If your class compiled a table in Step 3 that includes the number of faces, edges, and vertices in their polyhedra, then students have information they can use to explore Euler's formula ($V - E + F = 2$, where V = the number of vertices, E = the number of edges, and F = the number of faces). Ask them to analyze the table and look for a pattern in the relationship between the number of edges, vertices, and faces in a three-dimensional shape.

  Once they have found a pattern, have them copy down Euler's formula. Then, have students choose values for two of the three variables, figure out the value of the third variable, and try to build a structure that would fit those values. Is it possible or impossible to build? As a further extension, ask them to try to build a structure for which the formula is not true.

- Have students find and draw examples of famous buildings that have prisms, pyramids, or both in their construction. They can create a poster that defines prisms and pyramids for other students by using real-world examples.

- Let students experiment with building prisms and pyramids to determine what shapes can be combined to make each. Some questions to ask: What shapes cannot form a pyramid? a prism? Can you explain why?

Lesson 12

Drawing Tricks— Prisms and Pyramids

What techniques can you use to show depth when you are drawing three-dimensional objects? How can these techniques help you to represent prisms and pyramids?

In Lesson 3, students learned to make isometric drawings of cube structures. In this lesson, students explore techniques for showing depth in representations of polyhedra. They enhance their ability to visualize depth by drawing and comparing representations of objects from several different vantage points. They then learn specific techniques for drawing prisms and pyramids, which furthers their investigation of the properties of both kinds of structures. That investigation will help prepare students for Lesson 13, when they will need to visualize prisms and pyramids in order to solve clues based on their properties.

In Lessons 13 and 14, students will apply the drawing techniques they learn in this lesson.

Mathematical Goals

- Visualize and represent objects from different vantage points.
- Visualize and draw prisms and pyramids.
- Define, describe, and identify different types of prisms and pyramids.

Materials

Per Student	*Per Class*
Reproducible 33, *How to Draw a Prism*	Several identical pairs of objects for students to sketch, such as a book and a cup or mug (the pair of objects should represent different three-dimensional shapes, such as a cylinder and a prism)
Reproducible 34, *How to Draw a Pyramid*	
Reproducible 35, *Practicing Prisms and Pyramids*	
Reproducible 36, *Photo Sort* (optional)	

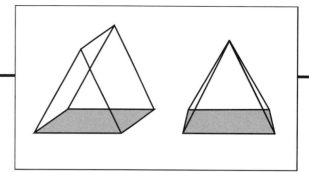

Preparation

Place two objects with different shapes, such as a cup and a book, on a desk so that they do not touch, and number the corners of the desk 1 through 4. Figure 1 is a top view of this arrangement.

Set up identical arrangements at several other desks around the classroom. Make one arrangement for every four to six students so that small groups of students can gather around the desks and get unobstructed views of the objects. All of the arrangements must be identical so that the class can make comparisons among drawings.

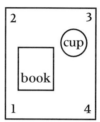

Figure 1.

Suggested Lesson Plan

▶ **From the Classroom**

I encouraged my students to study the arrangement very carefully before they began. I asked them to think about which object was in front, where lines intersected, and where the shadows fell. We discussed how the two-dimensional shapes might appear to change as students looked at them from a particular vantage point.

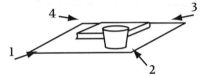

Figure 2.

1. Drawing: *Sketch objects from different vantage points.*

Students devise methods for sketching the three-dimensional arrangements (see Preparation) from one of four vantage points. When they compare these sketches in the next step, students will explore how the shape of the objects looks different from different vantage points, which is essential for learning how to show depth.

Assign each student one of the four vantage points, which are a few inches above each of the corners of the desk (see Figure 2).

It is important that the drawings be kept anonymous. In the next step, the class will try to identify the vantage point of some sketches; students should do this based on the sketch alone, rather than by knowing where the student was standing.

TO THE STUDENT

- Study the objects on the desk from your vantage point and make a sketch in which you show depth.
- Draw the shapes of the objects exactly as they look from your vantage point so that other students will be able to tell what your vantage point was.
- Other than showing depth, you don't need to include a lot of detail in your sketch.
- Write an identifying symbol on your sketches instead of your name so that only you can recognize which drawing is yours.

---

2. Sharing: *Compare techniques for showing depth.*

Gather as a class to discuss the different sketches. You may want to tape the sketches up around the room, or collect all the sketches and choose randomly from the pile. A comparison of ways to show depth will help prepare students for the next activity, in which they learn specific techniques for drawing three-dimensional structures.

Sample discussion questions include:

- What techniques were used in the drawings to show depth?
- Did any of the drawings use shading to show depth?
- Did the size of the objects vary to show depth in any of the drawings? For example, was the object in front drawn smaller or larger than the object behind?
- Which drawings were made from which vantage points? How do you know?

As an extension, students can order the sketches to represent the views seen as you move around the arrangement (see Figure 3).

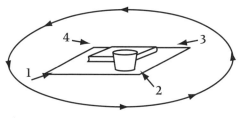

Figure 3.

3. Drawing: *Practice drawing prisms and pyramids.*

Reproducibles 33–35

Students are now shown a specific technique for drawing depth. *How to Draw a Prism* and *How to Draw a Pyramid* (Reproducibles 33 and 34, respectively) provide students with techniques for drawing the two kinds of polyhedra. As well as leading students to a deeper understanding of the differences between prisms and pyramids, the techniques teach students new ways to translate two-dimensional shapes into three-dimensional representations.

Demonstrate both techniques on the board or an overhead projector and then hand out *Practicing Prisms and Pyramids* (Reproducible 35).

Some students may find it difficult to match the corresponding vertices, especially on shapes with five or more sides. You can suggest numbering the vertices, starting at the same vertex in each shape.

You may want to review the definitions of *prism* and *pyramid* that the class created in Step 6 of Lesson 11. Ask students if the drawing techniques they've learned in this lesson change their understanding of the concepts in any way.

My students played around quite a bit with the kinds of prisms and pyramids they could draw. They ended up exploring a number of interesting questions: How would you draw a pyramid from a top down view? Can you use the same technique to draw a cylinder? How complicated a prism can you draw using this technique?

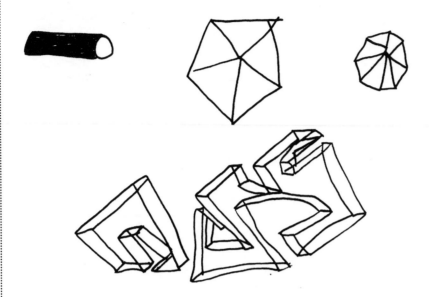

My students enjoyed learning a trick for drawing three-dimensional figures. They used this techniques to write their names in block letters.

Homework

Practice

Have students do the following activities:

1. Find three objects in your home that have the shape of a prism. Each object should be a different kind of prism. Draw each one and label what it is.
2. Draw three different kinds of pyramids. Write the name of the type of pyramid it is below it.
3. Try drawing your initials as three-dimensional block letters. You will need to draw an outline of each letter so that the letters do not have any curves in them.

   Then see if you can make them look three-dimensional by using what you have learned about drawing prisms.

Extension

Assign *Photo Sort* (Reproducible 36) for individual or small-group work.

Reproducible 36

Lesson 13

Mystery Structures

Can you visualize a prism with three sets of parallel faces and a square as its right side?

In Lessons 8 and 9, students visualized and created two-dimensional shapes on the basis of written descriptions of the shapes' properties. In this lesson, students solve similar clues for three-dimensional structures, which requires them to synthesize all of the geometric concepts they've learned in the unit. A final set of clues guides students in assembling the polyhedra they've made into a mystery structure.

After solving the clues, students create their own structures and clues. They then use their perspective drawing skills to create an answer key.

In Lesson 14, students will again create their own three-dimensional structures and perspective drawings when they build and represent a house made up of as many as twenty-four shapes.

Mathematical Goals

- Solve problems by:

  Identifying two-dimensional and three-dimensional shapes: triangle, square, rectangle, rhombus, trapezoid, hexagon, prism, and pyramid.

  Recognizing properties of shapes: equilateral; regular; parallel; symmetrical; number of faces, edges, and vertices.

  Interpreting orthogonal representations of polyhedra.

  Visualizing and building polyhedra.

  Create two-dimensional representations showing depth.

Materials

Per Student

Reproducible 40, *Mystery Structures: Game III— Edges and Vertices*

Per Group

Set of cardboard shapes from Lesson 11, with two extra squares and two extra rectangles per group

Masking tape or removable tape

Reproducible 37, *Mystery Structures Rules*

Reproducible 38, *Mystery Structures: Game I* (6 clue sets)

Reproducible 39, *Mystery Structure: Game II* (1 clue set)

Preparation

Mystery Structures: Game I includes six sets of clues (Reproducible 38, pages 1–3); *Mystery Structures: Game II* includes just one set of clues (Reproducible 39). Each group of three or four students will work with three or four of the clue sets for Game I, and with the clues for Game II. Copy and cut out the clues and then separate them into sets, using either envelopes or paper clips. You may want to laminate the clues to preserve them for use in future years.

Suggested Lesson Plan

1. Problem Solving: *Mystery Structures: Game I*

Divide the class into groups of three or four students and give each group:

- *Mystery Structures Rules* (Reproducible 37).
- A set of shapes.
- One set of four clues.

After the group has solved one set of clues, give them a second and then a third set of clues. Make sure that at least one group builds each of the six structures in Game I. In Game II, the six structures will be put together to form a house.

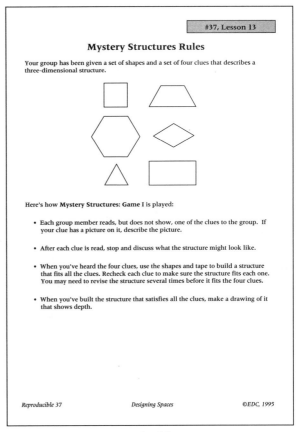

Reproducible 37.

The clues are read aloud, not shown, in order to maximize the communication and visualization students have to do to solve the clue set. If students are having trouble describing pictures

Reproducibles 37 & 38

in the clues, you can suggest that they use the shapes to help them. For example, they could hold up the hexagon shape and say, "The base of the structure looks like this."

Photos of the six polyhedra are included at the end of the lesson to serve as an answer key. The next time you teach the unit, you can use the student's perspective drawings as an answer key. That will give your students added incentive to make careful drawings.

2. Problem Solving: *Mystery Structures: Game II*

Reproducible 39

The six polyhedra built in Game I are used in Game II to construct a house. Collect one example of each of the six structures and ask for six volunteers to read the Game II clues for the class. You might designate a seventh student to serve as the class builder, following classmates' suggestions as the six clues are read.

A photograph of the final structure is provided in the answer key.

3. Discussion: *What strategies did you use to solve the Mystery Structures clues?*

Encourage students to reflect on the visualization they used to solve the mystery structures clues with questions such as:

- Did it matter which clue you started with? Why?
- How did you use the visual clues?
- How did you check that your structure worked with all the clues?

Students may find it helpful to look over the clues again as they answer the questions. Reflecting on the clues as they answer these questions will help prepare students to write their own clues in the next activity.

4. Writing: *Write your own set of clues for the Mystery Structures Game.*

TO THE STUDENT

- Build a closed, three-dimensional shape with up to twelve shape pieces. Make a structure that will be an interesting project for someone else to build.
- Write a set of four clues about your structure, with each clue on a separate piece of paper. Use at least one orthogonal drawing. From your four clues, someone else should be able to build your structure.
- Make a perspective drawing of the structure to serve as an answer key for other students who try to solve your clues.

This activity is appropriate for homework.

5. Problem solving: *Solve your partner's clues.*

Students exchange clue sets with a partner and then try to build from the partner's clues. After they've tried to solve the clues, partners exchange suggestions about improving the clue sets.

Some questions that students should think about as they give feedback on the clues include:

- Were there enough drawings?
- Were the drawings accurate?
- Were the notes easy to understand?
- What other information would have been helpful?

6. Practice: *Mystery Structures: Game III.*

Reproducible 40

Students match the three clue sets and perspective drawings on *Mystery Structures: Game III—Edges and Vertices* (Reproducible 40, two pages). To encourage visualization, you might want to suggest that students solve these clue sets without building the structure.

An answer key is provided at the end of this lesson. This activity works well for homework.

Homework Possibilities

Writing

Students can write their own mystery structures clues (Step 4) for homework.

Problem Solving

Students draw six different three-dimensional shapes in perspective drawings. Then, they write a set of four clues that leads to one of the six shapes. Encourage students to use some of the terms and concepts they have learned in the unit. They may use Mystery Structures: Game III as a guide to designing their own clue game.

Journal Writing

This lesson provides a good opportunity for students to reflect on what they've learned in Section 4 before they move on to the final project in Lesson 14.

Practice

Mystery Structures: Game III—Edges and Vertices (Step 6) can be used for homework.

Answer Key

1. The polyhedra.

Set 1

Set 2

Set 3

Set 4

Set 5

Set 6

2. The final castle.

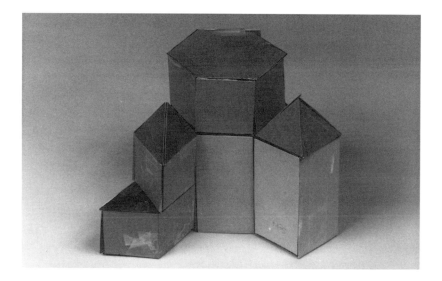

6. Set 1 is the hexagonal pyramid.

Set 2 is the cube with the square pyramid on top.

Set 3 is the octagonal prism.

Final Project—Putting the Pieces Together

How can you design and represent a house for a climate very different from your own? How would you describe the features of the house for potential buyers?

In this lesson, students complete a final project in which they (1) design a house for a specific climate, (2) create a set of building plans, and (3) write a detailed description of the features of the house. In their projects, students apply what they've learned in the unit—in particular the knowledge they've gained in the three previous lessons about visualizing, representing, and describing three-dimensional structures.

In Lesson 7, students designed a house for their own climate. In this lesson, students plan for a very different climate (either a cold, snowy one or a hot, rainy one). The final writing activity leads students to reflect further on the function and properties of shapes, as well as providing them with an opportunity to demonstrate their command of geometric terms and concepts.

The lesson ends with an assessment of the model houses, building plans, and design specifications. The final project is intended as a cumulative assessment of the material covered in the unit.

Mathematical Goals

Apply and extend knowledge of:

- Two-dimensional and three-dimensional shapes, their component parts, and their properties.
- Orthogonal and perspective representations of three-dimensional objects.
- Visualizing and building three-dimensional structures.
- Communicating a step-by-step building process.

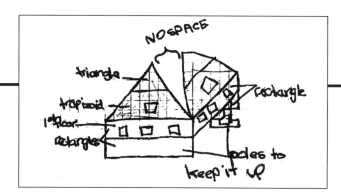

Materials

Per Student	Per Group	Per Class
Reproducible 41, *Memo 5 to House Designers*	Set of cardboard shapes from Lesson 11	Appendix A, *Designing Homes for Different Climates*
Reproducible 42, *Memo 6 to House Designers*	Masking tape or removable tape	
One fourth of a piece of large poster board (optional)	One sixth of a piece of large poster board, to use for making an additional shape (optional)	
	One fourth of a piece of large poster board, to use as a base for the house (optional)	

Preparation

Students will use the cardboard shape pieces to design their houses. You may be able to disassemble earlier structures that were made with the shape pieces in order to use the pieces in this lesson.

Decide whether you would like the students to build their houses in groups or individually. Individual projects require the preparation of many more shapes, but may give students a greater opportunity to express their knowledge and creativity. On the other hand, group projects may be richer since students will pool the design ideas of everyone in the group.

Suggested Lesson Plan

Reproducibles 41 & 42

► **From the Classroom**

Even though students were working on the second two parts of the project individually, I wanted them to apply what they had learned about giving feedback. So, I paired students up and gave them the responsibility of helping their partner do a good job on the project. After each of the three parts of the project, students would take on the role of Building Inspector and check each other's work to make sure that all of the pieces were complete and also to give each other suggestions. By this point, students understood the feedback process and needed only occasional reminders to critique the work, not the person.

1. Introduction: *Assign and discuss the final project assignment.*

Discuss the three parts of the final project assignment, as outlined on *Memos 5 and 6 to House Designers* (Reproducibles 41 and 42).

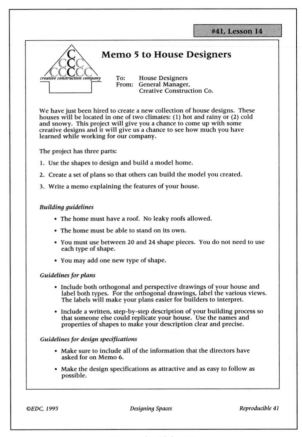

Reproducible 41.

If students are designing and building their houses in groups, make sure they understand that they will work individually on their plans and design specifications. These written assignments are designed to give each student the opportunity to demonstrate her or his knowledge.

2. Discussion: *Establishing quality criteria.*

Even if students haven't generated assessment criteria previously in the unit (for Lessons 6 and 10), you may want to have the class develop the criteria for the final project. At this point in the unit, students have designed, built, and described two houses so they should have a number of ideas about how to assess the assignment.

Here are three options for arriving at the quality criteria:

- Assemble the criteria that you used for the two earlier assessment lessons (Lessons 6 and 10). Have your class add criteria to the class list. Your list of criteria should address material from throughout the unit.
- Review the criteria provided with your class. You may want to ask students for suggestions on how to revise or add to the criteria.
- Have the class design quality criteria for the three parts of this project. Though this option may take longer than the others, it can give students a sense of ownership in the final project.

ASSESSMENT CRITERIA

- The model house is well built, can stand on its own, and fits the climate it was designed for.
- The plans are clearly written so that the house model can be replicated and include a step-by-step description of the building process.
- The plans and design specifications include geometric concepts and terms that help make the written description clear and precise.
- The correct terms for names of two- and three-dimensional shapes and the component parts of shapes are used. The work exhibits clear understanding of the properties of shapes.
- Geometric notation is used appropriately.
- The plans include both orthogonal drawings and drawings that show depth. Both types of drawings provide complete and accurate information about the structure.
- At least three orthogonal views have been drawn or described and labeled, and they are consistent with the drawings that show depth.

Since we live in a very cold, snowy climate, I had all of my students design a house for the hot, rainy climate. I read the article to them and then sent them off to brainstorm in their groups. Some groups decided to use slanted roofs so the rain would flow off. Others planned to leave openings in the walls for ventilation. One group decided to make their house on stilts so that their house wouldn't get flooded. Then they needed to figure out how to put the shapes together to get what they wanted.

3. Sharing: *Designing for a hot, rainy climate or a cold, snowy climate.*

Have small groups of students brainstorm design features for their houses. The students may want to start making some preliminary sketches of their ideas.

In Lesson 7, students designed houses for their own climate. In this lesson, students design houses suited for a climate that is different from their own: either a hot and rainy one or a cold and snowy one. This requirement encourages students to investigate building solutions that are different from the ones they pursued in Lesson 7.

Students can research the climate conditions at the library or by reading the article in Appendix A, Designing Homes for Different Climates. Students may also want to review the building solutions for different climates that they brainstormed in Step 1 of Lesson 7.

4. Building: *Create a home for a hot, rainy or cold, snowy climate.*

Review the building guidelines on *Memo 5 to House Designers* (Reproducible 41) with the students. Students can create one new type of shape for their house and can use as many copies of that shape as they can cut out of the sixth of a piece of posterboard. Students place their house model on the quarter piece of posterboard.

If students have extra time, they may want to add other elements to their models, such as furniture, illustrations, or colors inside the house or on the landscape.

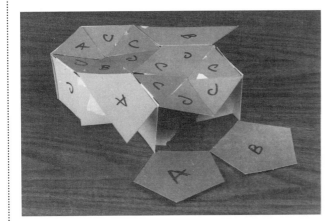

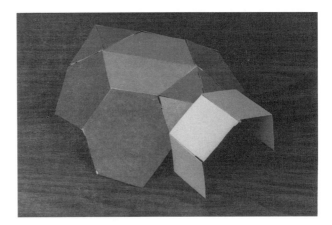

5. Drawing and writing: *Create a set of plans.*

Reproducible 41

As you review the guidelines for plans from *Memo 5 to House Designers* (Reproducible 41), remind students that they should work on the plans individually.

If students have built their houses with a group, most of the preliminary work on the plans will need to be done in the classroom so that students can refer to their house models. For homework, students can refine the plans by, for example, rewriting and editing their written description.

6. Writing: *Create design specifications.*

The design specifications should be written in the form of a memo to the directors, salespeople, and contractors of the Creative Construction Company as outlined on *Memo 6 to House Designers* (Reproducible 42). Explain that certain information about the house is needed so that the salespeople can sell the design and the contractors can build it. Tell students that they should also include any other information they think the directors need to know. They may want to include drawings in the memo if they think that will help explain the design.

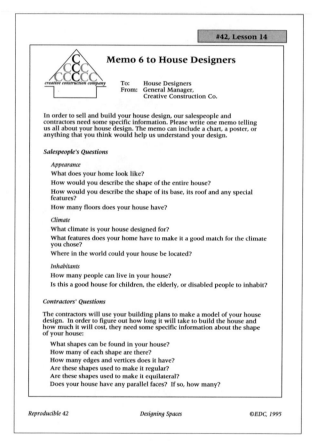

Reproducible 42.

Again, part of this assignment will need to be done at school because the students will need to look at their house. It may be added to and polished for homework.

My students were really interested in looking at one another's houses and learning about them. In the future, I might design a "mathematical scavenger hunt." I would create a list of questions and I would ask the students to compare the house models in searching for the answers to these questions. For example, I might ask students to look for the house model with the highest number of vertices or the most regular shapes. In this way, my students could study one another's houses and I could see which concepts they really understood.

► *Below are examples of one student's plans, along with notes about how they relate to the assessment criteria. See Appendix C for other sample student work on the final project.*

You need 4 hexagons ⬡ ,14 squares ⬜ , and 8 triangles △.

1.) Take two hexagons and six squares.
2.) Put one square on one side of one hexagon.

3.) Keep attaching squares on the sides of the hexagon until you have no more squares.
4.) When that is finished it should look like this:

5.) Then fold up the squares so that they are at a right angle from the hexagon. You should then put the other hexagon and place it on top of the folded up squares. It should look like this from the back, base view:

6.) Put that hexagonal prism down. Take the other two hexagons and 6 squares and make another hexagonal prism.
7.) Join two of the quare faces of the 2 hexagonal prisms together. It should look like this from the top:

8.) Take 1 square and 4 triangles. Put one triangle on one side of the square

9.) Put the rest of the triangles on the sides of the square so it looks like this

10.) Fold the triangles up so that they all meet at one vertex at the top. It should be a pyramid. It looks like this from the top.

11.) Take the leftover square and the rest of the four triangles and make another pyramid.
12.) Put one pyramid on top of one hexagonal prism. Put it on so that the sides of the square are parallel to two of the edges of the hexagonal prism. Put the other pyramid on top of the other hexagonal prism the same way. It should look like this from the front.

This student has fulfilled all of the guidelines for plans, including labeled orthogonal and perspective drawings and a clear description that uses geometric terms. She has visualized and described the building process so that someone else could build the structure from this set of building plans.

She has correctly identified some of the geometric terms and concepts in the unit. She has correctly used hexagon, square, triangle, right angle, hexagonal prism, vertex, and pyramid.

Homework

Parts of the project may be done outside of class. Remind students that they need to leave the house in the classroom so that all members of their group can look at the house.

Journal writing

Students write in their journal about the final project and the unit as a whole. Some questions they might answer include:

1. Describe the work you did for the final project of this unit. How well do you think you did on this final project? Why?
2. How do you feel about the final project? Did you enjoy doing it?
3. How would you describe this unit to someone else?
4. How did you feel about the unit? Was it easy? difficult? boring? fun? Why? What were your favorite and least favorite parts of the unit?

Entries from two students' journals are included on page 137.

Extensions

- Students build from each other's plans and give each other feedback on how they could improve their plans, as they did in Lessons 6 and 10. Though this will require additional class time, it will give you a sense of how students have grown in their ability to give feedback to each other.
- Have students present their completed project to the class. If you have a large class, you may want to break the group down into two or three smaller groups so that the presentations don't take too much class time. As each group is presenting, have other students think of one or two questions about the project. This will encourage a good discussion of the projects.

I would discribe this by saying, first you had to figure out what you wanted your house/building to look like then you should draw a picture of what your building looks like so your next step will be easier. Your next step and the step after can be done either way. You need to write clearly directions using math terms on how to build the stucture, then you need to discribe the house and then draw a orthagonal (2-D) and an I simetric (3-D) drawing. I really enjoyed this unit because it's not sitting down and doing math problems it's fun hands on math. It was fun and not too easy but not so hard. I'm really frusterated trying to do it.

1. The unit has taught us how to look at, (physical shapes and features) of 3-d or 2-d shapes. It has taught us to physically visualize different and various shapes, 3-d and 2-d.

Designing Homes for Different Climates

Fig. 1: A house of the Kirdi people in Cameroon

Fig. 2: An adobe in Southwest United States

Designing Homes for Different Climates

How could a house made of snow help keep you warm? Or a house made of dirt and grass keep you cool? Why is a dome-shaped house better on a windy day than a cube-shaped one? Why would someone build a house with walls, or even floors, that don't touch the ground? Or a house that can be folded up and moved from place to place?

After centuries of doing battle with the weather, people around the world have discovered some surprising ways to keep heat, cold, rain, and snow outside of their houses. Some of the house design features can be found in many parts of the world—like the circular floor plan that is used in igloos of the Arctic, yurts of Central Asia, tipis made by some Native Americans, and Norwegian laavu tents. Other design features are suited to a particular part of the world. For example, roofs made of thick leaves can provide great protection from the heat, but that won't help if you live in a desert where no thick leaves grow.

The houses described below show how people around the world have used available materials to design shelter suited to their climate.

Hot Climates

There are two main types of hot places: hot and wet places, such as a rain forest, and hot and dry places, such as a desert. The daytime temperature in a hot climate will usually be in the 80s or 90s and can often be over 100 Fahrenheit (38 Celsius). Deserts are hotter than rain forests during the day, but they get much cooler at night. That's because the heat from the sun doesn't move as well through wet air. The heat that does reach the ground is trapped there at night. The difference between daytime and nightime temperatures in the desert can be 50 or 60 degrees.

Insulation: Keeping heat out

Some building materials are good *insulators*. On a hot day, a good insulator helps block out the heat from the sun. On a cold night, insulation helps keep warm air from a furnace, stove, or fire inside the house.

In Cameroon, for example, the Kirdi tribespeople put thick roofs of leaves and grass on their houses to absorb the heat of the sun (Fig. 1). Other kinds of thick materials are used in desert houses to provide protection from the daytime sun and to retain warmth at night. In Mexico and Southwest United States, many houses are made of adobe bricks (Fig. 2). The clay in the bricks stores up the heat from the sun during the day and then releases the heat at night when the temperature falls.

The shape of shade

The shape and design features of a house can help cool a house by creating shade. For example, some houses in the Syrian Desert are built in the shape of beehives (Fig. 3). The small, rounded tops and curved walls mean that there is little surface area exposed to direct sunlight. The tall, sloping roofs of some Indonesian houses keep much of the house in the shade for much of the day (Fig. 4). Many houses in the United States have shutters or shades on the windows to block the midday sun; others have trellises over porches or patios.

Bringing wind in

There's nothing like a cool breeze on a hot day. But how can you design a house to bring the wind in and keep the sunlight out? The Quechua Indians of Peru have built bamboo houses with open sides to let the breezes blow through the house. In Japan, some traditional houses have sliding walls that can be opened on hot days, or kept closed for privacy and warmth.

Fig. 3: Houses in the Syrian Desert

Fig. 4: A house from Indonesia

Fig. 5: A house in Pakistan

Fig. 6: A tent home of the Tuareg people in the Sahara Desert

Fig. 7: A thatched roof house in Central America

Many Spanish houses have open-air courtyards that bring the wind into the center of the house. Fountains and shady spots in the courtyard help to cool the breeze.

Some houses bring wind down from the roof or up from the floor. In Pakistan, some houses have windscoops on the roof that catch the breezes and bring them down into the house (Fig. 5). House designers in Africa, South America, and Asia have built houses on stilts. The raised, bamboo floors let the cool breezes blow underneath the house and keep poisonous animals outside. The wind also blows under and into the tents made by the Tuareg tribespeople, who live in the Sahara Desert (Fig. 6). The walls of the tent can be rolled up to provide some air during the day and then rolled down for warmth during the cool, desert nights.

Cold and Wet Climates

In hot places, house designers hope to catch the wind and dodge the sun. In cold places, the opposite is true. People design houses that capture as much sun and avoid as much wind as possible. In some places, like Antarctica, the temperature in the winter can fall to -70 or -80 Fahrenheit (that's 70 or 80 degrees *below* zero; -57 to -62 degrees Celsius). In the Arctic, the temperatures can stay below zero even on a sunny summer day.

Insulation: Keeping warmth in

Throughout the world, people have used many kinds of materials to keep houses warm when it's cold outside. Thousands of years ago, people discovered that dirt and sod (strips of dirt covered with grass) are great insulators. There are still houses with sod roofs in places as far apart as Denmark and New Guinea. Thatched roofs (roofs covered with reeds, straw, or leaves) are used in houses throughout the Americas (Fig. 7). In Mexico, for example, the Native American Huichol tribe build huts with adobe walls and thatched roofs.

Animal skins are another good insulating material. The Native Americans tipi is covered with the hides of buffalo (Fig. 8). In the winter, the Kazakhs wrap the wooden frames of yurts with eight layers of felt (made from sheep's wool) and then cover them with a cane mat

(Fig. 9). In the summer, only the cane mats are used.

In the United States, many homes are insulated with man-made materials, like fiberglass. The material is placed between the inside and outside walls and between the ceilings and the roofs.

The most surprising insulator may be the material the Inuit people of the Arctic use to build their igloos: ice. The walls and ceiling of the igloo are made from blocks of snow. The Inuits make a fire inside the igloo, which melts the bottom layer of the snow walls and ceiling. When the fire goes out, the melted snow freezes to form a solid ice structure that keeps out the cold and wind (Fig. 10).

Shapes that keep the wind out

House designers in cold, windy places think a lot about making their houses *streamlined,* or wind-resistant. Aerodynamic structures direct the wind over and around them. For example, the dome shape of the igloo is very aerodynamic, because there are no flat faces or edges for the wind to hit.

What about cube-shaped houses, which are so common in the United States? How aerodynamic are they? Not very. Houses made up of flat, rectangular faces are easy targets for the wind. They are common because they can be built from straight pieces of wood and steel, which are simple to manufacture. The strong frame of these houses doesn't keep the wind out, but it does keep the structure standing even in strong winds (Fig. 11).

For cutting down on wind resistance, the next best thing to a circular floor plan may be an octagonal one. Several octagonal houses were built in the cold, foggy San Francisco Bay Area of California in the 1850s. Cone-shaped houses, like the Norwegian laavu tents and Native American tipis, are also aerodynamic (Fig. 12).

Using the sun

In order to get the most out of the sun's warmth, house

Fig. 8: A Native American tipi

Fig. 9: A yurt of the Kazakh people of Central Asia

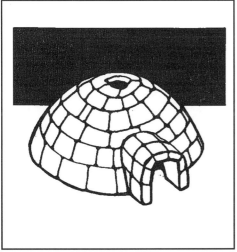
Fig. 10: An igloo of the Inuit people in the Arctic

designers have to know a lot about the way the sun moves around the earth at different times of the year. In the Northern Hemisphere, house designers try to place most of the windows on the south side of the house, which gets the most winter sun. In the Southern Hemisphere, the north-side windows get the most sun.

Some new houses in the United States have solar panels on the roof that catch the sunlight and produce heat and electricity (Fig. 13). Some solar panels are connected to water pipes. The panels heat up the water, which is then carried by the pipes to the hot water heater where the water can be stored for use in sinks, showers, and baths. Other solar panels convert the sun's heat into electricity.

Rain

Parts of the world get several feet of rain in a year. Keeping the inside of houses dry in that much rain, or even half that much rain, is quite a challenge. Waterproof roofs and walls are only half of the solution. You've also got to think about the floor. If rainwater doesn't drain away from your house, it can start to form a rising river under your floor.

Fig. 11: A home in the United States

Roofs made of waterproof materials, such as thick layers of leaves, keep the inside of houses dry in tropical places like Peru and Cameroon. Other houses are built using waterproof animal skins and hair. Native Americans use buffalo hides for their tipis, while the Bedouins of the Middle East weave their tents from goat hair.

Fig. 12: A Norwegian laavu tent

The chalets of Europe use roofs made of wood or stone slabs to keep water from getting inside. Many chalets, like many American houses, have slanted roofs made of overlapping shingles that direct the water down off the roof. Eaves extend the roof beyond the outside walls to keep the rainwater away from the house. Some houses also have gutters and down spouts, which collect the rainwater from the roof and carry it away from the house.

If possible, many house designers try to put their houses on a little hill, so that the rain water will drain away instead of flooding the first floor or basement. In places where floods are common, such as Thailand in Southeast Asia, some people build houses on stilts. There are even whole villages and cities that have been built on stilts—like Venice, Italy, where people travel from place to place on canals rather than streets.

Snow

Many features designed for rain also work for snow—waterproof material, slanted roofs, eaves. Unlike rain water, though, snow doesn't always drip right off the roof; it can stay where it falls, even on slanted roofs. And many feet of snow can put a lot of pressure on roofs and walls.

That's why houses in snowy climates need very strong roofs. Wood and stone are materials that are both strong and waterproof. The other parts of these houses also have to be strong. The same strong frames that keep houses standing in stiff winds help to *disperse*, (spread out) the weight of the snow.

Fig. 13: A house with solar panels in the United States

Changeable Houses

People in many parts of the world have to adjust to a lot of different climate conditions. Hot days and very cool nights. Snowy winters and very warm summers. Long dry seasons and short rainy seasons. How can you design a house to suit a changing climate?

Several of the houses described above have features that are designed to deal with different conditions. Some insulators, like adobe, provide protection from both heat and cold. The walls of many houses can be moved or rolled up to let the wind in or keep the cold out. In Southern Iraq, the Ma'dan (Marsh Arabs) build houses on swamps. The thick walls, covered with reeds, can be rolled back in the hot summer.

Fig. 14: An aqaal from Somalia

In the United States, many people use electricity, natural gas, and oil to keep their houses comfortable in a changing climate. Electric fans and air-conditioning systems provide cool breezes in the summer. Furnaces burn oil or gas to keep the house warm in the cold winter. Some houses even have electric humidifiers or dehumidifiers to make the air in the house wetter or drier as the weather changes.

Instead of changing the house, you can change the weather. Some of the houses described in this article are designed to be movable. When the weather changes, people can pack up the house and move someplace else. In the Somalia desert, for example, people move frequently in search of water or grasses where their animals can graze. They build dome-shaped houses from animal hides and grass mats called aqaals, which can be easily packed and moved (Fig. 14). Yurts, tipis, and tents are other examples of movable houses. And so is a mobile home—a combination house and automobile which can contain beds, a kitchen, and bathrooms (Fig. 15).

Of course, climate isn't the only thing you need to think about when you design a house. Take Jim Bierman's experience, for example. A few years ago, Jim decided to design and build his own house on the West Coast of the United States. To keep the house warm in the winter and cool in the summer, Jim built part of the house underground and covered the wood roof with pieces of sod that were a foot thick. The sod turned out to be the perfect insulation material. That is, until Jim came home one day to find a cow eating part of his roof. Maybe he should have used something less tasty—like cane mats or wooden shingles.

Fig. 15: A mobile home in the United States

Sources:

Hoffman, Eric. *Renegade Houses*. Philadelphia: Running Press, 1972.

James, Alan. *Homes in Hot Places*. Minneapolis: Lerner Publications Company, 1989.

———*Homes in Cold Places*. Minneapolis: Lerner Publications Company, 1989.

Pratt, Richard. *Houses, History and People*. New York: M. Evans, 1965.

Salvadori, Mario. *Why Buildings Stand Up: The Strength of Architecture*. New York: W.W. Norton, 1980.

Fig. 1

Fig. 2

Diseñar viviendas para climas diferentes

¿Cómo podría mantenerte caliente una casa hecha de nieve? ¿O mantenerte fresco una casa hecha de tierra? ¿Por qué una casa en forma de cúpula es mejor que una casa en forma de cubo en un día de viento? ¿Por qué construiría alguien una casa con muros, o incluso suelos, que no tocan la tierra? ¿O una casa que se puede plegar y trasladarse de lugar?

Después de siglos de batallar con el clima, las gentes de todo el mundo han descubierto algunas maneras sorprendentes de mantener el calor, el frío, la lluvia y la nieve fuera de sus casas. Algunas de las características del diseño de la vivienda se pueden encontrar en muchos lugares del mundo—como el suelo de planta circular que se usa en los iglús del Ártico, las yurtas de Asia Central, los tipis de los indios norteamericanos y las tiendas laavu noruegas. Otros rasgos de estos diseños se adaptan a una parte determinada del mundo. Por ejemplo, los tejados hechos de hojas gruesas pueden proporcionar gran protección contra el calor, pero no servirán si vives en el desierto, donde no crecen hojas gruesas.

Las casas descritas más abajo muestran cómo las gentes de alrededor del mundo han usado materiales a su disposición para diseñar cobijo apropiado a su clima.

Climas cálidos

Hay dos tipos principales de lugares cálidos: lugares cálidos y húmedos, como el bosque tropical, y lugares cálidos y secos, como el desierto. La temperatura por el día en un clima cálido será normalmente de 80 o 90 grados, y a menudo puede pasar de los 100 grados

Farenheit (38 Celsius). Durante el día, los desiertos son más calurosos que los bosques tropicales, pero por la noche se enfrían mucho más. Eso pasa porque el calor del sol no atraviesa tan bien el aire húmedo. El calor que llega al suelo se queda atrapado ahí por la noche. En el desierto, la diferencia entre la temperatura diurna y la nocturna puede ser de 50 o 60 grados.

Aislamiento: mantener fuera el calor

Algunos materiales de construcción son buenos *aislantes*. En un día caluroso, un buen aislante ayuda a mantener fuera el calor del sol. En una noche fría, el aislamiento ayuda a conservar dentro de la casa el aire caliente de un horno, una estufa o un fuego.

Fig. 3

En Camerún, por ejemplo, los miembros de la tribu Kirdi ponen gruesos tejados de hojas y hierba en sus casas, para absorber el calor del sol (Fig. 1). Otras clases de materiales gruesos se usan en las casas del desierto para protegerse del sol diurno y retener calor por la noche. En México y en el suroeste de los Estados Unidos, muchas casas están hechas de ladrillos de adobe (Fig. 2). La arcilla de los ladrillos almacena durante el día el calor del sol y suelta ese calor durante la noche, cuando baja la temperatura.

La forma de la sombra

Fig. 4

La forma y el diseño de la vivienda pueden contribuir, al crear sombra, a refrescar una vivienda. Por ejemplo, algunas casas en el desierto Sirio se construyen en forma de colmena (Fig. 3). Los pequeños techos redondeados y los muros curvos significan poca superficie expuesta a la luz directa del sol. Los techos altos e inclinados de algunas casas indonesias mantienen a la sombra la mayor parte de la casa durante casi todo el día (Fig. 4). Muchas viviendas en los Estados Unidos tienen contraventanas y persianas en las ventanas para impedir la entrada del sol de mediodía; otras tienen plantas trepadoras en el porche o el patio.

Dejar que entre el viento

No hay nada como una brisa refrescante en un día caluroso. Pero, ¿cómo puedes diseñar una casa que deje pasar el viento y mantenga fuera la luz solar? Los indios

Fig. 5

Fig. 6

Fig. 7

quechua del Perú han construido viviendas de bambú con los lados abiertos para que la brisa corra libremente por la casa. En Japón, algunas viviendas tradicionales tienen paredes correderas que se pueden abrir en los días calurosos, o cerrar si se desea intimidad y conservar el calor.

Muchas casas españolas tienen patios abiertos que permiten que el viento llegue al centro de la casa. Las fuentes y los rincones de sombra del patio ayudan a enfriar la brisa.

Muchas viviendas traen viento del tejado hacia abajo o del suelo hacia arriba (Fig. 5). En Pakistán, algunas viviendas tienen recogevientos en el tejado, que atrapan la brisa y la conducen hacia el interior de la casa. En África, Sudamérica, y Asia, los diseñadores de viviendas han construido casas sobre soportes. El suelo elevado de bambú permite que la brisa fresca sople por debajo de la casa, e impide la entrada de animales venenosos. El viento sopla también dentro y por debajo de las tiendas de los tuareg, que viven en el desierto del Sáhara (Fig. 6). Las paredes de la tienda se pueden enrollar para proporcionar aire durante el día, y desenrollar durante las frías noches desérticas para conservar el calor.

Climas fríos y húmedos

En los lugares cálidos, los diseñadores de viviendas esperan poder atrapar el viento y eludir el sol. En los lugares fríos, lo opuesto es cierto. La gente diseña viviendas que capturen el sol y eviten el viento tanto como sea posible. En algunos lugares, como la Antártida, la temperatura en invierno puede bajar a -70 o -80 Fahrenheit (eso es ¡70 u 80 grados *bajo* cero¡; -57 a -62 grados Celsius). En el Ártico, las temperaturas pueden permanecer bajo cero incluso en un día soleado de verano.

Aislamiento: mantener el calor dentro

En todo el mundo, la gente ha usado diversas clases de materiales para mantener sus casas calientes cuando hace frío afuera. Hace miles de años, los humanos descubrimos que la tierra y el césped (franjas de tierra cubiertas de hierba) son excelentes aislantes.

Hay todavía casas con tejados de césped en lugares tan distantes como Dinamarca y Nueva Guinea. Los tejados de paja (tejados cubiertos de cañas, paja u hojas) se usan en viviendas en todas las Américas (Fig. 7). En México, por ejemplo, la tribu india de los huicholes construye cabañas con muros de adobe y tejados de paja.

Fig. 8

Las pieles de animales son otro buen material aislante. El tipi de los indios norteamericanos está cubierto con cueros de búfalo (Fig. 8). En invierno, los Kazajos envuelven los armazones de madera de las yurtas con ocho capas de fieltro (hecho con lana de oveja) y luego los recubren con una estera de caña(Fig. 9). En verano sólo se usan las esteras de caña.

En los Estados Unidos, muchas viviendas están aisladas con materiales hechos por el hombre, como la fibra de vidrio. El material se coloca entre las paredes interiores y exteriores y entre el tejado y el techo.

Fig. 9

El aislante más sorprendente puede que sea el que usan los inuit para construir sus iglús en el Ártico: hielo. Las paredes y el techo del iglú están hechas con bloques de nieve. Los inuit encienden un fuego dentro del iglú que funde la capa inferior de las paredes y el techo de nieve. Cuando el fuego se apaga, la nieve fundida se congela y forma una estructura sólida de hielo que impide el paso del frío y el viento (Fig. 10).

Formas que impiden el paso del viento

Los diseñadores de viviendas en lugares fríos y ventosos piensan mucho en cómo hacer sus casas *aerodinámicas*, o resistentes al viento. Las estructuras aerodinámicas hacen que el viento pase por encima y alrededor suyo. Por ejemplo, la forma de cúpula del iglú es muy aerodinámica, porque no hay caras o aristas planas expuestas al viento.

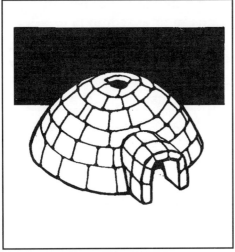

Fig. 10

¿Qué pasa con las viviendas que tienen forma de cubo, tan comunes en los Estados Unidos? ¿Son aerodinámicas? No mucho. Las casas con superficies planas y rectangulares son un blanco fácil para el viento. Son comunes porque se pueden construir con piezas convencionales de madera y acero que son fáciles de fabricar. El fuerte armazón de esas casas no impide el paso del viento, pero permite que la estructura continúe en pie incluso bajo vientos fuertes (Fig. 11).

Para reducir la resistencia al viento, lo mejor después de una planta de suelo circular es una planta octogonal. Varias casas octogonales se construyeron, hacia el año 1850, en la fría y brumosa zona de la bahía de San Francisco, en California. Casas con forma de cono, como las tiendas laavu en Noruega y los tipis de los indios norteamericanos, también son aerodinámicas (Fig 12).

Usar el sol

Para aprovechar al máximo el calor del sol, los diseñadores de viviendas tienen que conocer muy bien cómo se mueve el sol alrededor de la Tierra en las distintas épocas del año. En el Hemisferio Norte, los diseñadores de viviendas tratan de colocar la mayoría de las ventanas en el lado sur de la vivienda, que en invierno recibe la mayor parte del sol. En el Hemisferio Sur, las ventanas del lado norte reciben la mayor parte del sol.

En los Estados Unidos, algunas casas nuevas tienen paneles solares en el techo, que atrapan la luz solar y producen calor y electricidad (Fig. 13). Algunos paneles solares están conectados a tuberías de agua. Los paneles calientan el agua, que es transportada por las tuberías hasta el calentador de agua, donde se almacena para ser usada en fregaderos, duchas y baños. Otros paneles solares convierten el calor del sol en electricidad.

Lluvia

Algunas partes del mundo reciben varios pies de agua en un año. Mantener el interior de las viviendas seco cuando llueve tanto, o incluso con la mitad de lluvia, es todo un reto. Tejados y muros impermeables son sólo la mitad de la solución. También hay que pensar en los suelos. Si el agua de lluvia no se desagua fuera de tu vivienda, puede empezar a formar un río creciente bajo tu suelo.

Los tejados hechos con materiales impermeables, como gruesas capas de hojas, mantienen seco el interior de las viviendas en zonas tropicales como Perú y Camerún. Otras viviendas se construyen usando piel y pelo animal impermeable. Los indios norteamericanos usan cueros

Fig. 11

Fig. 12

de búfalo para hacer sus tipis, mientras que los beduinos de Oriente Medio tejen sus tiendas con pelo de cabra.

Los chalés europeos tienen tejados hechos de madera o de losas de piedra para impedir que entre el agua. Muchos chalés, como muchas casas norteamericanas, tienen tejados inclinados hechos de tejas de madera superpuestas que conducen el agua hacia abajo, fuera del tejado. Los aleros extienden el tejado más allá de los muros, para que el agua de lluvia se mantenga alejada de la casa. Algunas casas también tienen canales de desagüe y goteras, que recogen el agua de lluvia del tejado y la vierten lejos de la casa.

Fig. 13

Si es posible, muchos diseñadores tratan de situar la vivienda en una pequeña colina, para que la lluvia se vierta lejos, en vez de inundar la planta baja o el sótano. En lugares en los que las inundaciones son corrientes, como Tailandia, en el sureste asiático, algunas gentes construyen casas sobre soportes. Hay incluso pueblos y ciudades enteras que se han construido sobre soportes— como Venecia, Italia, donde la gente va de un sitio a otro por canales en vez de calles.

Nieve

Muchas de las características diseñadas para la lluvia también son adecuadas para la nieve—material impermeable, tejados inclinados, aleros. Sin embargo, a diferencia del agua de lluvia, la nieve no siempre gotea del tejado; puede quedarse donde ha caído, incluso en los tejados inclinados. Y muchos pies de nieve pueden ejercer mucha presión sobre tejados y paredes.

Por esa razón, las viviendas necesitan tejados muy resistentes en climas donde nieva mucho. La madera y la piedra son materiales fuertes e impermeables a la vez. Las otras partes de estas casas también tienen que ser fuertes. Los mismos armazones sólidos que hacen que las casas resistan los vientos fuertes ayudan a *dispersar* (repartir) el peso de la nieve.

Viviendas que cambian

Las gentes de muchas partes del mundo tienen que adaptarse a muchas condiciones climáticas diferentes.

Días calurosos y noches my frías. Inviernos nevados y veranos muy cálidos. Largas estaciones secas y temporadas cortas de lluvia. ¿Cómo puedes diseñar una vivienda para que se adapte a un clima variable?

Varias de las casas descritas arriba tienen características diseñadas para adaptarse a condiciones diferentes. Muchos aislantes, como el adobe, protegen tanto del frío como del calor. Las paredes de muchas viviendas pueden enrollarse o correrse para dejar que pase el viento o impedir el paso del frío. En el sur de Iraq, los Ma'dan (árabes de los pantanos) construyen viviendas en los pantanos. Los gruesos muros, cubiertos de cañas, pueden enrollarse en el caluroso verano.

En los Estados Unidos, mucha gente usa electricidad, gas natural y petróleo para hacer de sus casas lugares agradables en un clima variable. Los ventiladores eléctricos y los sistemas acondicionadores de aire proporcionan aire fresco en verano. Las estufas queman petróleo o gas para mantener la casa caliente en el frío invierno. Algunas casas incluso tienen humedecedores o deshumedecedores eléctricos para hacer que el aire de la casa sea más húmedo o más seco conforme cambia el tiempo.

En lugar de cambiar la vivienda, puedes cambiar el clima. Algunas de las viviendas descritas en este artículo están diseñadas para poder ser transportadas. Cuando el tiempo cambia, la gente puede recoger la casa y mudarse a otro lugar. En el desierto de Somalia, por ejemplo, la gente se traslada frecuentemente en busca de agua o hierba para que pasten los animales. Construyen viviendas en forma de cúpula con cueros de animales y franjas de césped, llamadas aqaals, que se pueden recoger y trasladar fácilmente (Fig. 14). Las yurtas, los tipis y las tiendas son otros ejemplos de viviendas movibles. Y también lo es una casa móvil—una combinación de casa y automóvil que puede tener camas, cocina y baño (Fig. 15).

Fig. 14

Por supuesto que el clima no es en lo único que necesitas pensar cuando diseñas una vivienda. Analiza la experiencia de Jim Bierman, por ejemplo. Hace unos años, Jim decidió diseñar y construir su propia casa en la Costa Oeste de los Estados Unidos. Para mantener la casa caliente durante el invierno y fresca en el verano,

Jim construyó parte de la casa bajo tierra y cubrió el tejado de madera con piezas de césped de un pie de grosor. El césped resultó ser el material aislante perfecto. Bueno, hasta que Jim llegó a casa un día y vio a una vaca que se estaba comiendo parte de su tejado. Quizá debería haber usado algo menos sabroso, como esteras de caña o tejas de madera.

Fig. 15

Sources:

Hoffman, Eric. *Renegade Houses.* Philadelphia: Running Press, 1972.

James, Alan. *Homes in Hot Places.* Minneapolis: Lerner Publications Company, 1989.

———*Homes in Cold Places.* Minneapolis: Lerner Publications Company, 1989.

Pratt, Richard. *Houses, History and People.* New York: M. Evans, 1965.

Salvadori, Mario. *Why Buildings Stand Up: The Strength of Architecture.* New York: W.W. Norton, 1980.

Scoring Rubric

Level 6 **Superior response**	**Exemplary response that goes beyond the requirements of the assignment.** Work shows complete understanding of the mathematical concepts and processes; clear identification of all important elements; a well-written mathematical argument that may include examples; and creativity and thoughtfulness in communicating the results, and the interpretation of those results, to an identified audience using dynamic and diverse means.
Level 5 **Competent response**	**The response accomplishes the prompted purpose with high quality.** Work shows good understanding of the mathematical concepts and processes; identification of most of the important elements; and clear, successful communication with an identified audience.
Level 4 **Satisfactory with minor flaws**	**The response accomplishes most of the prompted purpose but revisions are needed.** Work demonstrates an understanding of most of the mathematical concepts and processes; identification of the important elements even though some less important ideas are missing; and adequate communication with an identified audience but with limited clarity and variety.
Level 3 **Complete, but with serious flaws**	**The response addresses the prompted purpose, but contains serious flaws.** Work shows an understanding of some of the mathematical concepts and processes, but there is evidence of gaps; an identification of some of the important elements, but assumptions about some of the elements are flawed; communication of some ideas, but the identified audience is not addressed, and there is difficulty in expressing mathematical ideas.
Level 2 **Fragmented response**	**The response demonstrates purposeful effort but little progress.** Work shows only fragmented understanding of the mathematical concepts and processes, accompanied by disorganized, incomplete results; identification of few or no important elements; and attempts to communicate that are incoherent, muddled, or incomplete.
Level 1 **Little attempt**	**Little evidence of communication or attempt to address the prompted purpose.**

Sample Final Projects

Description Of House

1.   My house has two stories and is made up of fifteen pieces. The first step when building it is to put together the main part of the house. First, you take two rectangles (blue) and two squares (orange.) Then you put one edge of a square, and one end of a rectangle together. Repeat this step for the other half of the main area. When you have the other side finished, put the two pieces together by making sure that the edges of the pieces are rectangle to square (fig. 1.) You should have a rectangular prism without top or bottom faces.

Figure 1

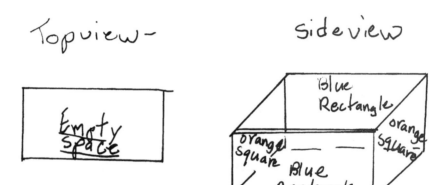

Topview –

Empty Space

side view

Blue Rectangle

orange Square

Orange Square

Blue Rectangle

2. (Optional) The next piece that you put on raises the amount to sixteen pieces. The extra step is a reinforcement piece. You attach another rectangle (blue) to one of the two open sides of the part that you just made. The piece should be the same shape and size as the empty space. Now you should have a rectangular prism that has only one face missing (Fig. 2.)

Figure 2
(optional)

Blue Rectangle –

Base rectangle (optional.)

3. The next step is to attach two triangles (neon pink) on either end of the main space. They go on the ends, on top of the squares that are on the piece that you just did. Do that twice. Make sure that the rienforcement piece, if you decided to use it, is on the opposite side of the house that the triangles are on. Now attach two rectangles (blue) to the sides of the triangles that you just put on. This makes the roof (Fig. 3.)

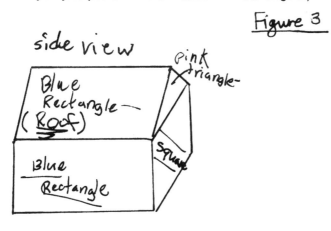

Figure 3

side view

Blue Rectangle — (Roof)

Blue Rectangle

pink triangle

Square

Top view

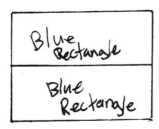

Blue Rectangle

Blue Rectangle

4. The next step is to make the entrance to the house. Make sure that on one side of the house, it is attached to the rectangles-the part that you did first. To make this, take two squares (orange) and one triangle (neon pink.) Attach the two squares, one edge to another, making sure that the edges line up. Then take the triangle and connect one side to one of the free sides of the squares. Make sure that you can mold the angle that you made with the squares around the triangle. Then do so, and secure it. Now you should have a triangular shaped entrance to the house. Position the entrance on one side of the main part of the house. Make sure it is on one of the blue rectangles. (Fig. 4.)

Top View <u>Figure 4</u>

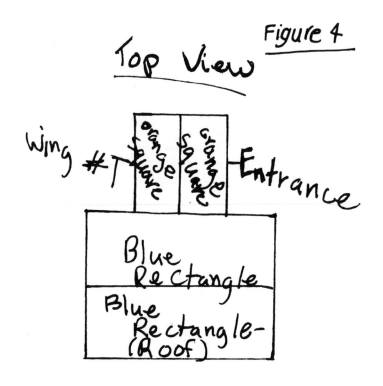

Wing #1 | orange square | orange square | orange square | Entrance

Blue Rectangle

Blue Rectangle (Roof)

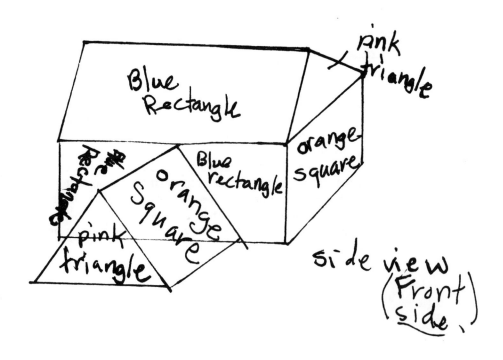

pink triangle

Blue Rectangle

Blue rectangle

orange square

Blue Rectangle

orange Square

pink triangle

side view (Front) side.

5.   The next step is to make the other wing. This requires four squares (orange.) remember to put the squares together so that the sides line up next to each other. First, make a line of three squares, one next to another. Bend them into a semi cube shape, without a bottom or two paralell faces. Then, put the left over square on one side of the three other squares that made the semi cube. Then, holding them together, attach this part to the other side from the entrance- on the rectangle on the other side. (fig. 5.)
    Now your house is complete.

Figure 5

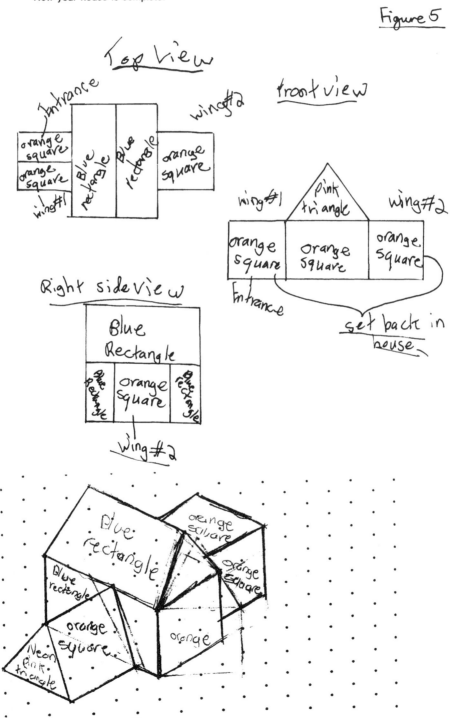

Top View

Front view

Right side view

MY HOUSE IS FOR THE HOT AND RAINY CLIMATE.I THINK THIS
HOUSE IS VERY GOOD FOR THIS CERTAIN CLIMATE . MY
REASONS ARE:

      1.) MY HOUSE HAS COLUMNS SO THAT AIR CAN
GO UP AND CIRCULATE THOUGH THE FLOOR.

      2.) MY HOUSE HAS A POINTED TOP SO THAT IT
CAN ACT LIKE A DRAINAGE TO THE WATER THAT GETS TO THE
ROOF.

      3.) MY HOUSE IS MADE WITH MUD (MUD
WOULD BE THE WALLS WERE THE TRAPEZOID WOULD BE ON
MY STRUCTURE) WALLS TO KEEP THE INSIDE COOL.

      4.) MY HOUSE HAS A TENT LIKE SUBSTANCE AT
THE VERTEX OF MY HOUSE SO YOU CAN FOLD IT UP AND LET
AIR, AND BREEZE IN ON THE VERY HOT NIGHTS.

      5.) MY HOUSE IS ABOVE THE GROUND SO IT
WONT GET WET AND DAMP FROM THE MOIST GROUND.

      THOSE ARE MY REASONS. NOW HERE IS MY HOUSE.

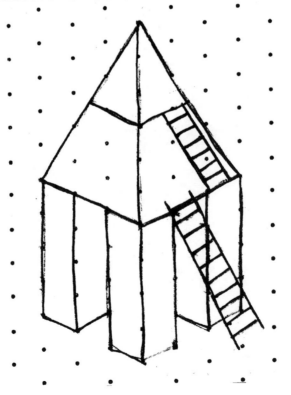

HOUSE FOR A HOT AND RAINY CLIMATE

This house consists of 24 pieces:

        8 Triangles
        3 Trapezoids
        1 Square
        12 Rectangles
        1 more trapezoid and 4 triangles are used during
construction but will not end up on the final structure.

1. Take 4 equilateral 4cm triangles (hot pink) and tape them together to
make a pyramid. (The pyramid is missing a square base.)

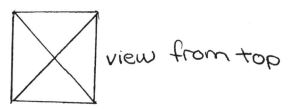

2. Take 4 trapezoids (florescent green) and attach one to each side of the
pyramid so that the pyramid gets twice as tall as it was in step one. What
you have so far is a pyramid that is made of 8 shapes and is still missing its
square base.

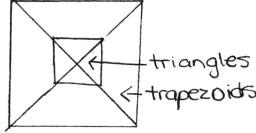

3. Take a square and attach it to the base of the pyramid. The square will
be roughly 8 cm square. All sides of the pyramid will be completely
enclosed. There will be 1 vertex.

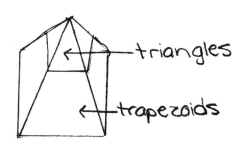

4. Now take off one side of the pyramid (made up of 1 triangle and 1 trapezoid) and replace it with one large triangle that fits. Since this house must have between 20 and 24 pieces, this step is needed to reduce the completed house from 25 to 24 pieces.

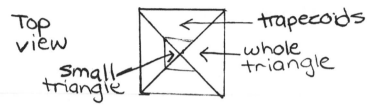

5. Take 6 rectangles and cut them in half along their longest length. Now you'll have 12 rectangles that are half as skinny than the original 6.

6. Make a prism out of 3 rectangles and 2 triangles. The sides of the triangles match the short side of the rectangles and should fit the open ends of the prism once the rectangles are put together.. Make 3 more of these prisms so you have a total of 4. Once you have the 4 prisms made, take away one triangle from the end of each prism.

7. Now it is time to attach the prisms to the pyramid. The pyramid will be the main house and the 4 prisms will be the columns holding the house up at each corner.. Put the open end of each prism up and tape it to the square base of the pyramid where each 90 degree corner is located. Tape each prism so that one rectangular face is parallel to the bottom edge of the pyramid's square base. One face of each column will line up with the bottom edge of the pyramid on one side and will slant back under the pyramid on two sides. Now you are done.

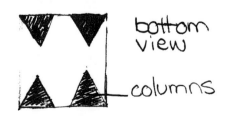

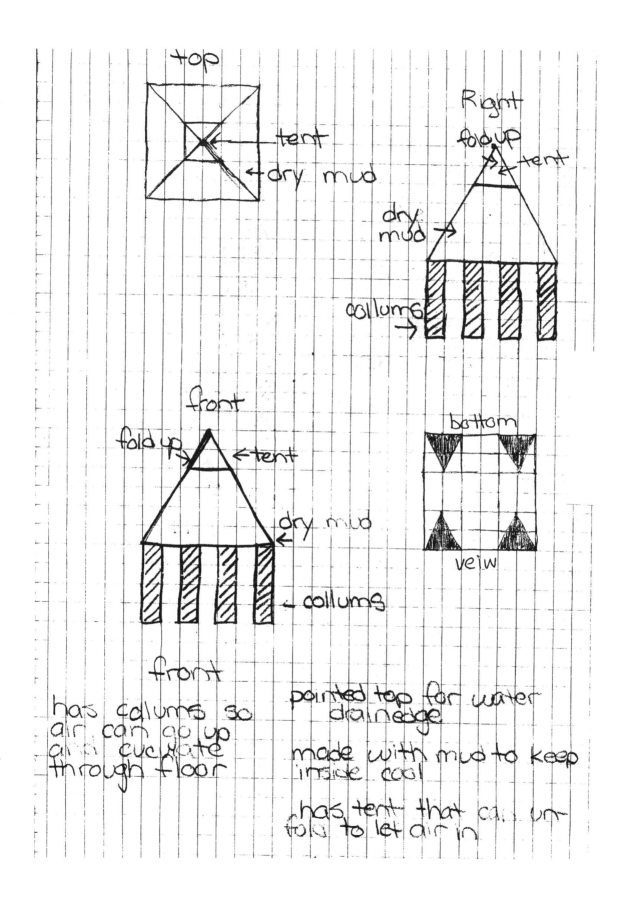

top

tent
dry mud

Right
fold up
tent
dry
mud
collums

front
fold up
tent
dry mud
collums

front

bottom
veiw

has collums so
air can go up
and cuculate
through floor

pointed top for water
drainage

made with mud to keep
inside cool

has tent that can un-
fold to let air in

Building Structures Unit

Math Assessment Test

My house has, in total, 14 pieces. It has 10 orange equilateral squares, 2 green trapezoids and 2 pink equilateral triangles. It's for a climate around Brookline, sometimes cool, sometimes warm. It doesn't often have hurricanes or floods, which can wreck the house.

Here are the steps to build my house.

1. Take two equilateral squares and tape them on there sides together. Place them in a horizontal line in front of you. See below.

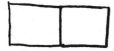

2. Repeat step 1. Now you have two sets of two squares taped together.

3. Place them horizontally parallel to each other, one equilateral square apart. See below.

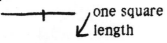

4. In that one square length between the parallel squares, put one square on each side.

New just put in square →   New just put in square

Here is a 3-D drawing of what it looks like so far.

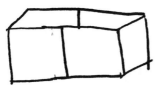

5. Place your 3-D rectangle on a flat surface, so that one of the sides with two rectangles taped together is facing you. *} What's it called?*

6. You are now going to make a 3-sided cube. First you will make it, then I will tell you how to attach it.

7. To make a complete cube, one will need 6 squares. We will use 4 squares only. It will have no bottom and one side missing.

perpendicular to eachother

8. Assemble the cube. Keep the open bottom down.

9. Face the cube toward you, so the missing side is facing the rectangle.

10. On the long side of the rectangle, center the cube.

11. Tape the cube in place.

12. For the roof you are going to build a prism, with a rectangular bottom. You will need two trapezoids and two equilateral triangles.

13. First you will build it then I will tell you how to attach it.

14. Take two trapezoids and stand them vertically upright.

15. Start leaning the tops in until the tops touch each other.

16. It will now look like this:

17. In the spaces on the sides, on each side place an equilateral triangle. Lean it in towards the center of the trapezoids.

18. When the sides of the triangles touch the sides of the trapezoids, tape all of them until there are no holes. This is a leak-proof roof.

19. Now take the prism, and the rectangle bottom will be attached to the open top of the 3-D rectangle with the cube attached.

20. Now you are done. Here's what it looks like.

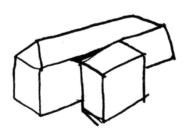

Orthogontal Drawings

Top

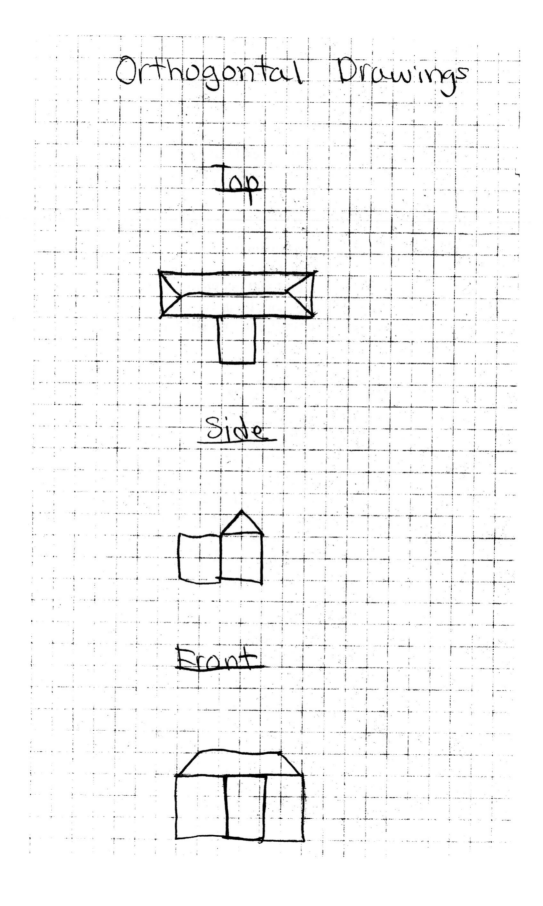

Side

Front

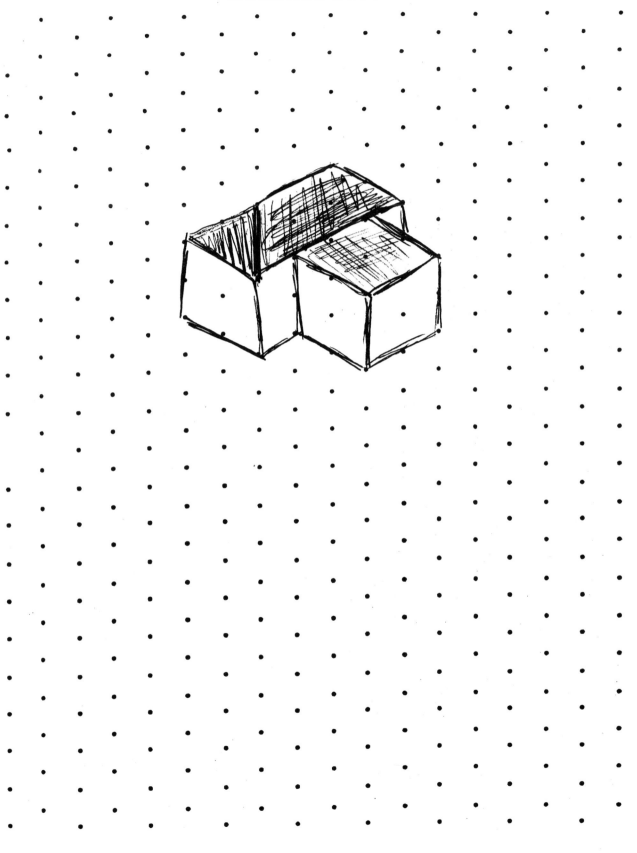

Shape Templates

Squares

Rectangles

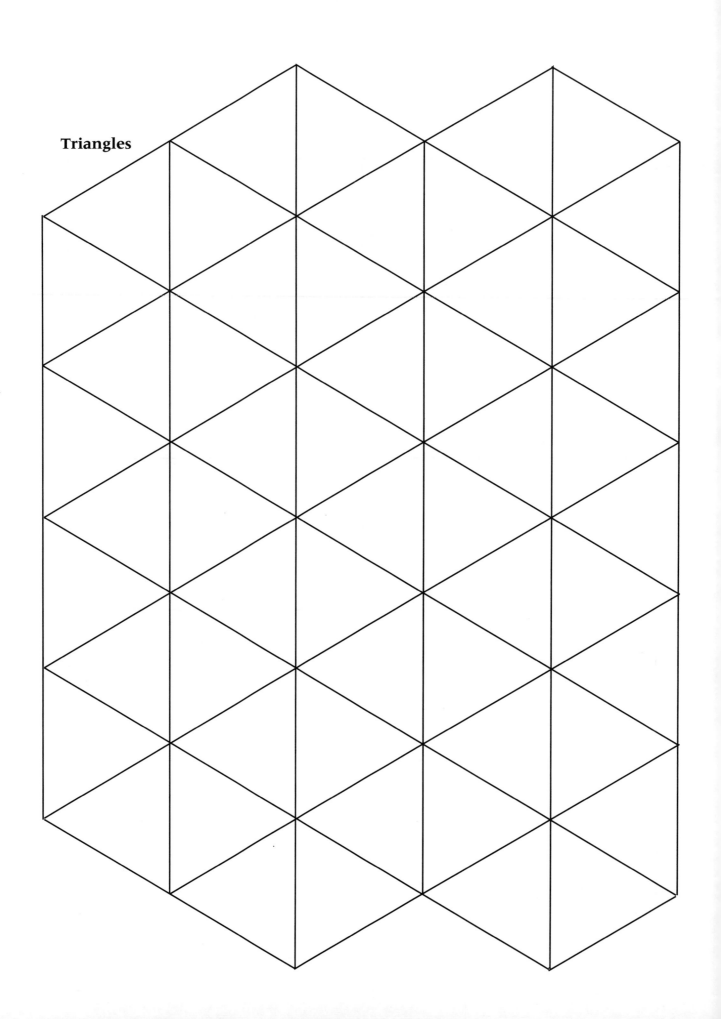

Triangles

Rhombi

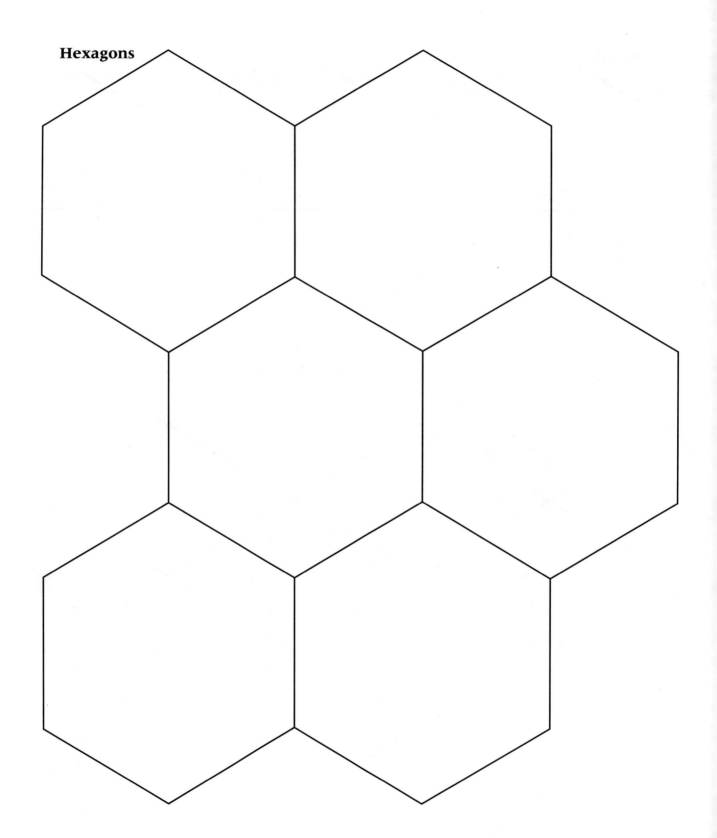

Hexagons

Trapezoids

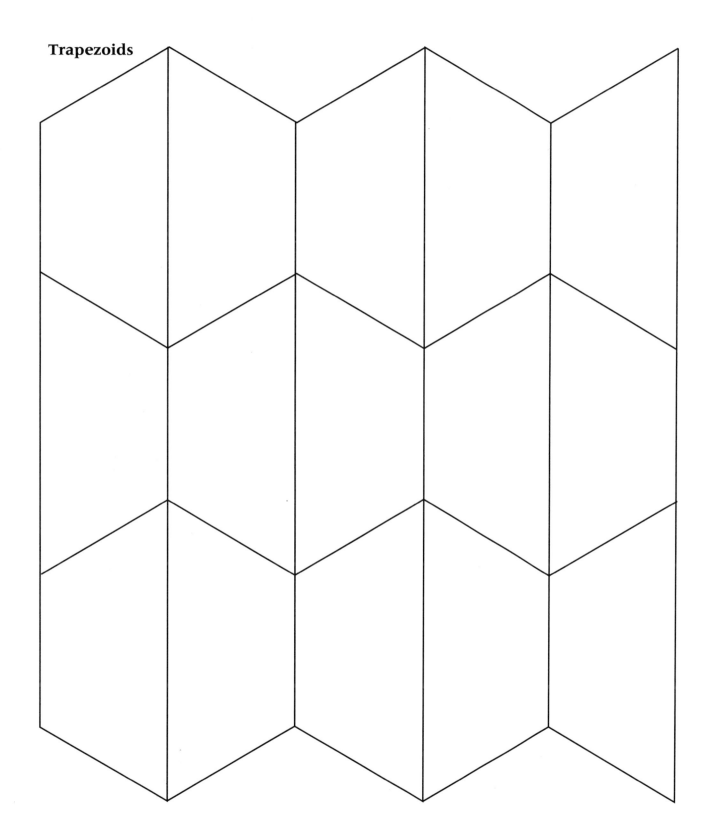

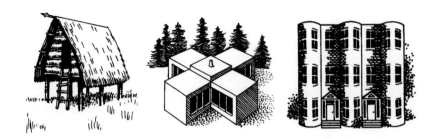

Dear Family,

Our class will soon be starting a mathematics unit called *Designing Spaces: Visualizing, Planning, and Building*, which addresses some of the key geometric topics recommended for middle school students by the National Council of Teachers of Mathematics. In this unit, students will take on the role of "house designers." They will design and construct models of homes for people around the world using the mathematics of geometry and spatial visualization.

In addition to experimenting with shapes to create their models, students will explore several methods for communicating about their home designs. For example, they will learn to represent their designs using isometric drawings, which show depth, and orthogonal drawings, which show the building from front, top, and/or side views.

Top   Front   Right Side

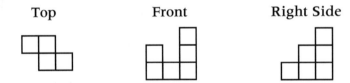

They will also learn to write precise building instructions using key geometric concepts—parallel, equilateral, prism, pyramid, opposite angles—so that others can build a replica of the structures.

You can help your child with the *Designing Spaces* unit in these ways:

- If you have traveled or lived in another country or in another area of this country, share pictures or descriptions of houses you have seen and discuss how they are different from those in your area.

- Explore the shapes of the houses in your neighborhood with your child. What shapes can you see in these structures when you look at them from different viewpoints?

- Try some of the school activities your child is doing in which visual representations and properties of shapes are explored. Discuss with your child the strategies that might be used to complete the activities.

- Encourage your child to share with you the model houses, building plans, and design specifications he or she is creating and revising.

Sincerely,

Homes Puzzle: Homes

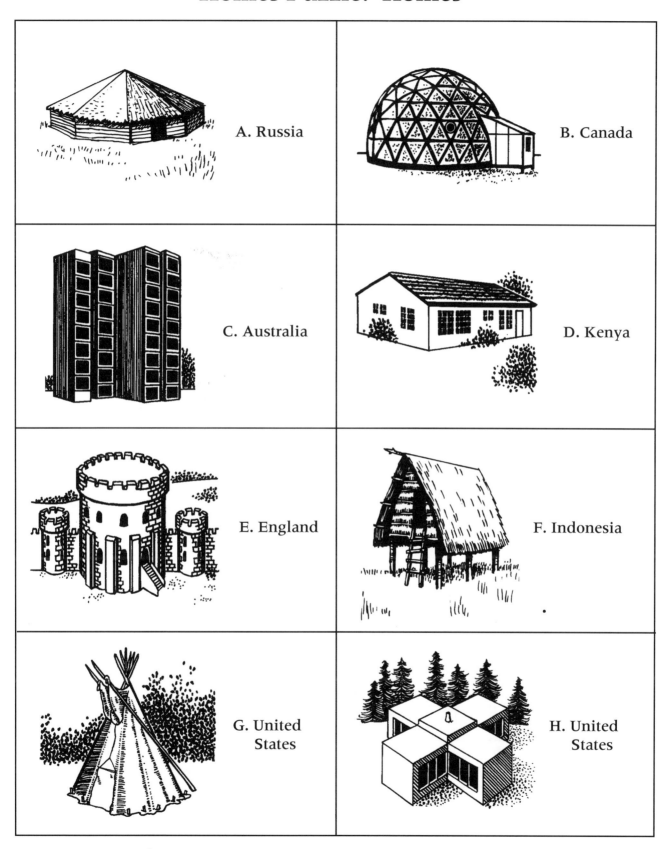

A. Russia

B. Canada

C. Australia

D. Kenya

E. England

F. Indonesia

G. United States

H. United States

Designing Spaces

Homes Puzzle: Views

View a

View from the top:

View b

View from the top:

View c

View from the top:

View d

View from the front:

View e

View of the base:

View f

View from the side:

View g

View of the base:

View h

View from the top:

Homes Puzzle: Descriptions

Description 1 Homes like mine were built a long time ago throughout Europe for kings and queens. It is large and has thick walls for protection.	**Description 2** At a factory, they make cube-shaped rooms for houses. They bring the rooms to the land, bolt them together, and cover them in cement. My house could be located in almost any climate.
Description 3 My home has thick wooden walls and only one level, to protect us from strong winds that are found in this cold climate. The shape of the home gives us a lot of floor space.	**Description 4** Buildings like mine are located in cities around the world because a lot of people can live in them and they don't take up a lot of land.
Description 5 My home is great for the extremely cold weather I live in. It is dome-shaped so that there is a large space inside, while only a small outside area is exposed to the cold.	**Description 6** In the past, Native Americans made homes like this one from animal hides and wood. These homes could be built quickly and were easy to move.
Description 7 My home protected me from floods. Since I live in a hot climate, the walls of my home are made from sticks and allow the breezes to blow through.	**Description 8** My one-story home is a good size for a family and is easy to build. That's why homes like mine are common in my neighborhood and all around the world.

Homes Puzzle: Shapes

Shapes I

Homes like mine are in buildings that are usually made up of rectangular parts.

Shapes II

Parts shaped like rectangles and triangles are needed to put my home together. My home is held up by six parts shaped like very thin cylinders.

Shapes III

Homes like mine are made from cube-shaped parts that are bolted together.

Shapes IV

The roof of my house is made up of parts shaped like triangles.

Shapes V

The main structures in my home are shaped like cylinders.

Shapes VI

My home has rectangles and pentagons as building shapes.

Shapes VII

The floor plan of my home is circular. My home is constructed with triangular parts.

Shapes VIII

My home looks like a cone or a pyramid with many triangular sides.

Rules for the Homes Puzzle

Preparing to play

1. Divide a blank sheet of paper (turned horizontally) into four columns.

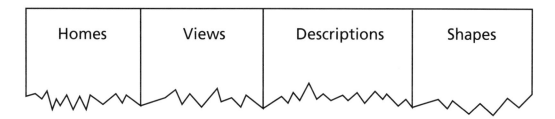

2. Cut out and divide the clues on the Homes Sheet so that each group member gets pictures of at least two homes. Group members place their pictures in the first column of the chart they've drawn.

3. Cut out all the clues on the other three puzzle sheets. Shuffle the clues and then stack them face down, like a deck of cards.

Putting the puzzle together

1. Take turns picking a clue from the stack. Read or show the clue to the group. Discuss which home matches the clue. The group member who has that home adds the clue to his or her sheet.

   Tip: If the group cannot agree on where to place a clue, put the clue aside and come back to it later.

2. Continue taking turns until all the homes are matched with views, shapes and descriptions.

3. When you've gone through all the clues, tape or glue the clues to the appropriate sheet.

   Tip: Don't glue or tape the clues to your sheet until you have finished the puzzle. You may change your mind about where to place some of the clues.

More Homes

My home is attached to other homes that look just like it. Since they are attached, there are fewer outside walls exposed to the sun. This keeps us cool in the hot summer.

I can move my home whenever I want since it is on wheels. Homes like mine cannot be more than ten feet wide so that they can travel on roads.

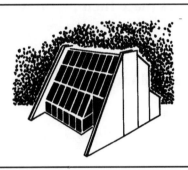

My solar home has glass panels to colllect heat from the sun. The heat can then be transformed into energy in the home for heating water or supplying electricity.

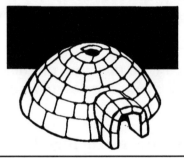

In the past, *igloos* were made by the Inuit people of the Arctic region. The climate is very cold and snow is an abundant building material. The dome shape provides a large inside space while exposing a small area to the bitter cold outside.

Homes like mine are called *saltboxes*. They are popular in New England because the long roofs protect people from the cold north winds.

I live in a brick rowhouse. It contains many apartments and does not take up a lot of land.

creative construction company

Memo 1 to House Designers

To: House Designers
From: General Manager,
          Creative Construction Co.

Welcome to Creative Construction Company! In your new job as a house designer, you will be asked to design different kinds of homes for our customers.

One kind of home our company designs is a low-cost modular home, made from cube-shaped rooms, all of which are the same size. For your first assignment, use eight to ten cubes to design a modular house model. Each cube represents a room in the house.

The pictures below show you how modules can be arranged:

✔ The face of one cube must line up exactly with the face of at least one other cube.

✔ No house can have rooms that defy gravity. Each cube must rest on the desktop or directly on top of another cube.

After you design and build your house, you will be making a set of building plans that someone else could use to build a copy of your house design.

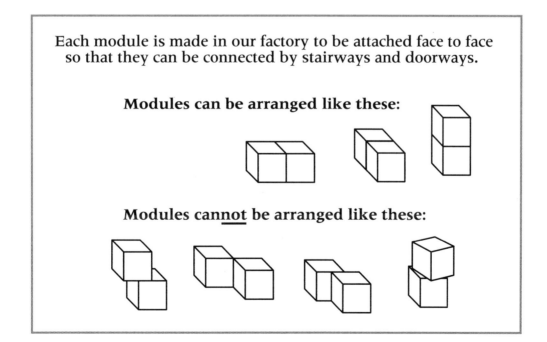

Each module is made in our factory to be attached face to face so that they can be connected by stairways and doorways.

Modules can be arranged like these:

Modules can<u>not</u> be arranged like these:

Many Modular Methods

There are many different ways to draw house plans so that someone else will understand how to build the house. In this assignment, you will experiment with different drawing techniques and think about which ones work the best.

Here is a drawing of a modular house that shows depth.

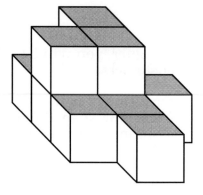

1. Show two other ways this house could be drawn. You may use methods you have seen or you may make up your own methods.

2. Choose one of the two ways you drew the house in (1). If your best friend had to build the house from looking at the drawing you chose, what are three different things that he or she should be able to figure out from the drawing?

3. Compare the sample drawing in (2) with the two methods you used in (1). Write your answers to these questions:

   a. Which method do you like better? Why?

   b. Which method do you think is more difficult to understand? Why?

4. Choose **either** (a) or (b):

   a. You may move *one* of the rooms in the house to a different location. Write a few sentences describing which room you moved and why. Draw the new house using whatever method you prefer.

Memo 2 to House Designers

To: House Designers
From: General Manager,
        Creative Construction Co.

Many of our customers are interested in building a simple, three-room house (living room, kitchen, and one bedroom/bathroom). You will be helping to prepare plans for these houses.

Design as many different houses as you can with three cubes. After completing a design, record it on paper so that someone else could build a house from it.

Design guidelines

✔ The face of one cube must line up exactly with the face of at least one other cube.

✔ No house can have rooms that defy gravity. Each cube must rest on the desktop or directly on top of another cube.

✔ The pictures below show you how to tell whether two houses are the same or different.

How to tell whether two houses are the same

Houses are the same if one can be rotated to look just like the other *without* lifting, raising, or lowering any modules.

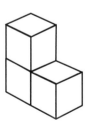 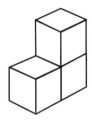   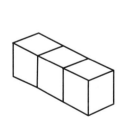 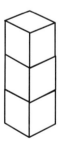

These two houses are the same. You can rotate one to be just like the other, without lifting it.

These two houses are different. You have to lift one house to make it just like the other.

Making Isometric Drawings

Isometric drawings are one way to represent cubes and three-dimensional shapes with rectangular faces. Isometric drawings show three faces of a structure in one sketch—two sides and either the top or the bottom.

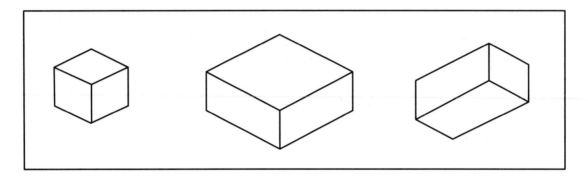

Special dot paper can be used to help you make these drawings.

Practice making isometric drawings

1. Using isometric dot paper, make copies of the examples shown above. Notice that one view shows the bottom of the object. How is the drawing that shows the bottom of the structure different from the ones that show the tops?

2. Draw a cereal box and a pizza box. How are your two drawings different? How are they alike?

3. Draw a three-dimensional letter L from different views.

4. Make an isometric drawing of a TV, videotape, bookcase, staircase, or other object in your home or classroom.

Isometric Dot Paper

Visual Glossary: Isometric Drawings

Look at the set of illustrations below and write a description
of what is meant by the the term *isometric drawing*.
Hint: Carefully compare the lengths of the sides and the
sizes of the angles in both kinds of drawings.

Which type of drawing more accurately shows the shape of
the actual object?

ISOMETRIC DRAWING

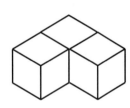
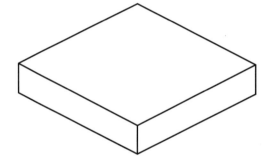

These are isometric drawings.

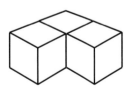
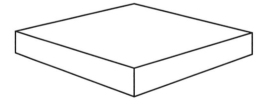

These are **not** isometric drawings.

Matching Rotations

Match each house on the left side with any house on the right side that could be a rotation of it. Rotations can be made by turning the house **or** by lifting it. Some of the houses on the left may match more than one of the houses on the right, and some may have no matches.

First try matching the structures in your head. Then you can check them using a set of four cubes.

1.

a.

2.

b.    f.

3.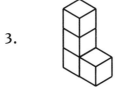

c.    g.

4.

d.

5.

e.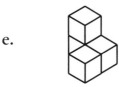

6. Choose two of the houses on the left and draw a different rotation of each one. Do not identify which of the houses you are using for your drawings. Other students may be asked to figure out the rotations you've drawn.

Reading Orthogonal Drawings

For each problem, you are given three views of a modular house. Your job is to build the house. Record the number of cubes you use for each house.

Orthogonal Drawings

Top	Front	Right Side

1.

2.

3.

4.

5.

6.

Making Orthogonal Drawings

For each problem, you are given an isometric drawing of a modular house. Your job is to make orthogonal drawings showing the top, front, and right side of the house.

1.

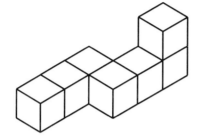

2.

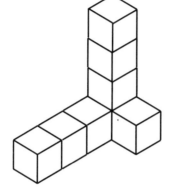

3.

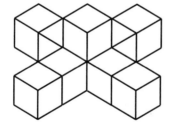

4.

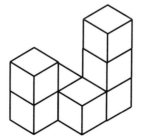

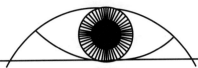

Visual Glossary: Orthogonal Drawings

Look at the set of illustrations below and write a description of what is meant by the the term *orthogonal drawing*.

ORGHOGONAL DRAWING

4 cubes

eyeglasses

coffee mug

These are orthogonal drawings.

---

4 cubes

eyeglasses

coffee mug

These are **not** orthogonal drawings.

Evaluating Plans

Students created the two sets of plans below. Read through the plans and underline or circle any parts that seem unclear to you. When you have read through the plans, answer the four questions for each set of plans.

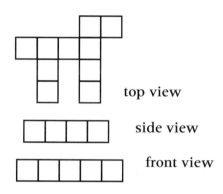

top view

side view

front view

Nathan's Plans

Lay down 2 cubes, one space apart from each other. To each cube, add 2 to each one behind it. Put one in between the two lines of cubes in the back so it makes a straight line across the back with 3 cubes. On the left side in the back, add one to the left. On the right side in the back, add one more behind the cube in the back corner, and one sticking off that on the right.

Maria's Plans

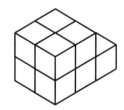

There are 10 cubes in the whole entire house. There are only two floors but it has big rooms. The whole entire house looks like a washing machine on its side.

1. Can you tell how many cubes were used in the structure? How do you know?

2. Can you tell how the cubes should be arranged? How would you make the drawings clearer?

3. Do the written plans include a step-by-step description of the building process? Are any steps missing?

4. What are one or two things that you think are done well in the plans? What are one or two things that you think need to be changed in the plans?

Giving and Getting Feedback

What is Feedback?

Feedback can be:

...advice

...suggestions

...opinions

When you ask someone,

"What do *you* think?"

they will give you feedback.

Feedback is suggestions and opinions that can help you improve your work. It is up to you to decide whether to use the feedback. Think about the feedback, and decide if you agree. If you don't agree, see if you can tell yourself why you don't agree.

If someone asks you,

"What do *you* think?"

how should you give feedback?

Remember, you are giving feedback in order to help someone else do a better job or to figure something out. Say what you have to say so that it will help the person solve their problem, not make him or her feel badly.

I really like how you did...

Some things you could improve are...

I had trouble understanding what you meant by...

The part that seemed unclear to me was when you said...

Hidden Cubes

For each set of drawings below, there is more than one possible house that can be built. (a) Visualize or build two different houses for each of the drawings. (b) Draw orthogonal views to show the difference between the two houses.

(Houses that are rotations of each other are considered the same house, and may only be counted once. The shaded faces represent the front view.)

1.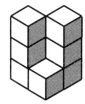

2.

3.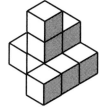

4.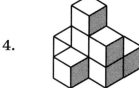

5.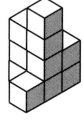

Make an **isometric** drawing of *at least two* houses that could be made from each drawing.

	Top View	**Front View**	**Right Side View**
6.	⊞	⊞	⊞
7.	⊞⊞	⊞⊞	⊞

Designing Spaces

Considering Climate in House Design

1	2
What features would you suggest for a house located in a desert?	What features would you suggest for a house located in an extremely cold place?
3	**4**
What features would you suggest for a house located in a climate that is warm in the summer and cool in the winter?	What features would you suggest for a house located in a climate that is warm all year round and has a lot of fog?
5	**6**
What features would you suggest for a house located in a climate that gets a lot of snow?	What features would you suggest for a house located in a climate that can be extremely windy, with occasional hurricanes?

Memo 3 to House Designers

To: House Designers
From: General Manager,
        Creative Construction Co.

Our company wants to develop a new line of houses that can be built using six shapes:

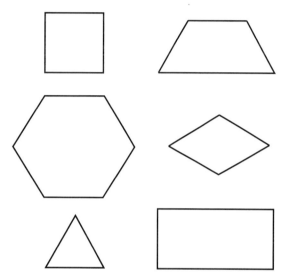

Use between 12 and 16 shape pieces to build a model home. You do not need to use each type of shape. The home must have a roof. Use tape to fit the shapes together so that the roof won't leak and the house can stand on its own.

When you have completed the model, create a set of plans so that others can build the model you designed.

Guidelines for plans

  ✔ Include at least one type of drawing of the whole structure in your plans. Decide whether you want to do orthogonal drawings, drawings that show depth, or both.

  ✔ Write a description of the building process so that someone else can follow it.

  ✔ Use names of shapes to make the plans as precise as possible.

Can You Make This Shape? Part 1

For each of the clues listed below, try to make the shape. You may use the string or you may do it with pencil and paper.

If you can make it, draw what you made and label the equal sides and the parallel sides. If you can't make it, write down that the shape is impossible.

Label the shape with a mathematical name. If you don't know a name for the shape, make up a geometrical name that you think fits. At the bottom of the page are some geometric parts of words that might help you.

Shape 1: An equilateral shape with more than 3 sides and no parallel sides.

Shape 2: A shape with 2 sides equal and 2 different sides parallel but not equal. (Hint: Your shape can have more than 4 sides.)

Shape 3: A quadrilateral with 2 pairs of parallel sides and only 2 sides equal.

Shape 4: A shape with at least 2 pairs of parallel sides that is not an equilateral shape. (Hint: Your shape can have more than 4 sides.)

Shape 5: A quadrilateral that is equilateral and has no parallel sides.

Shape 6: Make up a clue of your own and write it down. Test it to see if it can be done, and write a sentence telling why it can or cannot be done.

Parts of words that have geometric meanings

tri means 3	*quad* means 4	*penta* means 5
hexa means 6	*hepta* means 7	*octo* or *octa* means 8
equi means equal	*lateral* means side	*poly* means many

Animated Shapes

 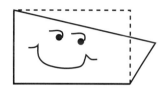 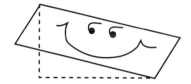

"Animated shapes" are shapes made with string when one of you moves while the rest of you stand still. As one of you moves, the shape will change according to where you move.

For each of the animated shapes described on the sheet:

First, try to visualize in your mind what will happen to the shape. Decide who will need to move to make the animated shapes. Think about whether you can make the shapes by moving different people, one at a time.

Next, make the animated shapes with your group.

Keep a record of how you made each shape. Include your starting positions, who moved, and where they moved. You may make a drawing or describe it in words. Use the correct marks for parallel and equal sides if you draw a picture.

Rules

- Only one person can move at a time; everyone else must stand still.

- Try to make the shapes by moving the *fewest* number of people.

- *For an extra challenge (optional)*: The starting shape for each question must be different from all the others; you cannot use the same starting shape more than once.

Animated Shapes

  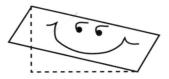

Clues

1. Start with a square. End up with a rhombus.

2. Start with a trapezoid. End up with a triangle.

3. Start with a rectangle. End up with a shape that has no parallel sides.

4. Start with an equilateral shape that has four sides. End up with a shape in which one side is longer than the side next to it.

5. Start with an equilateral shape with two pairs of parallel sides. It can be four-sided, but it does not *have* to be. End up with a shape in which only one pair of sides is parallel.

6. Start with an equilateral shape with no parallel sides. End up with a shape in which there is only one pair of parallel sides.

7. Start with an equilateral triangle. End up with a triangle in which only two sides are equal.

8. Start with a shape that has two pairs of parallel sides and no sides equal. It cannot be a four-sided shape. End up with an equilateral shape that still has two pairs of parallel sides. You may change the number of sides it has.

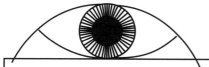

Visual Glossary: Parallel and Equilateral

Look at the set of illustrations below and write a description of
what is meant by the the terms *parallel* and *equilateral*.

PARALLEL

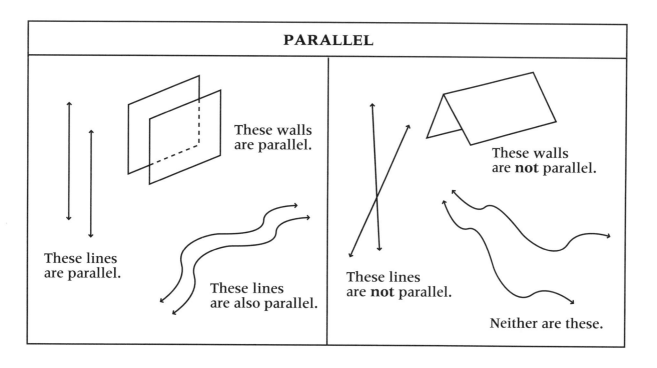

These walls are parallel.

These lines are parallel.

These lines are also parallel.

These walls are **not** parallel.

These lines are **not** parallel.

Neither are these.

EQUILATERAL

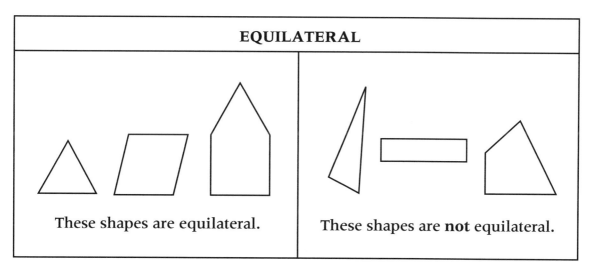

These shapes are equilateral.

These shapes are **not** equilateral.

Practice Shapes

Use string or paper and pencil to make the following shapes:

1. The first clue from *Can You Make This Shape? Part 1* is: *An equilateral shape with **no sides parallel**.* By changing one part of the clue, you get a completely new clue: *An equilateral shape with **only one pair of parallel sides**.* Try out this new clue and decide whether it is possible or impossible. If it is possible, draw a picture of a shape that fits the new clue. If it is impossible, try to explain why.

2. Take one of the clues from *Can You Make This Shape? Part 1* and change one part of it. Write down the new clue that you get. Is it possible or impossible? If it is possible, draw a picture of a shape that fits the clue. If it is impossible, try to explain why.

3. Write two clues of your own that use parallel sides, equilateral sides, or both. One of your clues must be impossible. Test each of your clues to be sure. For the clue that is possible, draw a picture of a shape that fits the clue. For the clue that is impossible, try to explain why.

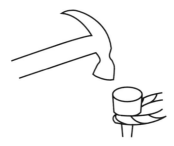

Roping It Off, Method 1

String or rope is often used in modern construction as a tool for marking off right angles. Read about the method and then complete the two problems below.

Method 1: When building a floor for a rectangular room, carpenters mark off the four corners of the room with stakes. Two pieces of rope are strung between corners to form a giant X. These ropes show the "diagonals" of the rectangle. The two pieces of rope are compared and the stakes are readjusted until the ropes are the same length. When they match, the floor will be a perfect rectangle with two pairs of parallel sides.

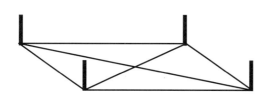   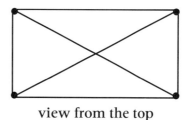

view from the top

1. Explain why this method works. What kind of shape do you get if the two ropes are not the same length?

2. Find examples of other shapes in which the diagonals are the same length. How many shapes can you find? Write a sentence or two for each shape you tried, describing what the shape was (you can also draw a picture), and what you found out.

What Is an Angle?

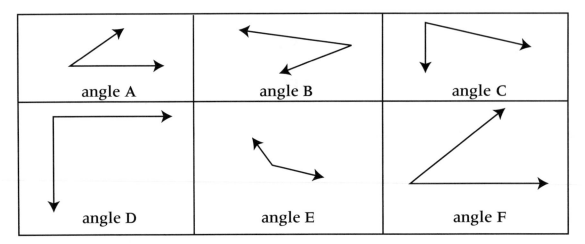

angle A	angle B	angle C
angle D	angle E	angle F

1. Circle the letter of the angle that is the largest. Then finish this sentence in your own words:

    *The way I can tell which angle is the largest is:*_____.

2. Read the three descriptions below. Which person's description of an angle do you think is the most accurate? Circle their name. Write a sentence for each of the other two choices, explaining why you did not pick them.

    Anna: "An angle is a line that goes on forever that is bent so that there is a corner."

    Lisa: "An angle is an amount of space that you turn between two sides."

    Luis: "An angle is the number of degrees when you measure with a protractor."

3. Finish this sentence in your own words:

    Measuring an angle of a shape is different from measuring a side of a shape

    *because*_____

    _____.

Can You Make This Shape? Part 2

For each clue, try to make the shape. You may use the string or you may do it with pencil and paper.

If you can make it, draw what you made and label the equal angles and right angles. Some of the clues might describe a shape that is impossible to make.

Label the shape with a mathematical name. If you don't know a name for the shape, make up a geometrical name that you think fits. At the bottom of the page are some geometric parts of words that might help you.

Shape 1: A quadrilateral with exactly two right angles.

Shape 2: A quadrilateral with exactly two right angles that are also opposite angles.

Shape 3: A shape with exactly three right angles.

Shape 4: A quadrilateral with only one pair of opposite angles that are equal.

Shape 5: A shape with five equal angles.

Shape 6: A quadrilateral in which each pair of opposite angles are the same size and at least one pair are right angles.

Shape 7: Make up a clue of your own and write it down. Test it to see if it can be made, and write a sentence telling why it can or cannot be made.

Parts of words that have geometric meanings		
tri means 3	*quad* means 4	*penta* means 5
hexa means 6	*hepta* means 7	*octo* or *octa* means 8
equi means equal	*lateral* means side	*poly* means many
angular means angle	*ortho* means right angle	*gon* means angle

Sides and Angles Game Cards

Side This shape is equilateral... **A**	**Angle** ...and has exactly two equal angles. **a**
Side This shape has two pairs of parallel sides... **B**	**Angle** ...and has two pairs of opposite angles. **b**
Side This shape is equilateral and has at least one pair of parallel sides... **C**	**Angle** ...and has at least one pair of opposite equal angles. **c**
Side This shape has no parallel sides in it... **D**	**Angle** ...and has at least two right angles in it. **d**

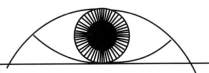

Visual Glossary: Types of Angles and Regular Shapes (1)

Look at the set of illustrations below and write a description of what is meant by the the terms *equal angles* and *opposite angles*.

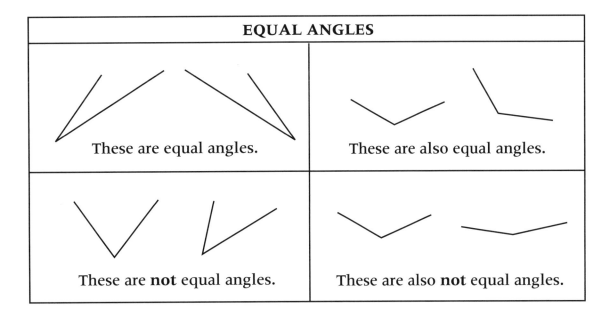

EQUAL ANGLES	
These are equal angles.	These are also equal angles.
These are **not** equal angles.	These are also **not** equal angles.

OPPOSITE ANGLES	
These are opposite angles.	These are also opposite angles.
These are **not** opposite angles.	These are also **not** opposite angles.

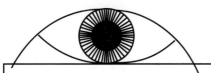

Visual Glossary: Types of Angles and Regular Shapes (2)

Look at the set of illustrations below and write a description of what is meant by the the terms *right angles* and *regular shapes*.

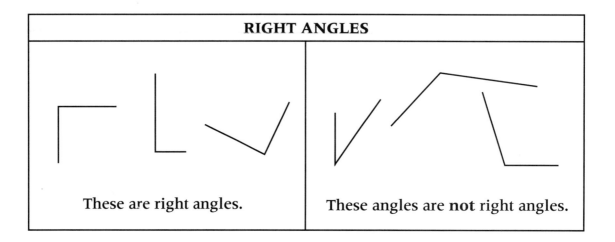

RIGHT ANGLES

These are right angles.

These angles are **not** right angles.

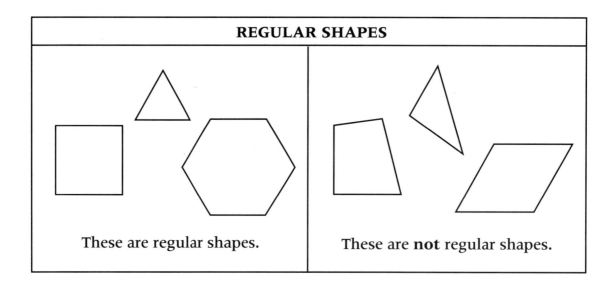

REGULAR SHAPES

These are regular shapes.

These are **not** regular shapes.

Designing Spaces

Roping It Off, Method 2

String or rope is often used in modern construction as a tool for marking off right angles. Read about the method and then complete the three problems below.

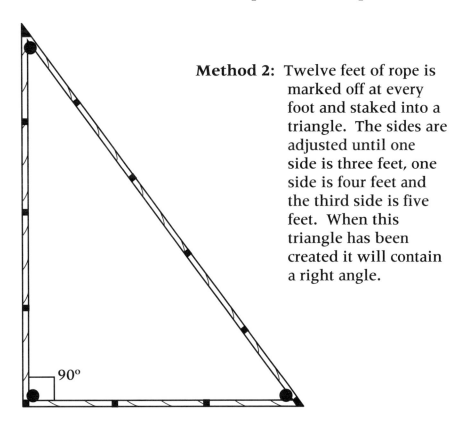

Method 2: Twelve feet of rope is marked off at every foot and staked into a triangle. The sides are adjusted until one side is three feet, one side is four feet and the third side is five feet. When this triangle has been created it will contain a right angle.

90°

1. Find another trio of side lengths that will create a right triangle. Explain how you know you have a right angle. Use string or rope either to build a small model or demonstrate it in class.

    Tip: An easy scale factor to use if you make a model is one foot of rope in the problem equals one inch of string in your model.

2. How many more feet must you add to the string or rope until you have a longer string that will still give you a new right angle? Cut a piece of string to this new length and find a new trio of side lengths using this longer string. What are the new side lengths?

3. Find two other trios of side lengths that will create a right angle in a triangle. There are patterns to some of these trios of side lengths. If you see a pattern, describe the pattern and make a prediction for how you would find other side lengths.

Memo 4 to House Designers

To: House Designers
From: General Manager,
        Creative Construction Co.

In order to sell and build your house design, our salespeople and contractors need some specific information. Please write design specifications telling us all about your house design. The specifications can include a chart, a poster, or anything you think would help us understand your design.

Salespeople's Questions

Appearance
What does your home look like?

Climate
What climate is your house designed for?

What features does your home have to make it a good match for the climate you chose?

Where in the world could your house be located?

Inhabitants
How many people can live in your house?

Is this a good house for children, the elderly, or disabled people to inhabit?

Contractors' Questions

The contractors will use your building plans to make a model of your house design. In order to figure out how long it will take to build the house and how much it will cost, they need some specific information about the shapes in your house.

What shapes did you use to design your house?

How many of each shape are there?

Which of the shapes are equilateral?

Which of the shapes have parallel sides?

Which of the shapes have equal angles, opposite angles, or right angles?

Sample House Plans

Review the following set of building plans, which were made by a sixth-grade student. Circle any places that seem unclear or incorrect to you and then answer the questions on the next page.

The "Tree" House

Part 1

a. Take three rectangles and put them together to form a 3-D triangle like this:

b. There will be two open ends that look like triangles. Get two triangles and put them in the empty spaces. Like this:

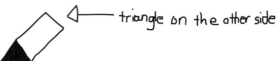

Part 2

c. Take a diamond and two triangles to form a big triangle. Like this:

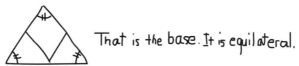

d. Take 3 of ◻ these and form them into a triangle. So, that the top of the triangle is shaped like another triangle. Like this:

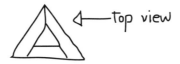

e. Get 3 triangles. Put them together to make another triangle. Like this:

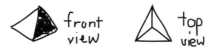

f. Put the 3 triangles and the 3 ◻ together. None of the sides should be parallel. Like this:

Sample House Plans (Continued)

g. Now, you are finished with the "tree house". The house should look like this:

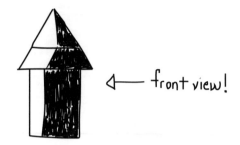

You know that you have it right if there are three ways that you can cut it from top to bottom so that the two pieces are symmetrical.

It is located on the banks of the Mississippi River. If the river ever floods, the people can go to the large, top floors and not get wet.

1. What do you like in the plans?

2. Can you tell how many shapes were used to make this house? Can you tell which shapes were used? If not, how would you redo the plans to make the shapes clearer?

3. What geometric concepts or notation could be added to the plans to make them clearer or more precise? Where would you add them?

4. Are there other drawings that could be included to make the plans easier to follow? What type of drawings should be included? Where would you put them?

5. What else do you need to know in order to build the "tree" house?

A Stack of Pennies

For each of the situations described below, draw the shape you would end up with and write answers to the questions on a separate sheet of paper.

1. Imagine a penny. Now imagine ten pennies stacked right on top of the first one so that the edges of each one line up perfectly with the one below it.

   Describe this shape. What would you call it? What properties does it have?

2. Imagine the shape you thought of in #1. Now imagine slicing that shape from top to bottom right through the middle. Open up the two halves of the shape.

   What two-dimensional shape is the face in front of you?

3. Imagine a rhombus-shaped piece of cardboard laying on your desk. Now imagine fifteen of them stacked on top of this shape so that all the corners and edges line up.

   Describe this shape. What would you call it? What properties does it have?

4. Imagine the shape that you thought of in #3. Now imagine that you sliced it from the top to the bottom through the center.

   What is the two-dimensional shape of the face?

5. Imagine a square. Imagine a point in space above the square. In your mind, draw a line from each of the corners of the square to the point. Now imagine this shape as a solid shape.

   Describe this shape. What would you call it? What properties does it have?

6. Imagine slicing the shape you made in #5 from top (the point) to the bottom (the square) right through the middle.

   What is the two-dimensional shape of the face?

How to Draw a Prism

First, draw the base of the prism. The base can have as many sides as you like. This example is a **pentagonal prism**, so the base is a pentagon.

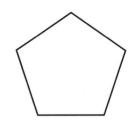

Next, draw the second base by making an exact copy of the shape (be careful to keep corresponding sides parallel). (The prism is easier to imagine if you draw the shapes diagonally apart from each other, rather than directly above or right next to each other.)

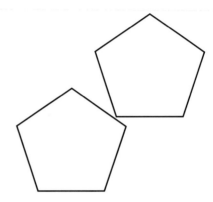

Third, connect the corresponding vertices of the two bases. This will produce a collection of parallel edges with the same length (in our case there are five).

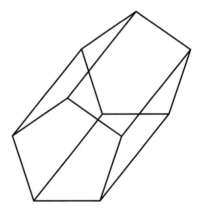

If the prism seems hard to see, you may want to try shading the front face, and erasing the edges that you would not see in a solid prism.

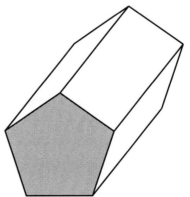

How to Draw a Pyramid

First, draw the base. It may have as many sides as you would like. This example is a **pentagonal pyramid**, so the base is a pentagon.

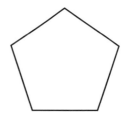

Second, choose any point outside the base.

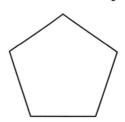

Third, draw line segments from each vertex of the base to the point.

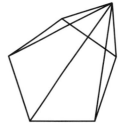

If the pyramid seems hard to see, you may want to try shading some of the faces and erasing the edges that you would not see in a solid pyramid.

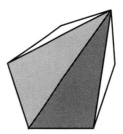

Practicing Prisms and Pyramids

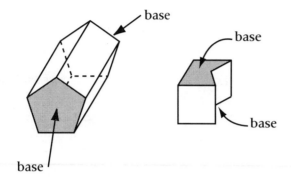

In a prism, there are two parallel faces that can be any shape. These are called the *bases*.

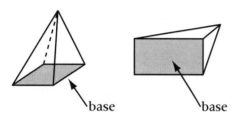

In a pyramid, one face can be any shape. All the other faces are triangles. The face that can be any shape is called the *base*.

A prism or pyramid gets its name from the shape of its base or bases; for example, if the base of a pyramid is a square, it is called a square pyramid.

Using the techniques shown on **How to Draw a Prism** and **How to Draw a Pyramid**:

- Draw a few prisms and pyramids on your own using the techniques you learned. For the pyramids, experiment with placing the point in different positions above and below the base.

- Draw a triangular prism, a hexagonal pyramid, and a rectangular prism.

Photo Sort

Imagine that you are walking around the group of buildings shown in the photos below. Choose one of the photos as a starting point and put the photos in order to show what you would see as you circle the buildings.

Mystery Structures Rules

Your group has been given a set of shapes and a set of four clues that describes a three-dimensional structure.

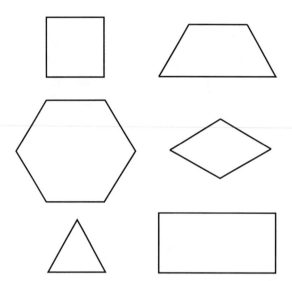

Here's how **Mystery Structures: Game I** is played:

- Each group member reads, but does not show, one of the clues to the group. If your clue has a picture on it, describe the picture.

- After each clue is read, stop and discuss what the structure might look like.

- When you've heard the four clues, use the shapes and tape to build a structure that fits all the clues. Recheck each clue to make sure the structure fits each one. You may need to revise the structure several times before it fits the four clues.

- When you've built the structure that satisfies all the clues, make a drawing of it that shows depth.

Mystery Structures: Game I

Clue Sets 1 and 2

Set 1 Game I The bottom view of this structure looks like this:	Set 1 Game I This structure has three sets of parallel faces. This structure is a prism.
Set 1 Game I Seven pieces are used to make this structure.	Set 1 Game I The right side of this structure is a square.

Set 2 Game I The number of rhombi in this structure is half the number of rectangles.	Set 2 Game I The bottom of this structure looks like this: left right
Set 2 Game I This structure is a prism. There are eighteen edges in this structure.	Set 2 Game I Eleven pieces are used to make this structure.

Mystery Structures: Game I

Clue Sets 3 and 4

Set 3 Game I This structure has no parallel faces.	Set 3 Game I The bottom view of this structure looks like: □
Set 3 Game I This structure is constructed with five pieces. All of the pieces are regular shapes.	Set 3 Game I The side view looks like this: △

Set 4 Game I This structure is made with three times the number of squares as hexagons.	Set 4 Game I This structure has twelve vertices. It is a prism.
Set 4 Game I The base looks like this: back left ⬡ right front	Set 4 Game I When this structure is cut from left to right through the center, the two resulting pieces are symmetrical.

Mystery Structures: Game I

Clue Sets 5 and 6

Set 5 Game I Three of the pieces in this structure are regular shapes.	**Set 5** Game I This structure is made with six pieces.
Set 5 Game I The base of this structure looks like this:	**Set 5** Game I This structure is a prism. It has two sets of parallel faces.

Set 6 Game I The view from the right side looks like this:	**Set 6** Game I The bottom view looks like this:
Set 6 Game I This structure is constructed with seven pieces. Only three of the pieces are squares.	**Set 6** Game I All of the pieces in this structure are equilateral shapes.

Mystery Structures: Game II

Game II The rectangular prism is attached to two other structures. It rests on one of its square faces. One of its rectangular faces is attached to the rectangular face from the hexagonal prism.	Game II The square pyramid is attached to the top of the rectangular prism.
Game II The hexagonal prism made with rectangles sits on its base made of rhombi. The hexagonal prism made with squares sits on top of it.	Game II On top of the trapezoidal prism sits the structure which looks like this... ...from the side.
Game II The base of the whole final structure looks like this:	Game II The trapezoidal prism is attached to the tall hexagonal prism. They are attached by joining a square face from the trapezoidal prism to the rectangular face from the tall hexagonal prism.

Mystery Structures: Game III
Edges and Vertices

Set 1   Which drawing on the next sheet matches these clues?

Clue a   This structure includes at least 1 regular hexagon.

Clue b   This structure has 7 vertices.

Clue c   When this structure is constructed you cannot find any rectangles.

Clue d   When this structure is constructed you can find at least 5 triangles.

Circle it on the next sheet and label it 1. Try drawing it here:

Set 2   Which drawing on the next sheet matches these clues?

Clue a   When this structure is constructed you can find 4 equilateral triangles.

Clue b   The base of this structure looks like this:

Clue c   When this structure is constructed you can find 2 more squares than equilateral triangles.

Clue d   When this structure is constructed you can find 16 edges and 9 vertices.

Circle it on the next sheet and label it 2. Try drawing it here:

Mystery Structures: Game III
(Continued)

Set 3 Which drawing below matches these clues?

Clue a This structure has more than 12 vertices.

Clue b The front view and the back view are the same.

Clue c When this structure is constructed you can find 4 times the number of squares as octagons.

Clue d When this structure is constructed you can find 2 regular octagons.

Circle it below and label it 3. Try drawing it here:

Shapes:

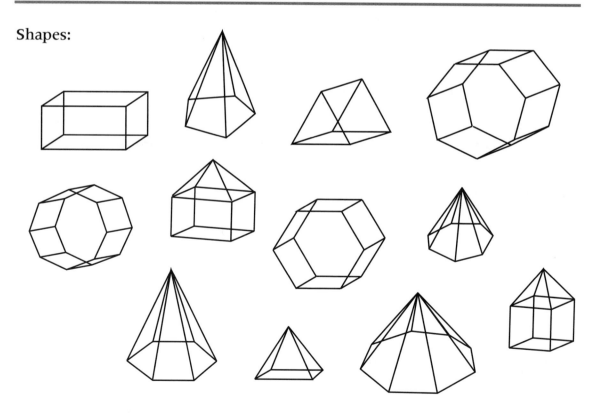

Memo 5 to House Designers

creative construction company

To: House Designers
From: General Manager,
         Creative Construction Co.

We have just been hired to create a new collection of house designs. These houses will be located in one of two climates: (1) hot and rainy or (2) cold and snowy. This project will give you a chance to come up with some creative designs and it will give us a chance to see how much you have learned while working for our company.

The project has three parts:

1. Use the shapes to design and build a model home.

2. Create a set of plans so that others can build the model you created.

3. Write a memo explaining the features of your house.

Building guidelines

- The home must have a roof. No leaky roofs allowed.

- The home must be able to stand on its own.

- You must use between 20 and 24 shape pieces. You do not need to use each type of shape.

- You may add one new type of shape.

Guidelines for plans

- Include both orthogonal and perspective drawings of your house and label both types. For the orthogonal drawings, label the various views. The labels will make your plans easier for builders to interpret.

- Include a written, step-by-step description of your building process so that someone else could replicate your house. Use the names and properties of shapes to make your description clear and precise.

Guidelines for design specifications

- Make sure to include all of the information that the directors have asked for on Memo 6.

- Make the design specifications as attractive and as easy to follow as possible.

creative construction company

Memo 6 to House Designers

To: House Designers
From: General Manager,
        Creative Construction Co.

In order to sell and build your house design, our salespeople and contractors need some specific information. Please write one memo telling us all about your house design. The memo can include a chart, a poster, or anything that you think would help us understand your design.

Salespeople's Questions

Appearance

What does your home look like?

How would you describe the shape of the entire house?

How would you describe the shape of its base, its roof and any special features?

How many floors does your house have?

Climate

What climate is your house designed for?

What features does your home have to make it a good match for the climate you chose?

Where in the world could your house be located?

Inhabitants

How many people can live in your house?

Is this a good house for children, the elderly, or disabled people to inhabit?

Contractors' Questions

The contractors will use your building plans to make a model of your house design. In order to figure out how long it will take to build the house and how much it will cost, they need some specific information about the shape of your house:

What shapes can be found in your house?

How many of each shape are there?

How many edges and vertices does it have?

Are these shapes used to make it regular?

Are these shapes used to make it equilateral?

Does your house have any parallel faces? If so, how many?

Estimada familia:

Nuestra clase pronto empezará una unidad de matemáticas que se titula *Diseñar espacios: visualización, planificación y construcción.* Esta unidad trata algunos de los principales temas geométricos recomendados por el *National Council of Teachers of Mathematics* (Consejo Nacional de Profesores de Matemáticas) para los estudiantes de grado medio. En esta unidad los estudiantes se convierten en "diseñadores de viviendas". Diseñarán y construirán maquetas de viviendas para gente de todo el mundo, usando la matemática geométrica y la visualización espacial.

Además de experimentar con formas geométricas para crear sus maquetas, los estudiantes examinarán distintos métodos para comunicarse información sobre sus diseños de viviendas. Por ejemplo, aprenderán a representar sus diseños por medio de dibujos isométricos, que muestran la profundidad, y dibujos ortogonales, que muestran la vista frontal, aérea (desde arriba) y/o lateral del edificio.

| Arriba | Frente | Lado derecho |

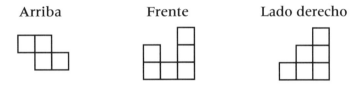

También aprenderán a escribir instrucciones específicas para la construcción, usando conceptos geométricos clave—paralelo, equilátero, prisma, pirámide, ángulos opuestos—para que los demás puedan construir una réplica de las estructuras.

Usted puede ayudar a su hijo(a) con la unidad *Diseñar espacios* de estas maneras:

• Si usted ha viajado o vivido en otro país, o en otra zona de este país, muéstrele fotografías o descripciones de las viviendas que usted ha visto y compare las diferencias con las de su área.

• Examine con su hijo(a) las formas que tienen las viviendas en su vecindario. ¿Qué figuras ven en esas estructuras cuando las miran desde distintos puntos de vista?

• Pruebe a hacer algunas de las actividades escolares que hace su hijo(a), en las que se examina la representación visual y propiedades de las formas geométricas. Discuta con su hijo(a) las estrategias que se pueden usar para completar las actividades.

• Anime a su hijo(a) a compartir con usted las maquetas de las viviendas, los planes de construcción y los datos específicos de diseño que esté creando y revisando.

Sinceramente,

Rompecabezas de las viviendas: Viviendas

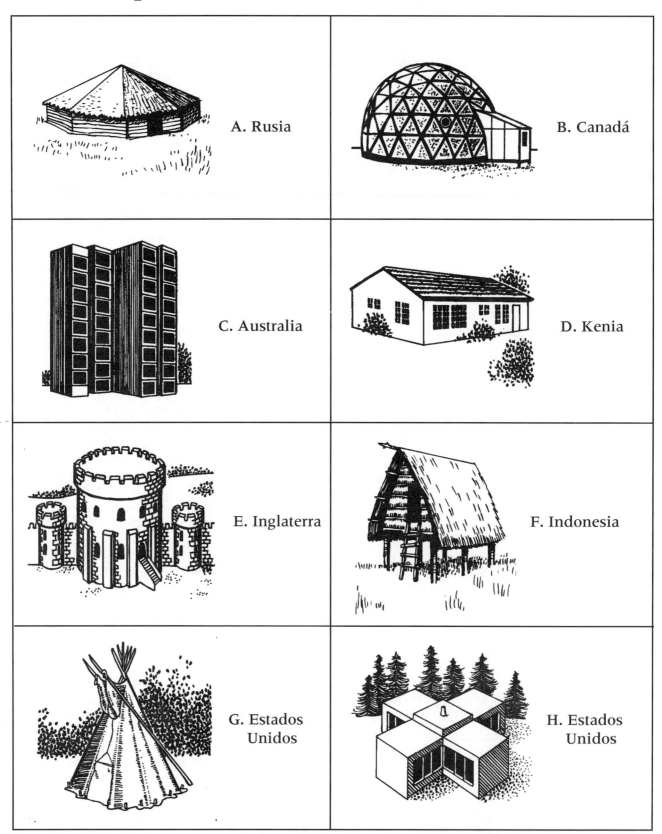

A. Rusia

B. Canadá

C. Australia

D. Kenia

E. Inglaterra

F. Indonesia

G. Estados Unidos

H. Estados Unidos

Rompecabezas de las viviendas: vistas

Vista a

Vista desde arriba

Vista b

Vista desde arriba

Vista c

Vista desde arriba

Vista d

Vista desde el frente

Vista e

Vista de la base

Vista f

Vista desde el lado

Vista g

Vista de la base

Vista h

Vista desde arriba

Rompecabezas de las viviendas: descripciones

Descripción 1

Casas como la mía fueron construidas en toda Europa por reyes y reinas hace mucho tiempo. Es grande y tiene muros de protección muy gruesos.

Descripción 2

En una fábrica hacen cuartos en forma de cubo para las casas. Ellos traen los cuartos al terreno, los atornillan entre sí y los cubren con cemento. Mi casa podría situarse en cualquier clima.

Descripción 3

Mi casa tiene gruesos muros de madera y sólo un piso, para protegernos de los fuertes vientos que hay en este clima frío. La forma de la casa nos proporciona mucho espacio.

Descripción 4

Edificios como el mío se encuentran en las ciudades de todo el mundo, porque mucha gente puede vivir en ellos y no ocupan mucho terreno.

Descripción 5

Mi casa es estupenda para el clima extremadamente frío en el que vivo. Tiene forma de cúpula para que haya mucho espacio dentro, mientras que sólo una pequeña área está expuesta al frío.

Descripción 6

En el pasado, los indios norteamericanos hacían viviendas como ésta, usando cueros de animales y madera. Estas viviendas se podían construir rápidamente y eran fáciles de trasladar.

Descripción 7

Mi casa me protegió de las inundaciones. Como vivo en un clima cálido, los muros de mi casa están hechos de palos y permiten que la brisa sople a través de ellos.

Descripción 8

Mi casa de una planta es de tamaño adecuado para una familia, y fácil de construir. Por esta razón, las casas como la mía son corrientes en el vecindario y en todo el mundo.

Rompecabezas de las viviendas: formas

Forma I

Casas como la mía están en edificios que usualmente están hechos de piezas rectangulares.

rectángulos

Forma II

Para montar mi casa son necesarias piezas de forma rectangular y triangular. Mi casa se sujeta sobre seis piezas que tienen forma de cilindros muy estrechos.

triángulo

Forma III

Casas como la mía están hechas de partes con forma de cubo atornilladas entre sí.

cubo

Forma IV

El tejado de mi casa está hecho de piezas en forma de triángulo.

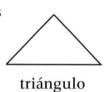

triángulo

Forma V

Las estructuras principales de mi casa tienen forma de cilindro.

cilindro

Forma VI

Mi casa se construye con piezas en forma de rectángulo y pentágono

pentágono

Forma VII

El plano del suelo de mi casa es circular. Mi casa está construida con piezas triangulares.

triángulo

Forma VIII

Mi casa parece un cono o una pirámide con muchos lados triangulares.

pirámide

Reglas del Juego de las viviendas

Prepararse a jugar

1. Divide una hoja de papel blanco (colocada horizontalmente) en cuatro columnas.

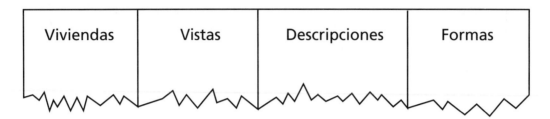

| Viviendas | Vistas | Descripciones | Formas |

2. Recorta y divide todas las pistas de la hoja de Rompecabezas de las viviendas de tal manera que cada miembro del grupo reciba por lo menos dibujos de dos viviendas. Los miembros del grupo colocan sus dibujos en la primera columna del cuadro que han dibujado.

3. Recorta todas las pistas de las otras tres hojas del puzzle. Mezcla las pistas y colócalas boca abajo en un montón, como una baraja.

Completar el rompecabezas

1. Por turnos, saquen una pista del montón de cartas. Lee o muestra la pista al grupo. Discute qué vivienda corresponde a la pista. El miembro del grupo que tiene esa vivienda añade la pista a su hoja.

   Consejo: si el grupo no puede ponerse de acuerdo sobre dónde colocar una pista, pongan la pista a un lado y vuelvan a ella más tarde.

2. Continúen con los turnos hasta que todas las viviendas estén emparejadas con las vistas, formas y descripciones.

3. Cuando hayas pasado por todas las pistas, pega las pistas con cinta o pegamento a la hoja apropiada.

   Consejo: No pegues las pistas a tu hoja hasta que hayas acabado el rompecabezas. Puede que cambies de opinión sobre dónde colocar alguna de las pistas.

Más casas

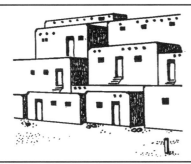

Mi casa está adosada a otras casas iguales a ella. Como están juntas, hay menos muros exteriores espuestos al sol. Esto nos mantiene frescos en el caluroso verano.

Puedo transportar mi casa siempre que quiero porque va sobre ruedas. casas como la mía no pueden tener más de diez pies de ancho para poder viajar por carretera.

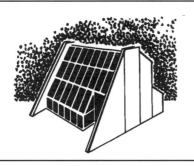

Mi casa solar tiene paneles de cristal para recoger el calor del sol. Después, el calor puede transformarse en energía para calentar agua o proveer electricidad a la casa.

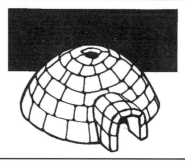

En el pasado, los *iglús* los hacían los inuit, un pueblo de la región ártica. El clima es muy frío y la nieve es un material de construcción abundante. La forma de cúpula proporciona un amplio espacio interior mientras que sólo expone una pequeña área al intenso frío exterior.

Las casas como la mía se conocen con el nombre de *saltboxes*. Son populares en Nueva Inglaterra porque sus largos tejados protegen a la gente de los fríos vientos del norte.

Yo vivo en un edificio de apartamentos hecho de ladrillos. Tiene muchos apartamentos y no ocupa mucho terreno.

Memo 1 a los diseñadores de viviendas

A: los diseñadores de viviendas
De: Director General,
        Compañía de Construcción Creativa

¡Bienvenidos a la Compañía de Construcción Creativa! En su nuevo trabajo de diseñador/a de viviendas se le pedirá que diseñe distintos tipos de viviendas para nuestros clientes.

Uno de los tipos de vivienda que diseña nuestra compañía es una casa modular económica, compuesta de habitaciones en forma de cubo, todas del mismo tamaño. Su primer encargo consiste en diseñar un modelo de vivienda modular usando 8-10 cubos. Cada cubo representa una habitación de la vivienda.

El dibujo de abajo le muestra cómo se pueden colocar los módulos.

✔ La cara de un cubo debe estar exactamente alineada por lo menos con la cara de otro cubo.

✔ Ninguna vivienda puede tener habitaciones que desafíen a la fuerza de gravedad. Cada cubo debe reposar sobre la mesa o directamente encima de otro cubo.

Después de diseñar y construir su vivienda, usted hará una serie de planos de construcción que otra persona podría usar para construir una copia del diseño de su vivienda.

Cada módulo se fabrica en nuestra factoría para ser adosado cara a cara y así poder conectarse con escaleras y portales.

Los módulos se pueden colocar como éstos

Los módulos <u>no</u> se pueden colocar como éstos

Métodos modulares diversos

Hay muchas maneras de dibujar planos de viviendas para que alguien más comprenda cómo construir la vivienda. En este encargo vas a experimentar con distintas técnicas de dibujo y analizar cuál es la mejor.

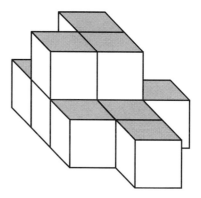

Aquí hay un dibujo de una vivienda modular que muestra profundidad.

1. Muestra otras dos formas en que se podría dibujar esta vivienda. Puedes usar métodos que hayas visto o puedes inventar tus propios métodos.

2. Elige una de las formas que usaste para dibujar la vivienda #1. Si tu mejor amigo/a tuviera que construir la vivienda mirando al dibujo que has elegido, ¿cuáles son tres cosas diferentes que él o ella debería ser capaz de figurarse al ver el dibujo?

3. Compara el dibujo de muestra en #2 con los dos métodos que has usado en #1. Escribe tus respuestas a estas preguntas:

   a. ¿Qué método prefieres? ¿Por qué?

   b. ¿Qué método crees que es más difícil de entender? ¿Por qué?

4. Elige **una**, (a) o (b):

   a. Puedes mover *una* de las habitaciones a un sitio diferente. Escribe algunas oraciones para describir qué habitación has movido y por qué. Dibuja la nueva vivienda usando el método que prefieras.

   b. La vista de la vivienda en (2) es desde el frente. Trata de dibujar cómo se vería la vivienda si estuvieras de pie detrás de ella. Puedes usar el método que prefieras.

Memo 2 a los diseñadores de viviendas

creative construction company

A: los diseñadores de viviendas
De: Director General,
 Compañía de Construcción Creativa

Muchos de nuestros clientes están interesados en construir una vivienda sencilla de tres habitaciones (sala de estar, cocina y un dormitorio/baño). Usted ayudará a preparar los planos de estas viviendas.

Con tres cubos, diseñe tantas viviendas diferentes como pueda. Después de completar un diseño, anótelo en papel para que alguien más pueda construir una vivienda fijándose en él.

Guía de diseño

✔ La cara de un cubo debe alinearse exactamente con la cara de otro cubo como mínimo.

✔ Ninguna vivienda puede tener cuartos que desafíen a la gravedad. Cada cubo debe apoyarse sobre la mesa o directamente sobre otro cubo.

✔ Los dibujos de abajo te muestran cómo identificar si dos viviendas son iguales o diferentes.

Cómo identificar si dos viviendas son iguales

Las viviendas son iguales si una se puede girar para que tenga la misma apariencia que la otra *sin* levantar, alzar o bajar ninguno de los módulos.

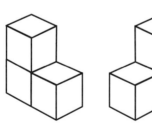
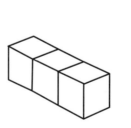
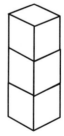
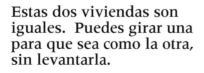

Estas dos viviendas son iguales. Puedes girar una para que sea como la otra, sin levantarla.

Estas dos viviendas son diferentes.

Hacer dibujos isométricos

Los dibujos isométricos son una manera de representar cubos y formas tridimensionales con caras rectangulares. Los dibujos isométricos muestran tres caras de una estructura en un boceto—dos caras y la parte superior o la inferior.

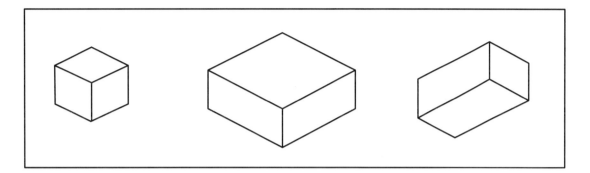

Puedes usar un papel punteado especial para ayudarte a hacer estos dibujos.

Practica el dibujo isométrico

1. Usando papel punteado isométrico, haz copias de los ejemplos que se muestran arriba. Observa que una vista muestra la parte inferior del objeto. ¿En aué se diferencia el dibujo que muestra la parte inferior de la estructura de los que muestran la parte superior?

2. Dibuja una caja de cereales y una caja de pizza. ¿En qué se diferencian tus dos dibujos? ¿En qué se parecen?

3. Dibuja una letra L tridimensional desde distintos puntos de vista.

4. Haz un dibujo isométrico de una TV, una cinta de video, una estantería, una escalera u otro objeto de casa o de la clase.

Nombre(s)

Papel punteado isométrico

Designing Spaces ©EDC, 1995

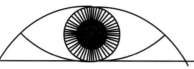

Glosario visual: dibujos isométricos

Mira el conjunto de ilustraciones de abajo y escribe una
descripción de lo que se quiere decir con el término *dibujo
isométrico*.

Consejo: compara cuidadosamente la largura de los lados y
el tamaño de los ángulos en las dos clases de dibujos.

¿Qué clase de dibujo muestra con más precisión la forma del
objeto real?

DIBUJOS ISOMÉTRICOS

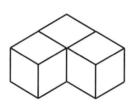 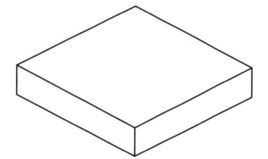

Éstos son dibujos isométricos.

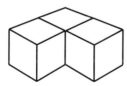 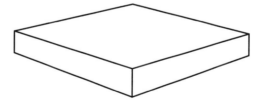

Éstos **no** son dibujos isométricos.

Emparejar rotaciones

Empareja cada vivienda del lado izquierdo con cualquier vivienda del lado derecho que pudiera ser su rotación. Puedes rotar la vivienda girándola **o** levantándola. Algunas de las viviendas de la izquierda puede que formen pareja con más de una vivienda de la derecha, y algunas puede que no tengan pareja.

Primero, trata de emparejar las estructuras mentalmente. Luego puedes comprobarlas usando un juego de cuatro cubos.

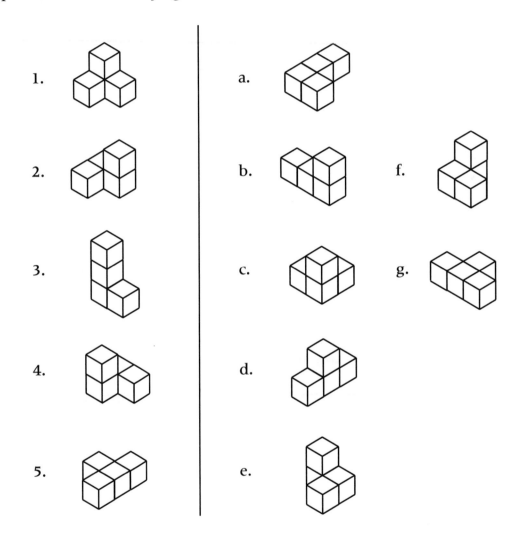

6. Elige dos de las viviendas de la izquierda y dibuja una rotación diferente de cada una. No identifiques qué vivienda estás utilizando en tus dibujos. Puede que se les pida a otros estudiantes que traten de figurarse las rotaciones que has dibujado.

Leer dibujos ortogonales

Para cada problema se te proporcionan tres vistas de una vivienda modular. Tu trabajo consiste en construir la vivienda. Apunta el número de cubos que empleas para cada vivienda.

Dibujos ortogonales

Arriba	Frente	Lado derecho

1.

2.

3.

4.

5.

6.

Hacer dibujos ortogonales

Para cada problema, se te proporciona un dibujo isométrico de una vivienda modular. Tu trabajo consiste en hacer dibujos ortogonales que muestren la parte de arriba, el frente y el lado derecho de la vivienda.

1.

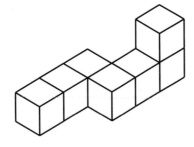

2.

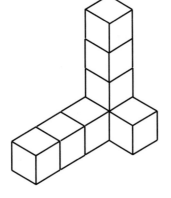

3.

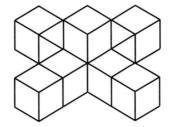

4.

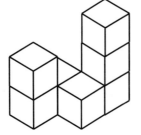

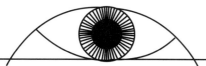

Glosario visual: dibujos ortogonales

Mira el conjunto de ilustraciones de abajo y escribe una descripción de lo que se quiere decir con el término *dibujos ortogonales.*

DIBUJOS ORTOGONALES

4 cubos

gafas

taza de café

Éstos son dibujos ortogonales.

---

4 cubos

gafas

taza de café

Éstos **no** son dibujos ortogonales.

Evaluar planos

Unos estudiantes crearon los dos conjuntos de planos de abajo. Lee las instrucciones de los planos y subraya o rodea con un círculo las partes que no te parezcan claras. Cuando hayas leído las instrucciones, responde a las preguntas para cada conjunto de planos.

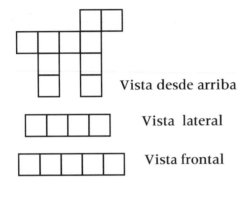

Vista desde arriba

Vista lateral

Vista frontal

Los planos de Nathan

Coloca dos cubos separados entre sí por un espacio. A cada cubo, añade dos a cada uno detrás suyo. Pon uno entre las 2 líneas de cubos en la parte de atrás para que formen una línea recta a través de la parte de atrás con tres cubos. En el lado izquierdo de la parte trasera, añade uno a la izquierda. En el lado derecho en la parte de atrás, añade uno más detrás del cubo del rincón del fondo y uno que sobresalga por arriba de ése en la derecha.

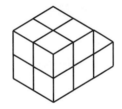

Los planos de Julia

En toda la vivienda hay 10 cubos. Tiene sólo dos pisos pero los cuartos son grandes. La vivienda completa parece una máquina lavadora tumbada.

1. ¿Puedes decir cuántos cubos se usaron en la estructura? ¿Cómo lo sabes?

2. ¿Puedes decir cómo deben colocarse los cubos? ¿Cómo harías los dibujos más claros?

3. Éstos planos por escrito, ¿incluyen una descripción paso a paso del proceso de construcción? ¿Falta algún paso?

4. ¿Puedes nombrar una o dos cosas que crees están bien hechas en los planos? ¿Y una o dos que necesiten ser cambiadas en los planos?

Dar y recibir opiniones

¿Qué es opinar?

Opinar pueden ser:

....consejos

...sugerencias

...pareceres

Cuando le preguntes a alguien:

"¿Qué te parece?",

te darán una opinión.

Las opiniones son sugerencias y consejos que pueden ayudarte a mejorar tu trabajo. Depende de ti el usarlos o no. Piensa sobre la opinión y decide si estás de acuerdo. Si no estás de acuerdo, mira a ver si puedes explicarte a ti mismo por qué no lo estás.

Cuando alguien te pregunte:

"¿Qué te parece?",

¿cómo debes opinar?

Recuerda que estás dando tu opinión para ayudar a alguien a mejorar su trabajo o a figurarse algo. Di lo que tengas que decir para ayudar a esa persona a resolver su problema, no para hacerla sentirse mal.

"Me gustó mucho cómo hiciste..."

"Algunas cosas que se pueden mejorar son..."

"Yo tuve problemas tratando de entender lo que quieres decir con..."

"La parte que no me quedó clara fue cuando dijiste..."

Cubos escondidos

Para cada grupo de dibujos de abajo se puede construir más de una vivienda.
(a) Visualiza o construye dos viviendas diferentes para cada dibujo. (b) Dibuja vistas ortogonales para mostrar la diferencia entre las dos viviendas.

(Las viviendas que sean rotaciones de sí mismas se consideran la misma vivienda y sólo se pueden contar una vez. Las caras sombreadas representan la vista frontal).

1.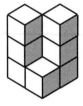

2.

3.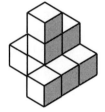

4.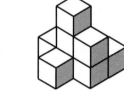

5.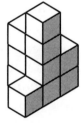

Haz un dibujo **isométrico** de *dos viviendas como mínimo* que se podrían hacer con cada dibujo.

	Vista aérea	**Vista frontal**	**Vista lateral derecha**
6.			
7.			

Tener en cuenta el clima en el diseño de viviendas

1 ¿Qué rasgos sugerirías para una vivienda situada en el desierto?	**2** ¿Qué rasgos sugerirías para una vivienda situada en un lugar extremadamente frío?
3 ¿Qué rasgos sugerirías para una vivienda situada en un clima cálido en verano y moderadamente frío en invierno?	**4** ¿Qué rasgos sugerirías para una vivienda situada en un clima cálido durante todo el año y que tiene mucha bruma?
5 ¿Qué rasgos sugerirías para una vivienda situada en un clima en el que nieva mucho?	**6** ¿Qué rasgos sugerirías para una vivienda situada en un clima extremadamente ventoso, con huracanes ocasionales?

Memo 3 a los diseñadores de viviendas

A: los diseñadores de viviendas
De: Director General,
Compañía de Construcción Creativa

Nuestra compañía quiere desarrollar una nueva línea de viviendas que se puede construir usando seis figuras geométricas:

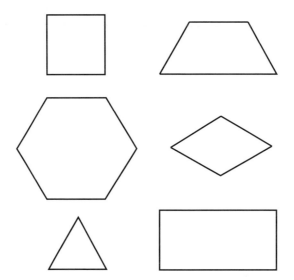

Use de 12 a 16 piezas de figuras geométricas para construir la maqueta de una vivienda. No necesita usar todos los tipos de figura. La vivienda debe tener tejado. Use cinta adhesiva para colocar correctamente las piezas, de tal forma que el tejado no tenga goteras y la vivienda pueda sostenerse sola.

Cuando haya completado la maqueta, cree un juego de planos para que otros puedan construir el modelo que usted ha diseñado.

Guía de diseño

✔ Incluya en sus planos por lo menos alguna clase de dibujo de toda la estructura. Decida si quiere hacer dibujos ortogonales, dibujos que muestran profundidad, o ambos.

✔ Escriba una descripción del proceso de construcción para que otra persona lo pueda seguir.

✔ Use los nombres de las figuras para que sus planos sean tan precisos como sea posible.

¿Puedes hacer esta figura? 1ª parte

Trata de hacer cada figura geométrica siguiendo cada pista que se da a continuación. Puedes usar la cuerda o puedes hacerlo con lápiz y papel.

Si puedes hacerla, dibuja la que hayas hecho y nombra las caras iguales y las caras paralelas. Si no puedes hacerla, escribe que la figura es imposible.

Nombra la figura con un nombre matemático. Si no conoces un nombre para la figura, invéntate un nombre geométrico que te parezca bien. Al final de la página hay partes de palabras geométricas que te pueden servir de ayuda.

Figura 1: una figura equilateral con más de tres caras y ninguna cara paralela.

Figura 2: una figura con dos caras iguales y dos caras diferentes paralelas pero que no sean iguales. (Pista: tu figura puede tener más de cuatro caras).

Figura 3: un cuadrilátero con dos pares de caras paralelas y sólo dos lados iguales.

Figura 4: una figura con un mínimo de dos pares de caras paralelas que no sea una figura equilátera. (Pista: tu figura puede tener más de cuatro caras).

Figura 5: un cuadrilátero que sea equilátero y no tenga caras paralelas.

Figura 6: haz una pista tú mismo y escríbela. Pruébala a ver si se puede hacer y escribe una frase explicando por qué sí o por qué no se puede hacer.

Partes de palabras que tienen significado geométrico

tri significa 3   *cuad* significa 4   *penta* significa 5

hexa significa 6   *hepta* significa 7   *octo* u *octa* significa 8

equi significa igual   *lateral* significa en el lado

poly significa numeroso, mucho

Figuras animadas

 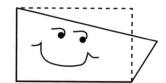 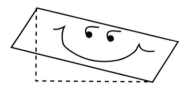

"Figuras animadas" son figuras hechas con cuerda, cuando uno de vosotros se mueve mientras los demás permanecen quietos. Al moverse uno de vosotros, la figura cambiará según a dónde os mováis.

Para cada una de las figuras animadas descritas en la hoja

Trata primero de formarte una imagen mental de lo que le ocurrirá a la figura. Decide quién tendrá que moverse para formar las figuras animadas. Piensa si puedes hacer las figuras moviendo personas diferentes, una cada vez.

A continuación, haz las figuras animadas con tu grupo.

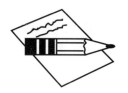

Haz anotaciones sobre cómo has hecho cada figura. Incluye vuestras posiciones al principio, quién se movió y a dónde se movieron. Puedes hacer un dibujo o describirlo con palabras. Si haces un dibujo, usa las marcas correctas para caras paralelas e iguales.

Reglas

- Sólo se puede mover una persona a la vez; todos los demás deben permanecer quietos.

- Trata de hacer las figuras moviendo el *menor* número posible de personas.

- *Para añadirle más dificultad (opcional):* la figura al comienzo de cada pregunta debe ser diferente a todas las demás; no puedes usar más de una vez la misma figura al empezar.

Figuras animadas

 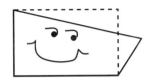 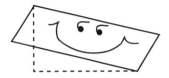

Pistas

1. Empieza con un cuadrado. Acaba con un rombo.

2. Empieza con un trapezoide. Acaba con un triángulo.

3. Empieza con un rectángulo. Acaba con una figura que no tenga lados paralelos.

4. Empieza con una figura equilátera que tenga cuatro lados. Acaba con una figura que tenga un lado más largo que el lado que le sigue.

5. Empieza con una figura equilátera con dos pares de lados paralelos. Puede tener cuatro lados, pero no *tiene* que tenerlos. Acaba con una figura que sólo tenga un par de lados paralelos.

6. Empieza con una figura equilátera que no tenga lados paralelos. Acaba con una figura que sólo tenga un par de lados paralelos.

7. Empieza con un triángulo equilátero. Acaba con un triángulo que sólo tenga dos lados iguales.

8. Empieza con una figura que tenga dos pares de lados paralelos y ningún lado igual. No puede ser una figura de cuatro lados. Acaba con una figura equilátera que todavía tenga dos pares de lados paralelos. Puedes cambiar el número de lados que tiene.

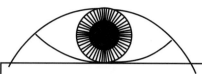

Glosario visual: paralelo y equilátero

Mira los grupos de dibujos de abajo y escribe una descripción de lo que se quiere decir con los términos *paralelo* y *equilátero*.

PARALELO

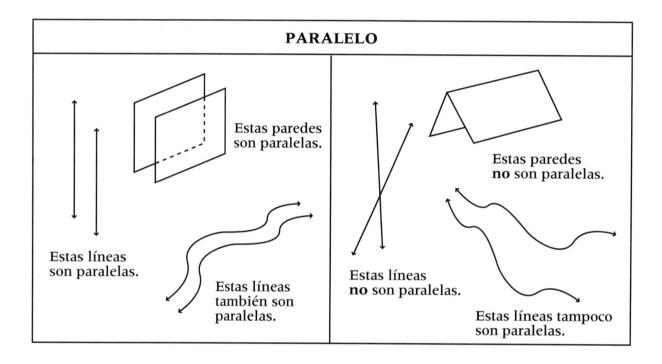

Estas paredes son paralelas.

Estas líneas son paralelas.

Estas líneas también son paralelas.

Estas paredes **no** son paralelas.

Estas líneas **no** son paralelas.

Estas líneas tampoco son paralelas.

EQUILÁTERO

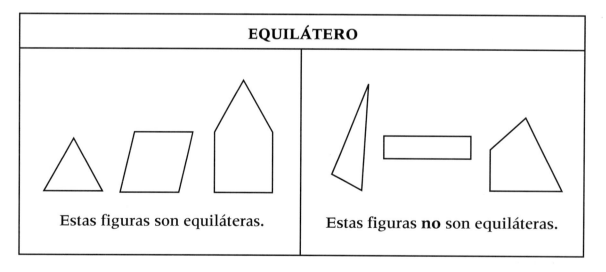

Estas figuras son equiláteras.

Estas figuras **no** son equiláteras.

Practica con figuras

Usa cuerda o papel y lápiz para hacer las siguientes figuras.

1. La primera pista en *¿Puedes hacer esta figura? 1ª parte* es: *una figura equilátera que **no tenga lados paralelos.*** Al cambiar una parte de la pista obtienes una pista completamente nueva: *una figura paralela con **sólo un par de lados paralelos.*** Prueba esta nueva pista y decide si es posible o imposible. Si es posible, dibuja la figura de acuerdo con la nueva pista. Si es imposible, trata de explicar por qué.

2. Toma una de las pistas de *¿Puedes hacer esta figura? 1ª parte* y cambia una parte. Escribe la nueva pista que has obtenido. ¿Es posible o imposible? Si es posible, dibuja una figura de acuerdo con la pista. Si es imposible, trata de explicar por qué.

3. Escribe tú mismo dos pistas usando lados paralelos, lados equiláteros o ambos. Una de tus pistas tiene que ser imposible. Prueba cada una de tus pistas para asegurarte. Para la pista que es posible, haz un dibujo de la figura que cumpla con los requisitos de la pista. Para la pista que es imposible, trata de explicar por qué.

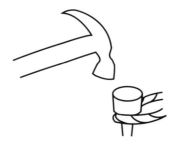

Marcándolo con cuerda, método 1

Cuerda o hilo se usan frecuentemente en la construcción moderna como herramienta para trazar ángulos rectos. Lee sobre el método y completa después los dos problemas de abajo.

Método 1: cuando construyen el suelo de un cuarto rectangular, los carpinteros señalan los cuatro rincones del cuarto con estacas. Dos trozos de cuerda se sujetan de rincón a rincón para formar una X gigante. Estas cuerdas muestran las "diagonales" del rectángulo. Los dos trozos de cuerda se comparan, y se reajustan las estacas hasta que las cuerdas son de la misma longitud. Cuando coincidan, el suelo será un rectángulo perfecto con dos pares de lados paralelos.

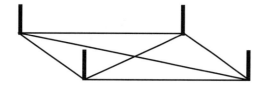   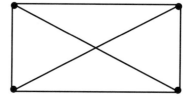

vista desde arriba

1. Explica porqué funciona este método. ¿Qué tipo de figura obtienes si las dos cuerdas no tienen la misma longitud?

2. Encuentra ejemplos de otras figuras que tengan diagonales de la misma longitud. ¿Cuántas figuras has encontrado? Escribe una o dos frases para cada figura que hayas probado, describiendo qué figura era (también puedes hacer un dibujo) y qué has averiguado.

¿Qué es un ángulo?

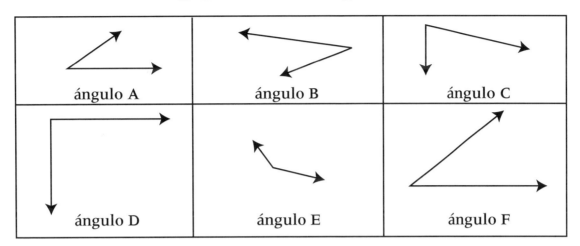

ángulo A	ángulo B	ángulo C
ángulo D	ángulo E	ángulo F

1. Rodea con un círculo la letra del ángulo más grande. Luego completa esta frase con tus propias palabras:

   *Yo digo que éste es el ángulo más grande porque:*_____.

2. Lee las tres descripciones de abajo. ¿Cuál de las personas describe un ángulo con más precisión? Rodea su nombre con un círculo. Escribe una frase para cada una de las otras dos selecciones, explicando por qué no las has elegido.

   Anna: "Un ángulo es una línea que no se acaba y que se dobla para que haya una esquina".

   Lisa: "Un ángulo es una cantidad de espacio que se hace entre dos lados".

   Luis: "Un ángulo es el número de grados cuando lo mides con un transportador".

3. Acaba esta frase con tus propias palabras:

   Medir el ángulo de una figura es diferente a medir el lado de una figura

   *porque*_____

   _____.

¿Puedes hacer esta figura? 2ª parte

Trata de hacer la figura para cada pista. Puedes usar la cuerda o hacerlo con lápiz y papel.

Si puedes hacerlo, dibuja lo que has hecho y nombra los ángulos iguales y los ángulos rectos. Algunas de las pistas puede que describan una figura imposible de hacer.

Nombra la figura con un nombre matemático. Si no conoces un nombre para la figura, invéntate un nombre geométrico que te parezca adecuado. Al final de la página hay partes de palabras geométricas que te pueden servir de ayuda.

Figura 1: un cuadrilátero con dos ángulos rectos.

Figura 2: un cuadrilátero con dos ángulos rectos que son también ángulos opuestos.

Figura 3: una figura con tres ángulos rectos.

Figura 4: un cuadrilátero con solo dos ángulos opuestos que sean iguales.

Figura 5: una figura con cinco ángulos iguales.

Figura 6: un cuadrilátero en el que cada par de ángulos opuestos tengan el mismo tamaño y por lo menos un par sean ángulos rectos.

Figura 7: inventa y escribe tu propia pista. Pruébala a ver si es posible y escribe una frase explicando por qué sí o por qué no puede hacerse.

Partes de palabras que tienen significado geométrico

tri significa 3	*cuad* significa 4	*penta* significa 5
hexa significa 6	*hepta* significa 7	*octo* u *octa* significa 8
equi significa igual	*lateral* significa en el lado	
poly significa numeroso, mucho	*angular* significa ángulo	
orto significa ángulo recto	*gon* significa ángulo	

Juego de cartas de los lados y los ángulos

Lado Esta figura es equilátera... **A**	**Ángulo** ...y tiene exactamente dos ángulos iguales. **a**
Lado Esta figura tiene dos pares de lados paralelos... **B**	**Ángulo** ...y tiene dos pares de ángulos opuestos. **b**
Lado Esta figura es equilátera y tiene por lo menos un par de lados paralelos... **C**	**Ángulo** ...y tiene por lo menos un par de ángulos opuestos iguales. **c**
Lado Esta figura no tiene lados paralelos... **D**	**Ángulo** ...y tiene por lo menos dos ángulos rectos. **d**

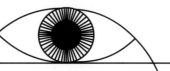

Glosario visual: tipos de ángulos y figuras regulares (1)

Mira el conjunto de ilustraciones de abajo y escribe una descripción de lo que se quiere decir con los términos *ángulos iguales* y *ángulos opuestos*.

ÁNGULOS IGUALES

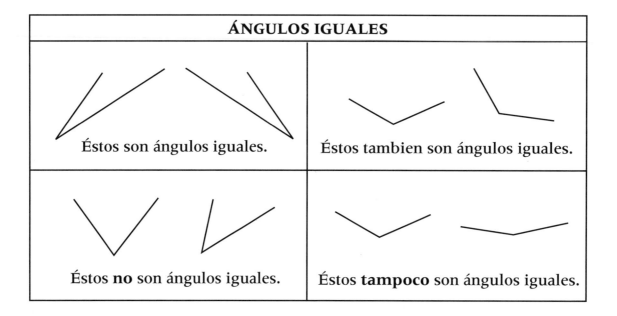

Éstos son ángulos iguales.

Éstos tambien son ángulos iguales.

Éstos **no** son ángulos iguales.

Éstos **tampoco** son ángulos iguales.

ÁNGULOS OPUESTOS

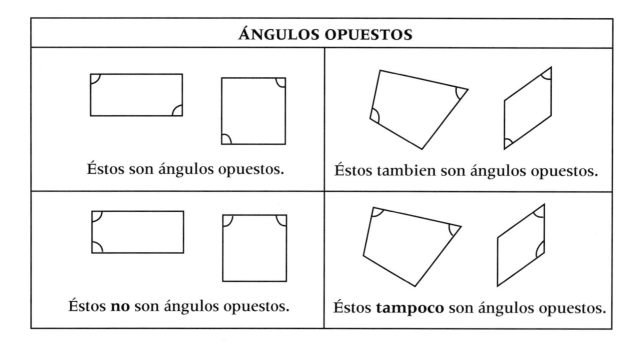

Éstos son ángulos opuestos.

Éstos tambien son ángulos opuestos.

Éstos **no** son ángulos opuestos.

Éstos **tampoco** son ángulos opuestos.

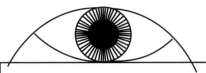

Glosario visual: tipos de ángulos y figuras regulares (2)

Mira el conjunto de ilustraciones de abajo y escribe una descripción de lo que se quiere decir con los términos *ángulos rectos* y *figuras regulares*.

ÁNGULOS RECTOS

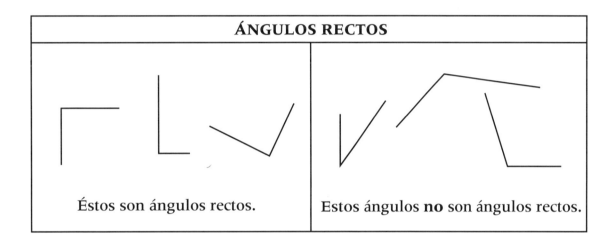

| Éstos son ángulos rectos. | Estos ángulos **no** son ángulos rectos. |

FIGURAS REGULARES

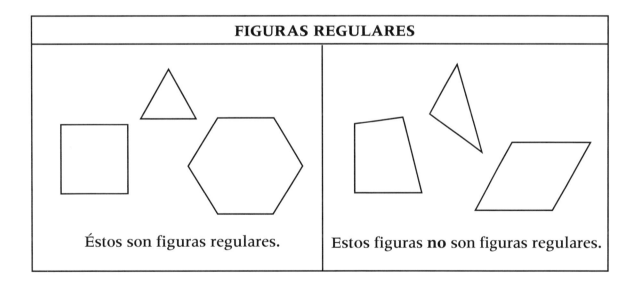

| Éstos son figuras regulares. | Estos figuras **no** son figuras regulares. |

Marcándolo con cuerda, método 2

Cuerda o hilo se usan frecuentemente en la construcción moderna como herramienta para trazar ángulos rectos. Lee sobre el método y completa después los dos problemas de abajo.

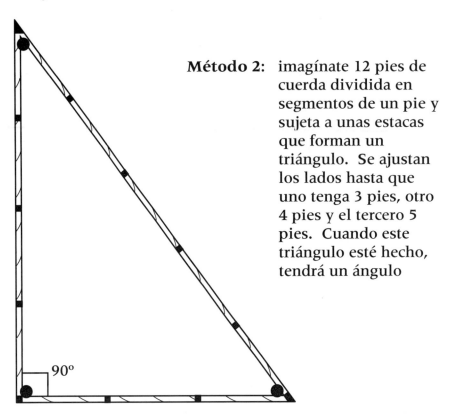

Método 2: imagínate 12 pies de cuerda dividida en segmentos de un pie y sujeta a unas estacas que forman un triángulo. Se ajustan los lados hasta que uno tenga 3 pies, otro 4 pies y el tercero 5 pies. Cuando este triángulo esté hecho, tendrá un ángulo

90°

1. Encuentra otro trío de longitudes de lado que formen un ángulo recto. Explica cómo sabes que tienes un ángulo recto. Usa hilo o cuerda para construir un pequeño modelo o para demostrarlo en clase.

   Consejo: un factor escalar que puedes usar si haces un modelo es 1 pie de cuerda en el problema equivale a una pulgada de hilo en tu modelo.

2. ¿Cuántos pies más debes añadirle al hilo o a la cuerda hasta que consigas un hilo más largo que todavía te proporcione un nuevo ángulo recto? Corta un pedazo de hilo de esta nueva largura y halla un nuevo trío de longitudes de lado usando este hilo más largo. ¿Cuáles son las nuevas longitudes de los lados?

3. Halla otros dos tríos de longitudes de lado que formen un ángulo recto en un triángulo. Hay patrones para algunos de estos tríos de longitudes de lado. Si ves un patrón, descríbelo y haz un pronóstico sobre cómo hallarás las longitudes de los otros lados.

   Designing Spaces ©EDC, 1995

creative construction company

Memo 4 a los diseñadores de viviendas

A: los diseñadores de viviendas
De: Director General,
    Compañía de Construcción Creativa

Para poder vender y construir su diseño de vivienda, nuestros vendedores y contratistas necesitan alguna información específica. Por favor, escríbanos una descripción detallada del diseño de su vivienda. Puede incluir un esquema, un cartel o cualquier cosa que usted considere pueda sernos de ayuda para entender su diseño.

Preguntas de los vendedores

Aspecto

¿Qué aspecto tiene su vivienda?

Clima

¿Para qué clima ha diseñado su vivienda?

¿Qué características hacen de su vivienda una buena elección para el clima que usted ha elegido?

¿En qué lugar del mundo podría situarse su vivienda?

Residentes

¿Cuánta gente puede vivir en su vivienda?

¿Es una buena vivienda para que la habiten niños, personas mayores o personas con impedimentos?

Preguntas de los contratistas

Los contratistas van a usar los planos de su vivienda para hacer una maqueta del diseño de su vivienda. Para que puedan calcular cuánto tardarán en construir la vivienda y cuánto costará, necesitan información específica sobre las figuras geométricas de su vivienda.

¿Qué figuras geométricas ha usado usted para construir su vivienda?

¿Cuántas unidades de cada figura ha empleado?

¿Qué figuras son equiláteras?

¿Qué figuras tienen lados paralelos?

¿Qué figuras tienen ángulos iguales, ángulos opuestos o ángulos rectos?

Planos de vivienda de muestra

Revisa a continuación el conjunto de planos de construcción hechos por un estudiante de sexto grado. Rodea con un círculo aquéllos lugares que te parezcan poco claros o incorrectos y responde a las preguntas de la página siguiente.

La casa "árbol"

Parte 1

a. Toma tres rectángulos y ponlos de tal manera que formen un triángulo 3-D como éste:

b. Habrá dos aberturas en los extremos, que tienen forma de triángulos. Consigue dos triángulos y colócalos en los espacios abiertos. Así:

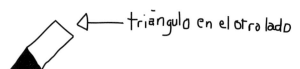 triángulo en el otro lado

Parte 2

c. Con un rombo y tres triángulos forma un triángulo grande. Así :

Ésa es la base
Es equilátero

d. Toma 3 de éstos 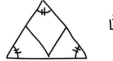 y forma con ellos un triángulo. De esta manera, la parte superior del triángulo tendrá la forma de otro triángulo. Así:

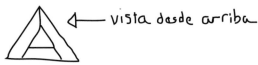 vista desde arriba

e. Toma 3 triángulos y júntalos para hacer otro triángulo. Así:

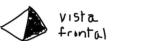 vista frontal

 vista desde arriba

f. Junta los 3 triángulos y los 3 . Ninguna de las caras debe ser paralela. Así:

Planos de vivienda de muestra (continuación)

g. Ahora has acabado la casa "árbol". La vivienda debería tener este aspecto:

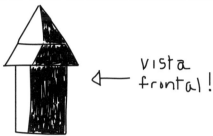

vista
frontal !

Sabes que la has hecho bien si puedes cortar de arriba abajo de tres maneras para que las dos piezas sean simétricas.

Se sitúa en los bancos del río Mississipi. Si el río se desborda, la gente puede subir a los espaciosos pisos superiores y no mojarse.

1. ¿Qué te gusta en los planos?

2. ¿Puedes decir cuántas figuras se han usado para hacer esta casa? ¿Puedes decir qué figuras se han usado? Si no, ¿cómo podrías rehacer los planos para hacer las figuras más claras?

3. ¿Qué conceptos geométricos o notación podrían añadirse a los planos para hacerlos más claros o más precisos? ¿Dónde los añadirías?

4. Se podrían incluir otros dibujos para hacer que los planos sean más fáciles de seguir? ¿Qué tipo de dibujos se deberían incluir? ¿Dónde los pondrías?

5. ¿Qué más necesitas saber para construir la casa "árbol"?

Un montón de centavos

Para cada una de las situaciones descritas a continuación, dibuja la figura que quieres obtener y escribe las respuestas a las preguntas en una hoja de papel aparte.

1. Imagínate un centavo. Ahora imagínate diez centavos apilados encima del primero, de tal manera que el canto de cada moneda esté perfectamente alineado con el de abajo.

   Describe esta figura. Cómo la llamarías? ¿Qué propiedades tiene?

2. Piensa en la figura que te has imaginado en el #1. Ahora imagínate que cortas esa figura de arriba a abajo justo por la mitad. Abre las dos mitades de la figura.

   ¿Qué figura bidimensional tiene la cara que tienes delante tuyo?

3. Imagínate que en tu escritorio hay una pieza de cartón en forma de rombo. Ahora imagínate quince más apiladas encima de esta figura, con los vértces y los lados alineados.

   Describe esta figura. ¿Cómo la llamarías? ¿Qué propiedades tiene?

4. Piensa en la figura que te imaginaste en el #3. Ahora imagínate que cortas esa figura de arriba a abajo justo por la mitad.

   ¿Qué figura bidimensional tiene la cara?

5. Imagínate un cuadrado. Imagínate un punto en el espacio por encima del cuadrado. Mentalmente, traza una línea desde cada una de las esquinas del cuadrado hasta el punto. Ahora imagínate que esta figura es una figura sólida.

   Describe esta figura. ¿Cómo la llamarías? ¿Qué propiedades tiene?

6. Imagínate que cortas de arriba (el punto) a abajo (el cuadrado) la figura que has hecho en el #5, justo por el medio.

   ¿Qué figura bidimensional tiene la cara?

Cómo dibujar un prisma

Primero, dibuja la base del prisma. La base puede tener tantos lados como quieras. Este ejemplo es un **prisma pentagonal**, así que la base es un pentágono.

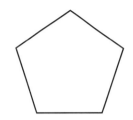

A continuación, dibuja la segunda base, haciendo una copia exacta de la figura (ten cuidado en mantener paralelos los lados correspondientes). (Es más fácil imaginarse el prisma si dibujas las figuras aparte diagonalmente, en vez de encima o al lado.)

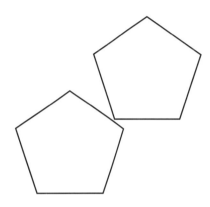

Tercero, conecta los vértices correspondientes de las dos bases. Esto producirá una colección de aristas paralelas de la misma longitud (en nuestro caso hay 5).

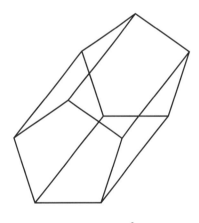

Si el prisma parece difícil de ver, puede que quieras sombrear la cara frontal y borrar las aristas que no verías en un prisma sólido.

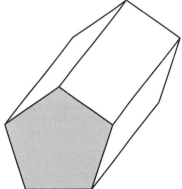

Cómo dibujar una pirámide

Primero dibuja la base. Puede tener tantos lados como quieras. Este ejemplo es una **pirámide pentagonal**, así que la base es un pentágono.

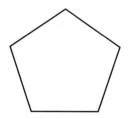

Segundo, elige cualquier punto fuera de la base.

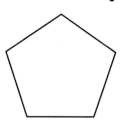

Tercero, dibuja segmentos lineales que vayan de cada vértice de la base al punto.

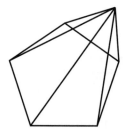

Si la pirámide parece difícil de ver, puede que quieras sombrear alguna de las caras y borrar las aristas que no se verían en una pirámide sólida.

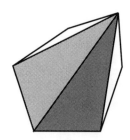

Designing Spaces ©EDC, 1995

Practicar con prismas y pirámides

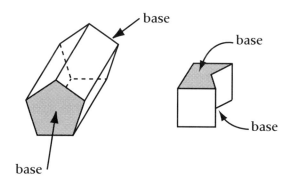

En un prisma hay dos caras paralelas que pueden ser cualquier figura. Éstas se llaman *bases*.

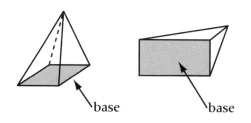

En una pirámide, una cara puede ser cualquier figura. Todas las otras caras son triángulos. La cara que puede ser cualquier figura se llama *base*.

Un prisma o una pirámide reciben su nombre de la figura que forma su base o bases; por ejemplo, si la base de la pirámide es un cuadrado, se llama pirámide cuadrada.

Usando las técnicas expuestas en **Cómo dibujar un prisma** y en **Cómo dibujar una pirámide:**

- Dibuja tú solo unas pirámides y unos prismas usando las técnicas que has aprendido. Para las pirámides, experimenta sitaundo el punto en posiciones diferentes por encima y por debajo de la base.

- Dibuja un prisma triangular, una pirámide hexagonal y un prisma rectangular.

Clasificar fotografías

Imagínate que vas caminando alrededor de un grupo de edificios como los de las fotografías de abajo. Elige una de las fotos como punto de partida y ponlas en orden según lo que vas viendo al rodear los edificios.

Designing Spaces ©EDC, 1995

Reglas de las Estructuras misteriosas

Tu grupo ha recibido un juego de figuras y una serie de cuatro pistas que describen una estructura tridimensional.

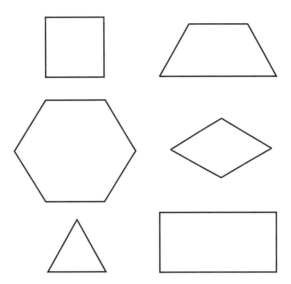

Así se juega a **Estructuras misteriosas: juego I:**

- Cada miembro del grupo lee una de las pistas al grupo, pero no muestra la pista al resto del grupo. Si tu pista tiene una foto, descríbela.

- Después de que se lea cada pista, para y discute qué aspecto podría tener la estructura.

- Cuando hayas oído las cuatro pistas, usa las figuras y cinta adhesiva para construir una estructura que cumpla con todas las pistas. Comprueba cada pista para asegurarte de que la estructura cumple con todas. Puede que necesites revisar la estructura varias veces antes de que cumpla con las cuatro pistas.

- Cuando hayas construido una estructura que cumpla con todas las pistas, haz un dibujo de ella que muestre profundidad.

Estructuras misteriosas: juego I

Series de pistas 1 y 2

Serie 1 Juego I La vista desde abajo de esta estructura tiene este aspecto:	**Serie 1** Juego I Esta estructura tiene tres grupos de caras paralelas. Esta estructura es un prisma.
Serie 1 Juego I Para hacer esta estructura hacen falta siete piezas.	**Serie 1** Juego I El lado derecho de esta estructura es un cuadrado.

Serie 2 Juego I El número de rombos en esta estructura es la mitad del número de rectángulos.	**Serie 2** Juego I La parte inferior de esta estructura tiene este aspecto: izquierda ⬡ derecha
Serie 2 Juego I Esta estructura es un prisma. Hay dieciocho aristas en esta estructura.	**Serie 2** Juego I Para hacer esta estructura se necesitan once piezas.

Estructuras misteriosas: juego I

Series de pistas 3 y 4

Serie 3 — Juego I Esta estructura no tiene caras paralelas.	Serie 3 — Juego I La vista desde abajo de esta estructura tiene este aspecto: ▢
Serie 3 — Juego I Esta estructura está construida con cinco piezas. Todas las piezas son figuras regulares.	Serie 3 — Juego I La vista lateral tiene este aspecto: △

Serie 4 — Juego I Esta estructura tiene tres veces más cuadrados que hexágonos.	Serie 4 — Juego I Esta estructura tiene doce vértices. Es un prisma.
Serie 4 — Juego I La base de esta estructura tiene este aspecto: atrás izquierda ⬡ derecha frente	Serie 4 — Juego I Cuando esta estructura se corta por el centro de izquierda a derecha, las dos piezas resultantes son simétricas.

Estructuras misteriosas: juego I

Series 5 y 6

Serie 5 Juego I Tres de las piezas de esta estructura son figuras regulares.	**Serie 5** Juego I Esta estructura se hace con seis piezas.
Serie 5 Juego I La base de esta estructura tiene este aspecto:	**Serie 5** Juego I Esta estructura es un prisma. Tiene dos grupos de caras paralelas.

Serie 6 Juego I La vista desde el lado derecho es así:	**Serie 6** Juego I La vista desde abajo tiene este aspecto:
Serie 6 Juego I Esta estructura se construye con siete piezas. Sólo tres de las piezas son cuadrados.	**Serie 6** Juego I Todas las piezas de esta estructura son figuras equiláteras.

Estructuras misteriosas: juego II

Juego II El prisma rectangular está adosado a otras dos estructuras. Se apoya en uno de sus lados cuadrados. Una de sus caras rectangulares está adosada a la cara rectangular del prisma hexagonal.	Juego II La pirámide cuadrada está adosada a la parte superior del prisma rectangular.
Juego II El prisma hexagonal hecho con rectángulos se apoya en su base hecha con rombos. El prisma hexagonal hecho con cuadrados se asienta encima suyo.	Juego II Encima del prisma trapezoidal se asienta la estructura que tiene este aspecto... ...desde el lado.
Juego II La base de la estructura final completa tiene este aspecto: 	Juego II El prisma trapezoidal está adosado al prisma hexagonal alto. Están adosados al juntar una cara cuadrada del prisma trapezoidal a la cara rectangular del prisma hexagonal alto.

Estructuras misteriosas: juego III
aristas y vértices

Serie 1 ¿Qué dibujo de la hoja siguiente cumple con estas pistas?

Pista a   Esta estructura incluye por lo menos un hexágono regular.

Pista b   Esta estructura tiene 7 vértices.

Pista c   Al construir esta estructura no puedes hallar ningún rectángulo.

Pista d   Al construir esta estructura encontrarás 5 triángulos como mínimo.

Rodéala con un círculo en la próxima hoja y numérala con un 1. Trata de dibujarla aquí:

Serie 2 ¿Qué dibujo de la hoja siguiente cumple con estas pistas?

Pista a   Al construir esta estructura encontrarás 4 triángulos equiláteros.

Pista b   La base de esta estructura tiene este aspecto: ☐

Pista c   Al construir esta estructura encontrarás 2 cuadrados más que triángulos equiláteros.

Pista d   Al construir esta estructura encontrarás 16 aristas y 9 vértices.

Rodéala con un círculo en la próxima hoja y numérala con un 2. Trata de dibujarla aquí:

Estructuras misteriosas: juego III
(Continuación)

Serie 3 ¿Cuál de los dibujos de abajo cumple con estas pistas?

Pista a Esta estructura tiene más de 12 vértices.

Pista b La vista frontal y la vista posterior son la misma.

Pista c Al construir esta estructura encontrarás cuatro veces más cuadrados que octágonos.

Pista d Al construir esta estructura encontrarás 2 octágonos regulares.

Rodéala con un círculo en la parte de abajo y numérala con un 3. Trata de dibujarla aquí:

Figuras:

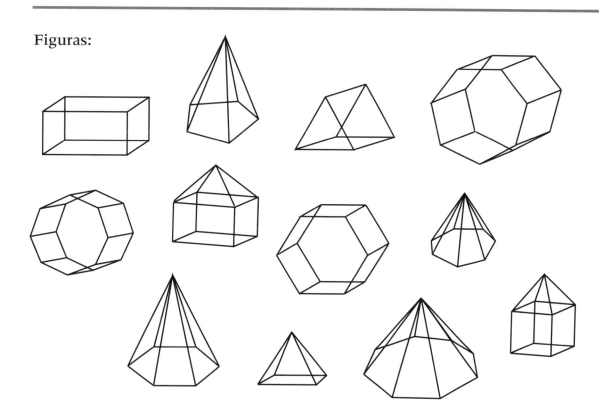

creative construction company

Memo 5 a los diseñadores de viviendas

A: los diseñadores de viviendas
De: Director General,
     Compañía de Construcción Creativa

Acabamos de ser contratados para crear una nueva colección de diseños de viviendas. Estas viviendas estarán situadas en uno de estos dos climas: (1) cálido y lluvioso o (2) frío y nevoso. Este proyecto le dará la oportunidad de presentar algunos diseños creativos y nos dará la oportunidad de ver cuánto ha aprendido usted trabajando para nuestra compañía.

El proyecto tiene tres partes:

1. Use las figuras para diseñar y construir una maqueta de la vivienda.

2. Cree una serie de planos para que otros puedan construir el modelo que Ud. ha creado.

3. Escriba un memo explicando las características de su vivienda.

Guía para la construcción

- La vivienda tiene que tener tejado. No se permiten tejados con goteras.

- La vivienda tiene que sostenerse sola.

- Tiene que usar entre 20 y 24 piezas de figuras geométricas. No es necesario que use cada tipo de figura.

- Puede añadir un nuevo tipo de figura.

Guía para los planos

- Incluya dibujos de su vivienda tanto ortogonales como en perspectiva, y nombre ambos tipos. Nombre las distintas vistas en los dibujos ortogonales. Estos nombres facilitarán la interpretación de sus planes a los constructores.

- Incluya una descripción escrita en la que se explique el proceso de construcción paso por paso para que, si fuera necesario, alguien más pueda reproducir su vivienda. Use los nombres y las propiedades de las figuras para hacer su descripción clara y precisa.

Guía para las especificaciones de diseño

- Asegúese de incluir toda la información que han solicitado los directores en el memo #6.

- Haga las especificaciones de diseño tan atractivas y fáciles de seguir como le sea posible.

creative construction company

Memo 6 a los diseñadores de viviendas

A: los diseñadores de viviendas
De: Director General,
        Compañía de Construcción Creativa

Para poder vender y construir su diseño de vivienda, nuestros vendedores y contratistas necesitan alguna información específica. Por favor, escriba un memo contándonos todo sobre el diseño de su vivienda. El memo puede incluir un esquema, un cartel o cualquier cosa que usted crea que pueda servirnos de ayuda para entender su diseño.

Preguntas de los vendedores

Aspecto

¿Qué aspecto tiene su vivienda?

¿Cómo describiría la forma de toda la vivienda?

¿Cómo describiría la forma de su base, su tejado y cualquier característica especial?

¿Cuántos pisos tiene su vivienda?

Clima

¿Para qué clima está diseñada su vivienda?

¿Qué características hacen de su vivienda una buena elección para el clima que Ud. ha elegido?

¿En qué lugar del mundo podría situarse su vivienda?

Residentes

¿Cuánta gente puede vivir en su vivienda?

¿Es una buena vivienda para que la habiten niños, personas mayores o personas incapacitadas?

Preguntas de los contratistas

Los contratistas usarán los planos de su edificio para hacer una maqueta del diseño de su vivienda. Para poder calcular cuánto tardarán en construir la vivienda y cuánto costará, necesitan alguna información específica sobre la forma de su vivienda.

¿Qué figuras se pueden encontrar en su vivienda?

¿Cuántas unidades de cada figura tiene?

¿Cuántas aristas y vértices tiene?

¿Se usan estas figuras para hacerla regular?

¿Se usan estas figuras para hacerla equilátera?

¿Tiene su vivienda caras paralelas? Si es así, ¿cuántas tiene?